To Cousin Scott & Yvette,

CHEERS!

Love,

C. L. Zie

Straight Whisky

Straight Whisky

A Living History of Sex, Drugs, and Rock 'n' Roll on the Sunset Strip

Erik Quisling and Austin Williams

Foreword by Henry Rollins

Afterword by Lemmy Kilmister of Motörhead

Chicago and Los Angeles

Interior book design by Eric Fulford
Layout by Michael Gorey
Color posters used with permission by Dennis Loren (*www.posterplanet.com, www.joeyjetsonmusic.com, www.bluemoonent.com*)

07 06 05 04 03   5 4 3 2 1

Library of Congress Cataloging-in-Publication Data

Quisling, Erik.
   Straight Whisky : a living history of sex, drugs & rock 'n' roll on the Sunset Strip / Erik Quisling and Austin Williams ; foreword by Henry Rollins ; afterword by Lemmy Kilmister of Motorhead.
      p. cm.
   ISBN 1-56625-197-4
   1. Whisky a Go-Go (Nightclub) 2. Rock music—California—Los Angeles—History and criticism. 3. Popular culture—California—Los Angeles. 4. Hollywood (Los Angeles, Calif.) I. Williams, Austin (Austin Lowry), 1970– II. Title.

   ML3534.Q57 2003
   306'.1'0979493—dc21
                                        2003007069

Bonus Books
160 E. Illinois St.
Chicago, IL 60611

Printed in Korea

for my sister Tori
—E.Q.

for my brother Stockton
—A.W.

STRAIGHT WHISKY

CONTENTS

CONTENTS

FOREWORD

I've done many shows at the Whisky A Go-Go and always had a really good time. The Whisky's great because you know there have been so many moments in that room. There used to be graffiti by Morrison and Hendrix on the dressing room's ceiling panels. That's pretty amazing.

I've got a tape of Van Halen, who were just barely signed to Warner Brothers at the time, playing the Whisky on New Year's Eve 1977-turning-into-1978. You hear this band on it . . . I mean, they were still just a club band, but you hear all that potential. They had all those songs together even back then, and they were just ripping it up at the Whisky. You think, "Wow, soon the rest of the world is going to find out about this band." I saw them a year later opening for Ted Nugent on a major tour. But there they were in 1977 on the same little stage that we mere mortals can be on.

When you think about who's been at the Whisky, it reminds you that L.A. actually used to have some culture. Now L.A. seems to be just sort of a cultureless, boob-jobbed, lifted-cheek wasteland. But, back then at the Whisky, I mean, there was a real scene. Something that I think is worth some real documentation.

Henry Rollins

INTRODUCTION

Memory, which is almost always based on personal interpretation as much as objective fact, tends to blur a bit when you're dealing with four decades of sex, drugs, and rock 'n' roll. As one of our interview subjects put it, "If you can remember it, you weren't really there."

The Sunset Strip boasts an unchallenged reputation as not only a hotbed of immortal music, but also a powerful magnet for the kind of freewheeling decadence with which rock 'n' roll is so often linked. No other stretch of real estate can lay claim to as many fabled live performances, nor as many trashed hotel rooms, wrecked limos, ravished groupies, smashed amps, and wasted lives. The sex, drugs, and rock 'n' roll lifestyle may not have been invented on the Strip, but there's no question it was perfected there and practiced by more people with more reckless abandon than on any other street in the world. Things happened there that simply could not have happened anywhere else.

The number of survivors still standing with sufficient gray matter left to tell the tale is rapidly diminishing. With the passage of time, there's a sense of myth gradually overshadowing reality, even in the minds of those who were either active participants or first-hand observers in this high-voltage, often outrageous rock 'n' roll tragicomedy that has been playing itself out on Sunset Boulevard since 1964.

But the story actually started well before then. Beyond its capacity for generating hazy legends, one of the Strip's most notable features is its sheer longevity. The ability to adapt to sweeping changes in culture and fashion has been a hallmark from the beginning. First making a name for itself in the roaring '20s, this two-mile path of glitter and asphalt serves as a bridge from the grimy kitsch of Hollywood to the emerald lawns of Beverly Hills and the Pacific coast beyond. It is a twisting pipeline of timeless dreams both realized and shattered. And as it rolls toward its centennial, the Strip shows little sign of losing its relevance or its mystique.

Each decade of the Sunset Strip's ongoing development could fill a detailed volume of its own. Rather than provide an all-encompassing history, this book focuses squarely on the legendary Whisky A Go-Go and its two sister clubs, the Roxy Theatre and the Rainbow Bar and Grill. Located within fewer than a hundred yards of each other, these three establishments constitute a rock block that has been the pounding heart of the L.A. music scene for forty years.

Under the management of the same small group of men, the Whisky, Roxy, and Rainbow have left an indelible mark on not only the evolution of popular music, but of pop culture in general. Elmer Valentine and Lou Adler have rightfully assumed positions of prominence in the rock 'n' roll pantheon for their roles in overseeing these nightclubs and launching the careers of innumerable artists.

In addition to those two visionaries, the Whisky's current sole owner, Mario Maglieri, stands as a towering (though largely unsung) hero who has quietly influenced the careers of many of rock's biggest names. The Doors, Jimi Hendrix, Led Zeppelin, Janis Joplin, Fleetwood Mac, Van Halen, Black Flag, Mötley Crüe, and Guns N' Roses represent only a sampling of the musical heavyweights directly affected by Mario's gruff good humor and salt-of-the-earth wisdom. Mario is the one man who has been on the front lines of this gloriously chaotic scene since the beginning (and still is, at least four nights a week), and it is impossible to imagine this story without his ever-present influence. His assistance has been crucial to the development of this book.

The biggest challenge we faced in writing *Straight Whisky* was how to construct a history of rock music on the Sunset Strip that was not only factually accurate, but also a compelling read. We felt strongly that a straightforward laundry list of band names and performance dates would quickly grow tiresome to all but the most die-hard rock historians. Our aim is to engage the casual music fan as well as the fanatic, and our approach is grounded in the belief that the enduring power of rock 'n' roll lies in not only *what happened,* but also *how it felt.* We wanted this book to capture both sides of the equation, from the immediate sensation of each iconic moment to a broader understanding of its significance. This is what led us to view the book as not simply a history, but, rather, a living history.

Each chapter begins with a re-creation by Austin Williams of an event that took place at the Whisky, the Roxy, or the Rainbow over the course of the past four decades. Drawing upon dozens of direct interviews and a wealth of secondary material, Williams has chosen sixteen incidents that exemplify their respective eras and fleshed them out into dramatic narratives. The main criterion for each selection was its ability to place the reader shoulder-to-shoulder with the people who were there when history was being made. Perhaps inevitably, certain gaps and inconsistencies cropped up in the recounting of the same incident by different sources. Although, as the saying goes, "there are three sides to every story: yours, mine, and the truth," these re-creations strive to depict the events as they might have appeared to a neutral observer.

The second half of each chapter offers a wide-ranging historical perspective by Erik Quisling that places the sixteen incidents within a broader context. Through copious research, Quisling has uncovered multiple connections that tie the history of rock 'n' roll on the Sunset Strip to the progression of music and culture in America at large. From the Monterey Pop

Festival to the Manson Family murders, from civil rights to acid rock, from the multibillion-dollar pornography boom to the rise of MTV, Quisling has unearthed causal relationships and coincidences that both directly and indirectly link what was happening on the national stage right back to L.A.'s notorious rock block.

Together, these two perspectives aim to provide a comprehensive look at a phenomenon that has shown remarkable durability in its capacity to inspire, appall, and amaze a worldwide audience. If a single prediction can be made from all that has happened on the Sunset Strip since 1964, it is that this story has surely not yet seen its final chapter. As long as rock 'n' roll retains its unique ability to stir people's imaginations and shake their bodies, the Whisky A Go-Go and its two companion nightclubs will continue to create history.

Erik Quisling and Austin Williams
Los Angeles
March 2003

THE PSYCHEDELIC STRIP

In the winter of 1963, there was no antidote for a nation trying to recover from the poison of President Kennedy's assassination. Barely a year removed from the Cuban Missile Crisis and the threat of all-out nuclear war, the United States found itself left with an unfamiliar leader facing escalating tensions in Vietnam. The Big Bopper and Buddy Holly were dead, and the Beatles had not yet hit America.

Today, driving down Sunset Boulevard on a cloudless summer day, it's easy to feel the laid-back vibe that permeates everything in Los Angeles. Sure, dire world problems still exist. But, snaking from Hollywood through Beverly Hills toward the beach, you get a sense that life is indeed good and that maybe things will find a way of working themselves out.

Perhaps it was a drive like this forty years ago that led Jan and Dean to pen the lighthearted "Surf City" in the midst of such turmoil. Perhaps it was a drive like this that spawned the carefree "Wipe Out" by the Surfaris. Perhaps it was a drive like this that our nation needed.

So maybe it was no accident that when Elmer Valentine opened the doors of the very first discothèque in the United States, it was an instant smash success. People needed to blow off steam, and here, amid the good vibes of Los Angeles, was the place to do it. The year was 1964. The club was the Whisky A Go-Go.

THE FIRST DISCO IN AMERICA

January 15, 1964

Caught up in the exertion of a heartfelt but somewhat spastic version of the Watusi, Cary Grant loses his footing on the tiled dance floor and stumbles into a man standing directly behind him. His broad right shoulder collides with a crystal martini glass clutched in the man's left hand, launching a shower of gin and vermouth all over Grant's unintended victim.

Grant is mortified by his gaffe. "Terribly sorry," he says with superbly crisp diction, struggling to be heard over the blare of the amplifiers while keeping his voice at a polite conversational level. It takes him a moment to recognize the owner of the drenched frilly shirt. It's Elmer Valentine, proprietor of this new nightclub that is in the act of noisily being born.

Valentine appears unfazed. "Forget it, Cary. My fault," he says in a salty Chicago brogue.

"Not a bit of it," Grant replies, managing to ooze confidence and class in the aftermath of his keenly awkward maneuver. "I should have seen you coming," he continues while extracting a silk handkerchief from his pocket to dab gingerly at Valentine's shirt.

Valentine grins with wolfish commiseration. "She's pretty

distracting, isn't she?"

Grant pauses, his hand hovering over Valentine's collar. "Who's that, old chum?"

Valentine's eyebrows reach lazily for the top of his forehead, creating a mien of richly amused incredulity. It's a common expression for him. When Grant continues to play dumb, Valentine points over the movie star's shoulder. Grant turns so that he faces the elevated stage at the back of the club, where a twenty-two-year-old Louisiana firebrand named Johnny Rivers is belting out a room rocking rendition of Chuck Berry's six-string classic "Roll Over Beethoven."

"Her," Valentine rasps.

Suspended above the stage, less than fifteen feet from Rivers's feverishly bopping head, is a cage about the size of two phone booths shoved together. Through its ornate gilded bars, a girl in a skintight pink miniskirt can be seen rocking to the infectious beat. Her name is Patty Brockhurst. She will come to be known as America's first go-go dancer.

Cary Grant nods slowly and says, "Oh. Her. Afraid I hadn't noticed her." He delivers the line with perfect deadpan, but a crooked leer gives him away. It's quite apparent that he, along with everyone else in the Whisky A Go-Go, has been staring at the imprisoned performer for most of the night. She's been putting on quite a show: arms swinging, hips pumping, strawberry-blonde hair tossed in a shape-shifting corona around her head and bare shoulders. She moves with thoughtless fluidity, like a dozen summer peaches in a terrycloth sack bumping along a badly paved road in the back of a pickup truck. It's a spectacle of sheer sensual abandon, the kind you rarely come across in nightclubs that don't require a back-alley entrance.

"Not bad for a last-minute replacement, eh?" Valentine says

with relish. "I only hired her to sell cigarettes."

Both men watch a few more gyrations and Grant nods again. "The girl possesses undeniable talent," he says.

"Like I say, she's just a stand-in. But I'm thinking I might keep her up there a while."

"Your instincts are entirely sound. I think it's best I return to my booth before I injure someone. Starting with myself." Grant twists around to scan the roiling sea of people for an open path that will lead him off the dance floor. None presents itself in the tits-to-tail crush pressing in from all sides. "You'll join me for a drink?" he asks with a trace of irritation.

Valentine laughs and pats his shoulder in a comradely way. "Sure. That last one didn't quite satisfy me."

"Splendid. I'll pick up this next round."

"Not on your life, pal." Valentine takes his elbow and steers him through the maze of whirling bodies. The Whisky will become known overnight as the premier spot in Hollywood where people come to dance to rock 'n' roll, yet the overall vibe is closer to that of an upscale supper club. Great attention has been paid to re-creating the refined continental atmosphere of the Champs Elysées, or at least the way most Americans might imagine it. Dark red velvet is the fabric of choice, draping the walls, tables, and any other immovable surface to which it can be attached. Gold paint finds a home on the cornices, the fixtures, even the ashtrays. Crystal abounds. As Valentine likes to say during guided tours, in press releases, and occasionally in his sleep: "This is a classy joint."

The clientele matches the venue. It's a well-heeled crowd, con-spicuously populated with the kind of people who make things happen in this town. Most of the men wear sharply tailored suits. Evening gowns and designer skirts adorn the ladies, many of whom smoke from elegant cigarette holders and apply lipstick between sips of greyhounds, gimlets, and other potables preferred by the Southern Californian upper crust.

In a word, the crowd is *respectable*.

But that doesn't stop them from dancing with the reckless zeal of true believers in the redeeming power of rock 'n' roll. Johnny Rivers works them up like a master, picking precisely the right moment to switch from ready-steady Motown covers to a breakneck medley of "La Bamba" and "Twist and Shout." The stuttering opening chords raise the roof and the Whisky A-Go-Go comes to life as a single unruly organism. It's a blur of dancing, cocktails, laughter, and sex appeal. High above it all, Patty Brockhurst casts a sultry spell with her improvised performance of pure caged heat.

This is a heady scene for 1964, and Elmer Valentine is clearly right at home. The man has an uncanny sense of direction in his own club; he navigates his way across the dance floor like an Apache scout tracking a runaway mare, always finding an open pocket and stepping into it without disrupting the rhythm of the people around him.

Cary Grant follows closely behind, admiring Valentine's facility at surfing the controlled chaos. Grant draws thrilled glances from all sides, but he's hardly the only celebrity in attendance. Just a few feet from the stage, Ann-Margret is on the verge of shimmying right out of her taffeta gown, an eventuality that looks like it might start a small riot. Johnny Carson is doing the twist with not one, but two, aspiring starlets whose careers in Hollywood will be a series of disappointments after tonight. Carson focuses on one young lovely for a few beats before spinning on his heel to groove with the other, keeping his turns frequent enough so that neither has a chance to feel neglected.

Elmer Valentine and Cary Grant finally arrive at a cluster of red Naugahyde booths forming a crescent around the lip of the dance floor. Tabletop candles offer glimpses of the faces huddled close by: some raptly focused on the band, others striking poses and hoping to be noticed. All of them look deeply satisfied with the knowledge that they are sitting at what is beyond doubt the hippest set of coordinates on the globe at this particular moment.

Valentine and Grant take a seat in the one empty booth. A waiter appears bearing a tray of fresh martinis, and Grant accepts his with gratitude.

"Hats off, Elmer," he says, raising his glass in a toast. "I don't think it's too early to call your venture a smashing success."

"I'll drink to that."

Their glasses clink. A pompadoured mountain of a doorman decked out in a velour monkey suit muscles his way over. He leans down to whisper in Valentine's ear. Valentine listens intently, nodding as he processes the information. Suddenly he's back on his feet.

"Excuse me a moment, will you?" he says with a rueful look at Grant.

"Another cigarette girl showing hidden talents?"

"I wish. Seems John Q. Law isn't happy with the line outside."

"Why not let them in?" Grant asks, holding a hand over his brow in a sort of salute. "I think I spy a few free inches in the far corner."

"Fire code violations. We're about fifty bodies over as is."

Grant shakes his head with mock reproach. "Only a few hours into your first night and already a neighborhood threat. Kudos."

Valentine walks away with the doorman. He's gone less than two seconds before a slender young thing with almond-shaped eyes peering out from under a towering bouffant slips into his vacated seat. Grant treats the girl to both barrels of the famed cleft chin and flawless smile. She blinks shyly. He casually pushes

Valentine's abandoned martini across the table and lights her cigarette with a monogrammed gold lighter, just as you'd expect Cary
Grant to do.

On the way to the front door, Valentine passes the bar, jammed
three deep with people waiting for drinks. Suede-skinned George
Hamilton pauses long enough while hitting on a ponytailed Sandra
Dee to slap Valentine on the back and offer some hearty congratula-
tions. Valentine can't make out what he says, but he acknowledges
Hamilton with a wave.

The doorman pauses at the entrance and takes a deep breath
before pushing on the door, as if to brace himself before facing
what awaits him on the other side. Valentine nods impatiently. The
front door swings opens to reveal a well-formed line of anxious
faces filling the narrow sidewalk that runs along Sunset. All are
dressed to the nines, wearing scowls in addition to their best
evening finery. None are on the guest list, nor did they arrive early
enough to talk their way in before the after-dinner rush. They are
uniformly well-behaved, but clearly less than pleased with their
current outsider status.

Two uniformed LAPD officers are holding the crowd of have-
nots at bay. Valentine shakes their hands cordially. "Evening, fellas.
What's the beef?"

The older of the two cops introduces himself. "Lieutenant
Gibson. I wanted to confirm that you wouldn't be letting anyone
else in tonight so we can send these folks home and clear the
sidewalk."

Valentine looks pained. "Well, shit. I'd love to let them *all* in,
but we're pretty well booked."

"That's what I thought," Gibson says. "Sorry to bother you."

He turns to share the unwelcome news with the crowd, but
Valentine lays a hand on his shoulder first.

"Tell ya what, I'd hate for them to go home empty-handed. How about I send out a few trays of drinks?"

Lieutenant Gibson, who has until now been regarding Valentine with a modicum of respect, gives him a look that a schoolteacher might reserve for an especially dim child. "You can't vend alcohol on the sidewalk, Mr. Valentine. I'd kind of expect you to know that."

Valentine lets it roll off his back. "Okay, fine. You've got a job to do."

The younger cop starts to clear out the crowd. Valentine steps closer to the lieutenant and lowers his voice. "What kind of beer you drink?"

Gibson pauses before answering. "Miller. When I'm off duty."

Valentine slaps the back of his hand against the doorman's chest. "Load a case of Miller into the lieutenant's car."

Gibson shakes his head, smiling. "That won't be necessary."

"My pleasure. I know how tough your job is, believe me."

Another pause, shorter than the last. "Have him carry it out the back. I'll pull around."

The doorman disappears back inside the club, leaving Valentine to deal with the heat and the crowd.

"Glad we're getting off to a friendly start, Lieutenant. I have a feeling we'll be seeing a lot of each other."

"Most clubs on the Strip shut their doors about six months after they open 'em," Gibson says, a good-natured taunt in his voice.

Valentine is as placid as ever. "I plan on sticking around a while."

They shake hands, and Gibson assists his somewhat over-whelmed partner in dispersing the crowd. Valentine stands outside for a few minutes, reveling in the intense interest his creation has generated. And it's only the first night! It promises to be a good year. Finally, Valentine turns away from the street with a shrug, looking genuinely disappointed to have turned away paying customers. Well-dressed ones, at that.

He steps inside the club, pulling the heavy black door behind him. And, with that, the Whisky takes its first small step toward earning a reputation as the most exclusive nightclub on the West Coast.

Paris Comes to America

Before that now-historic night of January 15, 1964, the club scene in the United States was facing a crisis. The champagne bucket–style lounge clubs that had dominated the 1940s and '50s were slowly dying along with the buttoned-down paranoia of McCarthyism.

Suddenly, from Greenwich Village to Hollywood, smaller folk clubs were starting to pop up with artists strumming a new brand of soul-searching, politically driven acoustic music. Rock 'n' roll was gaining momentum, and the big rooms and even bigger money of Las Vegas were beginning to hoard all of the country's most successful acts.

It was at this time in 1963 that Elmer Valentine, then co-owner of a moderately successful Los Angeles nightclub called PJ's, decided to re-evaluate his career choice.

A handsome, middle-aged transplant from the tough side of Chicago, Elmer had been a self-declared corrupt cop—AKA "captain's man"—who earned extra money moonlighting as a club manager for some of Chicago's most notorious mobsters. But, after narrowly avoiding a conviction on an extortion charge, Elmer had left Chicago and his failing marriage to start a new existence in the sunshine of Los Angeles.

He quickly put his nightclub expertise to use in L.A., starting a modest restaurant/lounge called PJ's, after his favorite New York pub. However, after achieving a small measure of fame and success when singer Trini Lopez's live album *Trini Lopez at PJ's* hit the American charts, Elmer cashed out.

Not entirely certain his fate was in Los Angeles, Elmer decided to move to France, open an American-style café, and enjoy the bohemian expatriate lifestyle. Little did he know, however, just how short this move to France would be. Late one night, soon after his arrival in Paris, Elmer chanced upon a popular new discothèque playing rock 'n' roll music. It was called the Whisky A Go-Go.

"They had these kids, young people, dancing like you wouldn't believe," says Elmer. "So I came back to Los Angeles and I wanted to open a discothèque. I wanted that badly 'cause I saw what was happening—the frenzy and the people and the lines."

So Elmer moved back to Los Angeles and, along with three minority business partners—Phil Tanzini, Ted Flier, and Shelly Davis—invested twenty thousand dollars into the refurbishing of a failing club called the Party, located in the former Bank of America building at the west end of the Sunset Strip. It was to be a slice of racy French culture in the heart of conservative America. He renamed it the Whisky A Go-Go.

Go-Go Girls

Importing ideas straight from the original Whisky in Paris, the new Whisky A Go-Go was designed as an upscale supper club featuring a large dance floor, a stage for a band, and a DJ booth.

Unfortunately, because of the club's relatively small size, there was little room for the booth. To solve this dilemma, Elmer struck upon the ingenious idea of rigging a cage with garishly painted bars that could be mounted and suspended over the dance floor. This led to another ingenious idea—that the cage should hold a beautiful female DJ.

Pouncing on the marketing potential, Elmer orchestrated a city-wide contest for this new female DJ position. Ironically, the winner of this contest failed to show up on opening night, so Elmer had to quickly give the position out to a sexy but shy cigarette girl named Patty Brockhurst.

"She had on a slit skirt, and we put her up there," says Elmer. "So she's up there playing the records. She's a young girl, so while she's playing 'em, all of a sudden she starts dancing to 'em! It was a dream. It worked."

In fact, Patty Brockhurst's hip-shaking was such a hit that night that she was given the position permanently. Within a week, Elmer added two more cages to be filled by what he now termed "go-go girls."

Elmer recalls actor and soon-to-be regular James Mason's reaction to first seeing the dancers:

"I remember this exactly," says Valentine, starting to imitate Mason's English accent. "He said, 'Oh, my gosh—how those girls jiggle so much with their titties while they're dahhn-cing.'"

But not everyone in L.A. was thrilled with Elmer Valentine's visionary endeavor. *Los Angeles Times* columnist Paul Coates promptly declared the end of an era. The headline read: SUN HAS SET ON THE SUNSET STRIP. Coates went on to write about the salad days when Hollywood royalty such as Humphrey Bogart, Jimmy Cagney, and Robert Mitchum partied hard "but with class" in the upscale clubs along Sunset. Coates also noted how they went to see "respectable" jazz acts like Joe E. Lewis, Sophie Tucker, and Pearl Bailey.

But, by 1964, according to Coates, what you were more likely to find was "a gaunt little lass doing a frantic Watusi or whatever it is they're doing currently." He further wrote, "It used to be a glittering boulevard in the silly old days. Now it is just a rather seamy street."

Indeed, rock 'n' roll did attract an entirely new segment of the population to the once exclusive Strip. But the Strip had been in a state of decline before the Whisky arrived. With this new offering of live rock 'n' roll, it was once again becoming a bustling and prosperous mecca for Hollywood nightlife.

Johnny Rivers

Two stars were actually born the night the Whisky A Go-Go opened its doors back in 1964. One was, of course, the Whisky, and the other was its opening-night act, Johnny Rivers.

Born John Ramistella on November 7, 1942, Rivers was a skinny, pompadoured white kid who had grown up in a predominantly black, extremely poor section of Baton Rouge, Louisiana.

"We weren't poor," says Rivers. "We were double poor."

Having learned to play guitar and mandolin at the age of eight by emulating his father, Rivers quickly discovered that copying the rural blues music native to the area made him popular around the neighborhood. Studying and learning the songs of his new musical heroes—B. B. King, Fats Domino, and Ray Charles, among them—his musicianship steadily improved, and, by age thirteen, he was earning money playing blues covers in local groups.

At age fourteen, he had saved enough money to finance his own summer trip to Nashville, where he found work as a studio musician. After graduating from high school in 1958, Rivers decided to move to Nashville permanently, where he quickly landed a dream job playing demo tracks for Elvis Presley and Johnny Cash.

But it was a trip to New York later that year that would decide Rivers's career path once and for all. It was there that he met legendary DJ Alan Freed, who took a liking to him and came up with the catchy moniker "Johnny Rivers." Freed also helped Rivers land a recording contract with Gone Records, which resulted in Rivers's first single, "Baby Come Back."

After catapulting this success into a position as a staff writer for the famed Hill and Range Songs music publisher, Rivers composed "I'll Make Believe," which was recorded in 1958 by teen heartthrob Ricky Nelson.

But chart success and subsequent financial success eluded Rivers, despite his streak of good fortune. Considering his options, Rivers decided it was time to save up his publishing earnings and make a move. In 1960, he set out for Los Angeles.

Once in L.A., Rivers spent the next three years hopping from label to label, recording a battery of tunes with little success. He was even groomed to become a teen heartthrob by Chancellor Records, home of teen superstars Frankie Avalon and Fabian, but this also failed.

Finally, after seeing stardom greet several of his friends, including the young Neil Sedaka and Jackie DeShannon, fate smiled on Rivers in the most unlikely of places.

It was one night late in 1963 that Rivers received an unusual proposition from Bill Gazzarri, then the owner of a small Italian restaurant/lounge in West Hollywood named Gazzarri's. The jazz trio Gazzarri had booked for a three-night stint had suddenly backed out, and he desperately needed someone to fill in at the last minute.

According to Rivers:

"Gazzarri said to me, 'You're a musician, why don't you come in here and play for a few nights?' I said, 'I don't play jazz. I'm a rock 'n' roll musician, I play the blues. I don't think you want that in here while people are eating.' But Gazzarri said, 'I don't care, just help me out until I can find another jazz band. Come in here and play anything.'"

So that's exactly what Johnny Rivers did.

Grabbing his electric guitar and the opportunity to play live rock 'n' roll, Rivers called his drummer friend, Eddie Rubin, and the two men set up their instruments at Gazzarri's. Playing without any rehearsal, they went straight to the songs they knew best and improvised upbeat versions of some of their favorite old blues tunes, as well as some popular Chuck Berry, Fats Domino, and Ray Charles covers.

What happened after that was pure magic.

As commonplace as live rock 'n' roll may be in the clubs of the twenty-first century, in the winter of 1963, it was unheard of. At the time, rock 'n' roll had been deemed a phenomenon for the *American Bandstand* teenybopper generation—in other words, unsuitable for the more mature nightclub scene, which relied on liquor sales for profit. Rivers proved just how wrong this assessment was.

That first night, Johnny Rivers was a hit with the crowd. The second night, the club was packed. By the third night, there were lines stretching around the block waiting for a chance to get in to see this live rock 'n' roll.

In a mere three nights, Johnny Rivers, with just an electric guitar and a drummer, had single-handedly turned Gazzarri's from a mellow Italian supper club into a bona fide word-of-mouth hotspot.

As Lou Adler, a then very young music-industry operator and new acquaintance of Elmer Valentine, recalls:

"When I first saw Rivers [at Gazzarri's], part of what interested me was the audience that I saw. They were adults dancing to rock 'n' roll—people in sports coats and ties. That showed the audience was getting really broad."

Elmer Valentine also witnessed the Rivers phenomenon at Gazzarri's:

"Johnny was like the Pied Piper. People were waiting in line to go in and dance. When I saw that, I said, I gotta get this guy."

That's exactly what Elmer did. Convinced by his new friend Lou Adler that Rivers was more than just a fly-by-night success, Valentine took a gamble and made Johnny Rivers an offer he couldn't refuse.

As Rivers recalls:

"Elmer Valentine said to me, 'You know, I've got a chance to purchase that club the Party up on Sunset. If you'll sign up with me for a year, we'll take over the Party and change the name to the Whisky A Go-Go. But we want you to play three sets per night. We are also going to play records during your set breaks to keep the people dancing. Let me know if you are interested and we'll sign a deal.'"

Needless to say, Rivers was interested and quickly accepted a full-year contract to be the marquee act at the brand-new Whisky A Go-Go, earning several times what he was being paid at Gazzarri's.

For Valentine, the gamble paid off. And then it paid off some more. And then some more.

From opening night on, the Whisky was a phenomenon and Johnny Rivers was the star attraction. With scantily clad go-go girls dancing and spinning records in between Rivers's sets, the club was sold out virtually every night that first year.

News of the club and its infectious boogie beat stretched from coast to coast. Within six months, the club was the subject of the cover story for *Life* magazine.

The biggest names in entertainment flocked to the club—from Cary Grant to Johnny Carson to the Beatles.

As Johnny Rivers recalls:

"I remember the Beatles coming and the Stones and Bob Dylan. And I didn't recognize half the celebrities. People'd say, 'That was Gina Lollobrigida dancing out there and Steve McQueen.'"

And Johnny Rivers's career hit unprecedented heights. His 1964 album *Johnny Rivers Live at the Whisky A Go Go* remained high on the charts for forty-five consecutive weeks with three gold singles; in fact, Rivers was soon considered one of the few American challengers to the Beatles. Spurred on by this success, Johnny Rivers would go on to sell more than twenty million albums in his career.

Lou Adler

By all appearances, Johnny Rivers was the first beneficiary of the platinum pixie dust that seemed to be sprinkled on every performer at the Whisky in the 1960s. However, look more closely, and it becomes apparent that the now legendary Lou Adler, the man Elmer trusted to help book the club in its early days, simply had an absolutely unprecedented ear for talent.

Having connected with Valentine and the Whisky while still barely thirty years old, Adler was already well on his way to making his mark on the new L.A. music scene.

A handsome charmer toughened by his impoverished East L.A. upbringing, Adler began his career as co-manager (along with Herb Alpert) of the California surf group Jan and Dean. He also cowrote (again with Alpert) such classics as Sam Cooke's "Wonderful World" and "Only Sixteen" and then founded the phenomenally successful Dunhill Records.

Earning his reputation as a playboy, he routinely showed up at clubs and parties with the likes of Ann-Margret and the beautiful Shelley Fabares, whom he later married, of *Donna Reed Show* fame.

All of this must have deeply impressed Elmer Valentine, a notorious womanizer in his own right because, from the start, what Adler said went at the Whisky. So, when Adler suggested that the Whisky begin booking some of the rising folk bands, ones that attracted a less-than-buttoned-down clientele, Valentine quickly agreed.

THE GREAT UNWASHED

July 23, 1965

Milwaukee Phil can't believe his eyes. He can't really be seeing what he thinks he's seeing. It's got to be a trick of the light. Or maybe just a gag. God knows it isn't funny, but who can say what passes for humor in the minds of these Southern California fruitcakes?

On this, his first night at the Whisky A Go-Go, Milwaukee Phil has already witnessed more than enough to confirm every dirty suspicion he's ever held about this godforsaken West Coast and the people who inexplicably choose to live here. That they are all doomed to perdition for their libertine ways was never in question, at least not in Phil's mind. But he had no idea just how depraved life in this modern-day Gomorrah really is.

Milwaukee Phil hopes what he's looking at is a joke, but a dull gnawing at the center of his gut tells him it isn't. He can't quite process the information that travels from his eyeballs to his weary, bourbon-soaked brain. It just doesn't add up.

There's no fuckin' way that's a man, Phil thinks to himself. I simply do not believe that person has a cock and balls.

Phil takes a two-gulp hit off his glass of Maker's Mark and

impatiently signals for a refill. The gesticulating makes him uncomfortable. He's accustomed to verbally calling out for beverage service or simply clapping his oily, manicured paws. The ear-shattering noise level in the Whisky tonight makes such methods of communication impossible. So Phil swings both arms as broadly as the tight tailoring of his sharkskin suit will allow. Finally convinced he's transmitted his message to an attentive waiter, Phil turns his gaze back to the apparition that has so unpleasantly held his attention for the past twenty minutes.

Which happens to be a waifish teen dancing with almost lunatic abandon up by the stage. Ostensibly male, spinning 'round and 'round like a top in the hands of a demented child, this androgynous creature seems to be occupying its own private planet. Head thrown back, unshorn locks whipping through the air, eyes shut, s/he is clearly having a hell of a time.

This is the first time Phil has seen a hippie up close. It's a nauseating experience. Before he set foot on the West Coast, he tended to dismiss the stories he heard about young men in California with shoulder-length hair as tall tales, like sightings of that sea monster in Scotland. At best, such accounts had to be wild exaggerations. Surely the unkempt coifs of those limey faggolas the Beatles represented the endpoint of subversively effeminate fashion acceptable in the Western world today.

But no. Tonight's encounter has proven all the stories to be true. And then some.

Meanwhile, what about the "music" being played tonight? The sonic jumble he's listening to is closer to auditory insanity than anything he would recognize as music. Such is Phil's critique of the Byrds, though he hasn't even bothered to learn the band's name.

Up on the stage, the Byrds crank through a mind-bending version of their enormously popular proto–drug anthem "Eight Miles

High." Frontman Roger McGuinn commands the room, howling out lyrics of alienation and transcendence that are received either as manna or gibberish, depending primarily on the age of the listener. At forty-three, Phil is hardly the target audience. But if he thinks the Byrds's music is garbage, he is almost certainly alone in that opinion tonight. Most of the people who have come to hear these electrified folk rockers seem to be die-hard fans. Almost everyone in the club is under the age of twenty-five.

This is not the A-list Tinseltown assemblage that showed up for the Whisky's opening night less than two years ago. Not by a long shot. This crowd is younger, rawer, and more fanatically devoted to the music. They are also a lot less concerned with personal hygiene than the audiences of days past. Clearly, a cultural shift has taken place.

Flustered, Phil turns to his companion, Shelly Davis, who sits across the table from him. A minority owner of the Whisky, Davis has been handed by default the task of entertaining Milwaukee Phil on his three-day trip to Los Angeles. Technically, Elmer Valentine should be playing the role of tour guide. But Elmer has been missing in action since last night. There's been no answer at his home phone all day, and, when Shelly dispatched a busboy to drive out to his house, he found it dark and empty. Shelly could worry about where his partner is right now, but he's not. Given Elmer's rather *eccentric* (to be diplomatic) behavior of late, Shelly is quite convinced that no foul play has befallen the founder of the Whisky A Go-Go. If he had to put odds on it, Shelly would wager Elmer is either lost in a dope haze or balls-deep in some curvaceous teeny-bopper right about now.

On the other side of the booth, Milwaukee Phil points to the androgynous hippie on the dance floor. "What the fuck *is* that?!" he bellows.

Shelly Davis pretends he can't hear. Holding a hand to his ear to imply deafness, he just shrugs and turns his eyes back to the stage. Davis has been trying to focus on the band all night, but his attention keeps being stolen by the antsy fidgeting of his guest. It burns Shelly up. The Byrds have been widely touted as the hottest live act to take the Strip by storm since Johnny Rivers, and he's been waiting all week to see for himself.

Much to Phil's chagrin, it's impossible to escape the distorted power chords of the Byrds as they switch from "Eight Miles High" to a deafening rendition of their biblically inspired ballad "Turn, Turn, Turn!" His ears throbbing painfully with each beat, Phil feels like he's been relegated to a dark pit of hell. At the very least, he's a long way from home.

In spite of his nickname, Phil hails not from the hometown of the Brewers, but from Chicago. Though he was born Felix Alderisio, everyone remotely connected to both the Illinois underworld and the FBI knows him as Milwaukee Phil. He earned the name about ten years ago, according to legend, when he whacked a stoolie at the behest of legendary mob boss Tony "Big Tuna" Accardo.

It was supposed to be no different than the two dozen murders Alderisio already had to his credit as one of the Chicago Outfit's most prolific hit men during the 1950s. Standard rub-out job. But it ended up requiring a two-day road trip that reached its grisly con-clusion in a fleabag hotel in downtown Milwaukee. The veteran trig-ger man was so pissed off at having to expend such effort that he literally filled the pigeon's gut with lead, unloading a staggering total of eighteen slugs into the man's torso. Upon returning to Chicago and relating the incident to the Big Tuna in stomach-churning detail, Alderisio was dubbed "Milwaukee Fill." Greatly pleased by the moniker, he changed the second half to "Phil," and the name stuck. That's one version of the story, anyway. As with many gangland biographies, it's probably at least partly apocryphal, but few would dare to challenge its veracity within Phil's earshot.

Ah, the good old days. Sitting in the Whisky's Naugahyde booth, Phil thinks about all the things he would gladly trade to be back in Sweet Home Chicago right now, sipping a real drink (not this watered-down insult) in some classy joint along East Lake Shore Drive and listening to the soothing sounds of a genuine artist like Dean Martin instead of this headache-inducing hippie crap. Alas, Phil has business out here and won't be able to catch a plane back east for at least another day or two.

He flew out this morning at the request of Elmer Valentine, an old contact from the Windy City. Though he counts Elmer as a friend, Phil immediately regretted saying yes. The two men were pretty tight during Elmer's days as a captain's man, often frequenting the same swanky establishments and chasing the same perfumed women. How much Elmer knew of Phil's line of work is the kind of topic that was never openly addressed in Chicago. In all likelihood, he probably didn't *want* to know too much. Knowledge could be a death sentence in certain circles on the South Side. So Elmer chose to just throw back the occasional drink with Milwaukee Phil and refrain from asking any stupid questions. They'd had their share of good times.

So, when Phil got the call from Elmer asking if he'd mind coming out to the coast for a weekend, he felt compelled to comply. Apparently Elmer had been getting some heavy pressure from rival club owner Bill Gazzarri about the booking rights to some of the more in-demand bands. Gazzarri, no stranger to the underworld himself, called in some muscle to add leverage to his position. Not wanting a turf war, but also not willing to be intimidated, Elmer decided that maybe his old pal Milwaukee Phil should come out and have a little chat with Gazzarri. No violence per se, just the very explicit threat of it. That should be enough to smooth things out. There was plenty of musical talent to go around on the Strip, if only everyone was willing to share.

Swallowing his distaste for all things Californian (based solely on the music of the Beach Boys and *Gidget* movies), Phil got on a plane at O'Hare and starting drinking with grim determination minutes after takeoff. In spite of his nonstop self-medication, he's been on edge ever since touching down in L.A. Everything about this place bothers him. The palm trees look fake. He's constantly sweating under the tireless sun. All the people seem so fucking healthy. It's awful.

As the Byrds continue to grind away with ever-increasing volume, Phil eyes Roger McGuinn with ever-increasing hostility. The little prick isn't even singing up there, he's fucking *screaming*. Phil's heard one-eyed alley cats that carried a better tune. Still, he has to admit that all the young tail in here tonight—and there's a king's ransom of it—seems to go for the act. They're packed up against the edge of the stage, oozing availability in the direction of McGuinn and his ill-groomed cohorts.

Big deal, Phil thinks angrily. They wouldn't be so impressed if a real man got his hands on him. The little creep's head would crack like a ripe melon with one well-placed kick. Then he'd really have something to scream about. Phil indulges in this pleasant fantasy for a few moments. As he pictures McGuinn's floppy purple shirt being doused with the singer's own gore, Phil unconsciously uses a finger to stir the ice cubes floating in his glass of Maker's Mark. Where the hell is Elmer?

And then things start to look up. The Byrds wind down their fuzzed-out jam and take a collective bow. The show appears to be over. Phil takes the opportunity to grill Shelly Davis.

"Where is he?"

Shelly reacts coolly. He's not intimidated by Phil, though that's only because he has no idea what he does for a living. "I'm as surprised as you, Phil. He should've been here an hour ago."

Phil stirs uneasily in the booth. "Fuckin' rude is what it is. Guy asks you to travel halfway across the fuckin' country, you fuckin' *be there* when he shows up."

"I couldn't agree more."

"So where *is* he? Any ideas?"

Davis has his ideas, but he doesn't feel like voicing them. "Tell you what," he says, standing. "Just relax for a few minutes. I'll send over another drink."

Immediately, Phil is on his feet. "Where the fuck *you* goin'?"

"Gonna run up to the office. Elmer might have left a note. I'll place a few calls and try to track him down."

Thinking he's made his case, Shelly steps out of the booth. He's dismayed to see Milwaukee Phil following close behind.

"I'm coming with you," Phil says in a tone that allows for no rebuttal. "Could've thought of this two hours ago, for Christ's sake."

Letting that slide, Shelly navigates to the rear of the crowded club and up the narrow stairway that leads to the second floor. After walking down a low-lit hallway, he enters an unpainted door at the far end.

The room is shrouded in darkness. Fumbling his hand across the wall, Shelly finally locates the light switch and flicks it on. Milwaukee Phil is nonplussed by what he sees. The executive offices of the Whisky A Go-Go are confined to an unpainted box of a room. It's small, cluttered, and thoroughly unimpressive. So, Phil thinks as they step inside, this is the inner sanctum of the most profitable nightclub in the United States.

Indeed, this is where the decisions are made, the deals brokered, and the careers launched. It's not exactly what he pictured.

First of all, the room absolutely *reeks* of pot. A collective exhalation seems to hang in the air, permeating the office with a THC-rich haze. Concert posters from some of the bigger recent shows paper the walls. Disorderly piles of documents are scattered across the floor. A small landfill's worth of empty bottles appears to be holding up the west wall.

Shelly starts rifling through some papers on the desk. He's not really looking for anything; the story about coming up here to find a note from Elmer was just bullshit to shake Phil. But now that he's being watched by the beady-eyed hit man who stands guarding the doorway, Shelly has no choice but to go through with the pantomime.

Just as Shelly is ready to shrug and say they're out of luck, Phil is shoved roughly from behind. Losing his footing, he falls painfully to one knee. An unruly parade of a half-dozen people comes charging into the office. They are hippies, one and all, five of the six being teenage girls in various states of groovy undress. The leader of the pack, a plump man with long, bushy hair, wearing love beads and flared suede bellbottoms, is the one responsible for inadvertently decking Phil. He leans down to help the sputtering gangster to his feet, muttering apologies.

Phil grabs him by his floral-patterned shirt and thrusts him up against the wall. "Watch where you're goin', hippie!" he screams.

The bushy-haired dude neither apologizes nor shows the slightest trace of fear. He only coughs faintly.

Milwaukee Phil is stunned to be staring into the face of Elmer Valentine.

"Ayyy," Elmer drawls casually, as a wide smile breaks free. "Who the fuck let *you* in here?"

Phil's too stunned to offer a prompt reply. The past eighteen months have made quite an impact on his old friend. Elmer's rough

Chicago exterior has been baked to a smooth softness by the Southern California sun. Abandoning his crisply tailored suits and wingtips for baggy pastels and sandals, letting his hair grow as it pleases, he seems to be a different person entirely. In place of the slick captain's man who commanded the respect of some of the South Side's scarier characters, Phil finds himself looking at a grinning, disheveled, middle-aged hipster who is obviously stoned out of his gourd.

"No way," Milwaukee Phil says finally. "There's no fuckin' way."

Richly amused by his old pal's astonishment, Elmer laughs and chucks him on the arm.

"Whassamatter, man? Got a turd in your pocket?"

Phil is sweating freely. Beads form on his brow and trickle south. "I *know* this is a fuckin' gag," he sputters. "Who put you up to it? Benny Bags? Sammy the Fish?"

"Okay, relax," Elmer says in his mellowest voice.

No sooner does he lay a hand on Phil's shoulder than it's knocked away like it belongs to a leper. Everyone in the room freezes. Outbursts of anger are anathema to the laid-back vibe that dominates the Whisky and its youthful patronage. Phil has broken a basic tenet of hippie decorum, and no one seems quite sure how to react.

"Forget 'relax!'" Phil barks. Out of instinct, his hand falls upon the snub-nosed .38 sitting securely in its shoulder holster. "I want answers."

One of Elmer's girls, a rail-thin gypsy with Day-Glo flowers painted on her cheeks, steps squarely into Phil's personal space and tells him that the only answers worth seeking are those found within oneself. Phil stiff-arms her away, hard enough to send her skull into a lacerating collision with the door.

The jolt of unexpected violence sobers Elmer up, pronto. As the girl clutches the back of her head in pain, Elmer briskly shoos her and the others out of the office. Then he turns to face Phil. Suddenly remembering what kind of creature he's dealing with, Elmer implores the apoplectic hit man to take a seat and hear him out.

It takes much of the night for Elmer to convince Milwaukee Phil that he is not the victim of an elaborate, cross-country practical joke perpetrated by his goombah buddies back home. Elmer's new look is just too ridiculous to be believed. For Phil, a person with an extremely closed worldview, it's a tremendous shock to see someone he thought he knew so radically transformed. All the more so because it's obvious Elmer's metamorphosis is not just skin-deep.

Valentine is no longer the razor-sharp businessman he was when he left Chicago. Continual exposure to loud music, a mild climate, sexually adventurous girls, and good drugs are bound to take the edge off a man. And the Whisky has started to suffer as a result. No major crises, just a series of small oversights. For example, this recent blowup with Bill Gazzarri that Phil has come out to fix; it could easily have been avoided if Elmer had been paying closer attention to his own club's booking policy.

Deep down, he knows he's at fault. It's clear, even to him, that the nuts-and-bolts operations of running the Whisky are probably better left to someone else. Though he would never use such an inflated term to describe himself, Elmer is a visionary. His strength lies in identifying promising possibilities and breathing life into them. Strict intendance of nightclub management (maintaining permits, balancing the books, stocking the bar, paying the bands, etc.) simply isn't his strong suit.

Thankfully Elmer is still sharp enough to realize that part of being a successful leader is knowing when to delegate. He knows just the right man to manage the club, an old friend from the Chicago police force who moved out here just months ago. As Elmer guides Milwaukee Phil back downstairs for a badly needed double shot of bourbon, he makes a mental note to call Mario Maglieri first thing Monday morning.

In the end, the business dispute with Bill Gazzarri will be settled without a drop of blood spilled. A simple sit-down is all it takes. After three torturous days in Los Angeles, leavened only by a brief and frenetic liaison with a shapely brunette go-go dancer, Milwaukee Phil will lumber back onto a plane at LAX and return to his beloved Chicago with a sense of dazed gratitude. He will resume his prolific career of wiping fellow human beings off the face of the Earth. He will even serve as head of the Chicago Outfit for a brief, turbulent period before being succeeded by the more even-tempered Joseph "Joey Doves" Aiuppa.

For the rest of his days, the last of which are destined to be spent in a federal penitentiary, Milwaukee Phil will relate to people in lurid detail his visit to that fucking lunatic asylum called California. But he will never set foot there again.

The Byrds

By 1965, the meteoric success of the Whisky combined with the "bigger-than-Jesus" arrival of the Beatles in America had every coffeehouse and supper club across the U.S. adding drums and electric guitars to their stages. Beat poets and political activists also started adding "electrified" music to their events to bring in bigger audiences. Even Bob Dylan had plugged in. The revolution was officially underway.

On the front lines of this revolution were Lou Adler and his perfect musical proving ground, the Whisky A Go-Go.

After making a small fortune by recording and producing *Johnny Rivers Live at the Whisky A Go-Go* and its follow-up release *Here We A-Go-Go Again,* Adler was eager to keep his success going by bird-dogging the best of the popular new crop of electric folk bands that were popping up in L.A.

The first of these bands to emerge was a trio called the Jet Set, who had recently moved to L.A. from New York City. Originally composed of Jim McGuinn (who later changed his first name to Roger), Gene Clark, and David Crosby, the group had been a regular on the L.A. coffeehouse circuit, playing a gentle blend of thoughtful, acoustic folk songs for as little as three dollars per night.

"It was kind of a square scene back then," recalls McGuinn. "The music scene in L.A. was not very happening compared to New York. L.A. seemed like a sleepy little town, with the Beach Boys, the radio DJs who talked real slow, and the light radio playlists . . . . There wasn't really any interesting rock 'n' roll happening at that point."

But, struck with the feverish obsession with the Beatles that was sweeping the globe at the time, the group decided to experiment by electrifying their sound and adding a bass player, Chris Hillman, and a drummer, Michael Clarke. To cap it off, the band grew their hair into long, flamboyant Prince Valiant–style hair-dos, à la the Fab Four, and completed the transformation by changing their name to the Byrds.

The formula worked.

In early 1965, the Byrds and their new high-energy act landed a weekly gig on the Sunset Strip playing Ciro's, the onetime legendary (but by that point fading) supper club just up the street from the Whisky. Before long, a steady new mix of beatniks and jazzers started frequenting the formerly coat-and-tie club.

"The scene got pretty wild at Ciro's," says McGuinn. "We had Steve McQueen and Marlon Brando and all kinds of movie stars hanging out there. And we had Zito's gang—they were these artists who lived in East Hollywood. We used to go over to their house before shows and rehearse and take LSD."

One new fan of the band was Benny Shapiro, a music industry executive earning acclaim as Miles Davis's agent. Having recognized the Byrds' originality after seeing them perform at Ciro's, he invited the band over to his house for a private audition.

"Gene Clark, David Crosby, and I sang some songs over a tape recording of backing tracks in Benny's living room," says McGuinn. "We didn't know it, but Benny had his teenage daughter upstairs listening. She was about fourteen or fifteen, and she came running down the stairs going, 'Daddy, Daddy, who's that?' You know, like somebody really cool was in her living room—like the Beatles or something. Well, the next day Miles Davis came over to see Benny, and Benny tells him the story of how his daughter flipped out over us. Miles told Benny that the group must be good, 'because kids know things like that,' and called up Columbia Records right then and told them they should sign us—and they did! So it was Miles Davis who discovered us."

Signed to a major recording house, McGuinn and the band were sent into the studio with Beach Boys producer Terry Melcher, and, in April 1965, the Byrds released their debut single, an electric cover of Bob Dylan's "Mr. Tambourine Man."

By May 1965, "Mr. Tambourine Man" and the Byrds were

number one in America.

Suddenly, the Byrds, with their long hair and strange mix of electric folk music, were stars of an entirely new musical genre—folk rock.

Of course, with this phenomenal success, the Byrds almost instantly outgrew Ciro's. So, after some prodding and courting by a determined Lou Adler, the band made the inevitable move to the hallowed hall up the street.

"The Whisky wouldn't touch us at first," recalls McGuinn. "We couldn't get a job there because we were not established. Johnny Rivers was playing there at the time, and there were a few other acts, but we weren't one of them until we got a hit with 'Mr. Tambourine Man.' And then I remember the Doors opening up for us there."

Hippies Invade the Strip

With Roger McGuinn's experimental sixteen-millimeter film of a lava lamp projected on the back wall, the Byrds' musical set at the Whisky hardly resembled the bombastic, Chuck Berry–style rock 'n' roll that was the hallmark of the Rivers era. This was electric Bob Dylan. But an even more dramatic difference was the audience the Byrds attracted.

No longer was it the well-dressed Hollywood glitterati dancing the Watusi and the frug. Instead, it was a much younger breed of beatniks with long hair and love beads. These hippies took their music very seriously and saw it as a way to inspire political change.

The voice of a new generation was beginning to emerge from the folk rock sound. From all over the country, college-age kids thinking about peace and love and skeptical of the warmongering government were descending upon the Sunset Strip to be near their new musical heroes.

A monumental groundswell soon surrounded the Byrds, and, for the first time, America was given a glimpse into the enormity of the so-called "counterculture movement" that was beginning to take hold.

As Terry Melcher recalls:

"The Byrds were the catalyst—they brought all the kids to the Strip. They took Dylan songs, electrified 'em, rock 'n' rolled 'em, and kids came from everywhere. It just happened. One day you couldn't drive anymore. It was, like, overnight—you couldn't drive on the Strip."

West Hollywood City Councilman Paul Koretz recalls the impact this had on the Strip's longtime residents: "The hippies just sort of drove out most of the fancier restaurants and night-clubs," he says. "That was really the start of the great rock 'n' roll clubs like the Whisky and Gazzarri's and Filthy McNasty's. And literally thousands of hippies all up and down the Sunset Strip."

Barely a year removed from Johnny Rivers's opening night extravaganza, the Whisky A Go-Go was again at the forefront of a new music revolution.

The Mamas and the Papas

If the incredible success of the Byrds in 1965 proved anything to aspiring folk rock stars, it was that the Sunset Strip was the place to make things happen.

One songwriting team particularly interested in what was happening in L.A. was the husband-and-wife duo of John and Michelle Phillips. Old friends of the Byrds who were still living in New York City at the time, they found themselves losing heart as they struggled to earn enough from their music just to eat. However, when the Byrds struck gold with "Mr. Tambourine Man," they knew there was hope. As Michelle Phillips recalls:

"We were astonished the Byrds got a record deal, let alone a hit. We thought, if the Byrds can do it, anyone can."

How true this sentiment turned out to be (at least for them). In August 1965, John and Michelle packed their bags and moved to California.

"We arrived in L.A at the end of the summer of '65," says John Phillips, "and we were living with a friend, three blocks from the Whisky A Go-Go. Elmer was one of the first people we met. He let us in for free, let us stand in the back for a couple of sets. We were nobodies, and we had no bodies we were so starved. Elmer just took a liking to us."

Thanks to a recommendation from their friend Roger McGuinn, John and Michelle Phillips took the stage along with their singing partners Cass Elliot and Denny Doherty in the Whisky's house band warm-up slot. They called themselves the Mamas and the Papas.

Almost instantly, they were a hit with the Whisky's unwashed crowd.

Within a month of this first performance, Lou Adler signed them to his Dunhill Record label and began producing their debut album, *If You Can Believe Your Eyes and Ears*. Less than nine months later, they had two Top Five singles—"Monday, Monday" and "California Dreamin'"—and the Mamas and the Papas' album was number one in the United States.

3

ACID, GRASS, BOOZE, AND THE END

October 2, 1966

"Ohmmmmm." The sound reverberates through the smoky air, slowly dying as the voice behind it runs out of breath.

"Cut that shit out, Ray." John Densmore is leaning against the dressing room door, as if to ward off a marauding army on the other side. Given John's beanpole ninety-eight-pound–weakling frame, it's a laughable proposition.

The Whisky's dressing room is located on the second floor, in a cramped converted loft that sits directly above and behind the stage. On a night like tonight, when the club is packed beyond capacity, the entire room vibrates slightly with the collective body movements and unfulfilled lust of the hordes of paying customers downstairs.

Tonight the vibrations are even heavier than usual. The pressurized atmosphere can be intimidating for artists waiting to storm the Whisky's stage. It makes Densmore, who's wrapped a little too tight even under the best circumstances, extremely nervous.

"Ohmmmmm," repeats keyboardist Ray Manzarek. He sits in the lotus position in the center of the incense-choked dressing room, hands on his knees, palms up. His nubile Japanese wife,

Dorothy, lies on her back with her head in his lap, hands raised high in a yogic pose that lifts her satin top to reveal her tan double-scoop soft-serve breasts to anyone interested enough to take a gander. No one bothers. Pretty much everyone in the Doors has seen their bandmates' old ladies in the raw by now, and they have more urgent matters to consider. Manzarek's eyes are sealed stubbornly shut. If he even heard his drummer's rebuke, he's not letting on.

Densmore turns to Robby Krieger, the trace of a snarl in his voice. "Doesn't that shit bother you, Robby? Tell him to stop."

Krieger, who's been totally absorbed with the process of tuning his Stratocaster for the past ten minutes, barely bothers to glance at Densmore. He just tweaks the tuning knobs and shrugs. "It worked last time. Give it a chance."

"What if it doesn't work this time? I'm not going down there without him. We're lucky they didn't charge the stage."

"What are you worried about, John?" Krieger asks casually. "They can only kill you once."

Densmore's groupie of the moment, a pneumatic brunette with a slight lisp who calls herself Persephone Moonglow (née Weinberger), tries to soothe him with a backrub, but Densmore shakes her off. The clock is creeping up on a quarter to ten on what has already been a rough night for the Doors. They had to fumble through the entire first set without their lead singer, who was hiding under the bed in his room at the Tropicana Motel a half-mile away. The crowd reacted with bored hostility to the instrumental set; they came to see Morrison. The only way the Doors got offstage without violence breaking out was to promise that the entire band would be present for the second set and would deliver the type of performance of which rock legends are made.

The gross amateurism of the experience ties Densmore's stomach in knots. Is this group a skilled outfit worthy of their success or, as some of their more vocal critics have claimed, a quartet of deep-fried acid casualties who can't be counted on to get through a sound check without some sort of chemical implosion? He's still trying to figure it out. Further irritating Densmore is the fact that he's the only one in the band who seems to care.

The Doors have played the Whisky forty or fifty times by now, going back to the spring of '66, when they were the underpaid house band whose sets would be over and done with well before the headliner's traffic started rolling in off the Strip. Back then it was easy to kill time in the dressing room before taking the stage — they'd get high, make claims on bedmates for the night, and generally not be bothered by the slightest case of nerves about their performance. No one was listening, anyway.

Tonight is an entirely different proposition. Though the Doors' eponymous debut album won't steal number one on the U.S. charts for another six months, the band is already a phenomenon. After spending the past few months touring the country, they're back in the cradle of Southern California rock for a triumphant victory lap on their home turf. It should be an exhilarating moment, and it is. But it's also laced with anxiety. Expectations, nonexistent in the old days, now hover in the upper stratosphere. The entire shaggy, denim-clad corps of the L.A. rock press is in attendance. Densmore realizes the only way to ward off career-ending screeches of "hype!" is to blow the lid off each and every person in the Whisky tonight. The drummer knows they have what it takes, but it's already forty-five minutes past their second curtain call. Will the Doors even get a chance to prove themselves?

Manzarek opens his eyes and removes the blissed-out Dorothy from his lap. She seems to have left the room via astral projection, not even noticing as her husband sets her head less than gently on the floor. Uncoiling out of his lotus pose like an anemic python from a wicker basket, Manzarek crawls across the shag carpet on his hands and knees.

His destination is the black leather couch that usually sits against the far wall. It is currently askew, sticking out into the center of the room at a thirty-five-degree angle. The space between the back of the couch and the far wall is a dark, enclosed wedge separated from the lava lamp glow and tension that permeate the rest of the dressing room. It's the farthest possible point from the stage down below. Jim Morrison is using that dark wedge behind the couch as a place to hide.

Front man of the hottest band to come out of L.A. since the Beach Boys, owner of the knee-knocking baritone rumble and Greek god–sculpted features, poster boy of the West Coast poet/rocker crowd, and martyr to hedonism in the making, Morrison is at present curled up against the wall in a drooling fetal ball. His greasy mane falls down in tangles over his chalk-colored face. His eyes are glazed basketballs of dilated shock. Not for the first time, not even the first time this week, he's deep in the throes of lysergic psychosis. And it's showtime.

Manzarek crawls within a few feet of the shell-shocked singer. "Jim? Can you hear me?" Manzarek asks in the mellowest voice he can muster. "It's Ray, Jim. I need to tell you something important."

Across the room, Krieger and Densmore are suddenly all ears, both waiting to hear the magic combination of words that will revive their leader from his deliberately induced vegetative state and save the most important gig of their career from assured disaster.

"How much did he take?" Densmore whispers to Krieger.

Robby can't conceal a look of awe as he makes the tally in his head. "Ahhh . . . about two dozen hits. It was incredible, man."

Morrison has been eating acid like popcorn for going on a year now, but tonight his intake has pushed him into a corner from which performing seems an impossibility. Densmore's fingers are crossed behind his back so Krieger won't mock him for being superstitious. Maybe Ray can pull it off; he's held Jim's hand through a number of near-meltdowns before.

A shudder of Morrison's head seems to suggest Manzarek is getting through. The keyboardist leans in closer. "There's something I want to say to you, Jim. Listen to me very carefully."

Manzarek takes a deep breath, searching for the proper cadence in which to deliver what Densmore hopes is a well-crafted speech of comfort and inspiration.

Manzarek closes his eyes and says, "Ohmmmmm."

"Oh, for Christ's sake!" Densmore almost shouts, kicking over a wastebasket full of empty beer cans and cigarette butts. He pivots toward the exit. "I'm calling it off."

He reaches for the door, but it flies from his grip as someone on the other side gives it a firm pull.

Almost losing his balance, Densmore opens his mouth to berate whoever had the temerity to approach their dressing room uninvited.

Until he sees who it is.

The man on the other side of the doorway is lighting the well-chewed stub of a Romeo y Julieta with a gunmetal lighter acquired in Sardinia during the waning days of World War II. This brand of cigar, along with his pinkie ring and colorful lexicon of incessantly foul language, is one of Mario Maglieri's trademarks. A mushroom cloud of blue smoke encircles Maglieri's head as he revives the cigar. Not until it's relit to his satisfaction does he deign to look up and acknowledge Densmore.

"Gonna invite me in, Johnny, or do I have to fucking kiss you first?"

Densmore steps aside, allowing Maglieri to enter, his cigar fumes trailing behind him. Everyone in the room except for the catatonic Morrison reacts with visible discomfort to his entrance. They all knew this was coming eventually if they failed to get the show going. It was just a matter of time.

In the wake of Elmer Valentine's abdication of daily operations, Maglieri has become the Whisky's hands-on manager. He deals directly with the staff and the talent, continually donning new hats to play the roles of cajoler, provider, enforcer, and occasional skull-cracker. One of his first moves was to relocate his office from the second floor to the ground floor, where he can keep a closer watch over the action. In four years, he will be part owner of this club. Three years after that, he'll have a major stake in the entire ridiculously well-trafficked 9000 block of Sunset, including two more clubs of world renown: the Roxy and the Rainbow Bar and Grill. But right now only two things are on Maglieri's mind: getting his superstar attraction to perform before the crowd turns ugly and keeping his cigar lit.

The man's appearance is striking for its incongruity to everything around him. His tailored pinstripe suit is pressed to perfection; it belongs to another era. His thick salt-and-pepper hair is slicked straight back in a style that hasn't been hip since Sinatra owned the Top Forty. A bushy black mustache makes it hard to tell if he's smiling or grimacing. He's old enough to have fathered everyone in the room, yet would clearly win an arm-wrestling match with any takers. An unmistakable twinkle in his eye belies his displeasure over the present situation.

Maglieri stands with his mirror-shiny loafers sinking into the shag. He puffs furiously, placing the onus of breaking the ice on someone other than himself.

Feeling uncharacteristically bold, Krieger decides to give it a shot. "No need to get uptight, man," the guitarist offers. "We're just about there."

Maglieri wheels on Krieger with unnerving speed.

"Just about there?" Maglieri repeats, savagely mimicking Krieger's nasal stoner twang. Then he shifts into his natural register: prewar South Side Chicago, poured from a cracked whiskey glass. "Just about where, Robby? Don't tell me you're just about ready to be onstage, where you should be, because if you were you wouldn't be jerking off in the fucking dressing room."

Thoroughly defeated, Krieger casts his eyes down and turns his attention back to tuning his six-string.

Maglieri navigates his way across the dressing room floor, careful not to step on any stains that look too fresh. He moves in a measured, unhurried gait. This is a man who never rushes anywhere, least of all inside his own club. People rush to him. Or away from him, depending on the circumstances.

Maglieri looms over the crouching Manzarek, who is still chanting in Morrison's general direction. He gets the keyboardist's attention with an ear-splitting whistle. Manzarek looks up.

"This piece of shit gonna sing tonight or what?" Maglieri asks, jabbing the cigar stub toward Morrison.

Manzarek pulls himself up to a standing position. He's a good three inches taller than Maglieri, but seems to wilt away from him. "I think he's coming out of it. Maybe another twenty minutes . . ."

"Twenty minutes?" Maglieri barks. "You gotta be shitting me. There's a riot in the works down there."

"I'm doing the best I can, Mario. Ten minutes ago I thought we'd have to cancel."

"Is that right?" Maglieri asks, his gravelly voice ripe with sarcasm. Back in goes the cigar. "Lemme steer you straight on something,

Raymond. No one's canceling shit. You cocksuckers are gonna get out and play, or I'm taking a giant dump on all of you."

A quick pause, in consideration of Dorothy and the groupies. "Ladies excepted, of course," Maglieri adds with a small bow. He takes a seat on the couch next to Densmore's chick and pats her bare thigh with his beefy pinkie-ringed hand. She smiles nervously.

"What a fucking night," Maglieri says, shaking his head. "Three fights at the front door already. Every goddamn lunatic in the business is busting my chops for a table. John Lennon's sitting down there with a fucking tampon on his head. Limey prick won't take the thing off—says it keeps his hair from falling out."

No one has a response to that. Densmore is a little stunned. John Lennon is here? Jesus, that's perfect. That's just what they need, to pull a no-show with a Beatle in the crowd. That will really secure the Doors' rep in the upper rungs of the rock hierarchy. Though from what Mario said, it sounds like Lennon might be just as badly twisted as Morrison is. Maybe he won't notice if the gig never happens.

All of a sudden, Morrison lurches to his feet. The sound of Maglieri's voice seems to have set off a tripwire somewhere in the recesses of his brain. Everyone holds their breath to see if Jim has in fact been revived or if it's just a passing flirtation with consciousness. For a few seconds it looks like he's about to face-plant into the glass-topped table Krieger's girl is using to roll some thick Berkeley bombers, but Morrison manages to win the fight with gravity.

The singer barrels across the room and falls in a heap at Maglieri's feet, wrapping his arms like a pair of amorous terriers around the manager's pinstriped left thigh.

"Maurio!" he belches, mispronouncing Maglieri's name as usual.

"Where ya been, Maurio?! We've been waiting for you!"

"You're wrinkling the fabric, asshole! Let go!" Maglieri shoves Morrison away firmly enough to encourage a semblance of composure.

The acid seems to have finally shifted gears. Unburdened of the gut-wrenching paranoia that's gripped him mercilessly for the last hour, Jim is edging back into his spotlight-hogging rock star persona. He claps his hands together in a tribal rhythm, frequently failing to make contact. "Let's go, let's go, let's go!" he squawks. "Music, I said! We gonna make some music!"

"Jesus, kid," Maglieri says, shaking his head. "Let me do you a favor and burn those pants."

Morrison's hands clutch at the striped bellbottoms that have been epoxied to his legs since early spring.

"What?! No way, Maurio! These are my good-luck charm."

"Those things can probably walk around on their own by now. Why don't you take a little pride in your appearance?"

"Like you?" Morrison asks in a smart-ass whine.

"Yeah, that's right, shithead. Like me." Maglieri starts to continue, but gives up with a shrug.

Densmore's grip on himself is disintegrating. He takes a monster hit off the joint proffered by Krieger's girl, ignoring a judgmental eye-fucking from Maglieri. Then he makes another pass at the exit, hoping to impart a sense of finality with his movements. "Okay, Doors," Densmore says in a voice betraying his uncertainty. "Let's show 'em what we're made of."

Amazingly, Morrison actually hears him. He brushes his hair out of his face and nods. "Sure, why not? I can't wait on you guys all night."

A palpable wave of relief rolls through the dressing room as the band makes their final preparations. Krieger slaps Jim on the back as he moves to the exit, Stratocaster slung across his concave chest. "I knew you'd pull it together, man." Morrison smiles and punches him on the arm, hard enough make Krieger lose his footing under the girth of the guitar.

Maglieri is the last person to rise. He's been through preshow shenanigans before, albeit none as egregiously frustrating as tonight. He isn't about to make a move until he's sure the band's departure is for real.

Morrison stops midstep, as if remembering something vital. "You guys go ahead," he says to the band. "I'll catch up in a minute."

Standing in the doorway, Densmore winces like he's been treated to a gut punch. Damn! They were so close. His anguish isn't lost on Morrison, who waves a reassuring hand at him. "It's cool, John. I just need a quick word with the old goat."

Realizing he has no choice but to hope for the best, Densmore allows himself to be pulled out of the room. Morrison and Maglieri are left alone.

"This better be good," the manager grumbles.

Morrison stumbles for words, suddenly the shy adolescent once more. "There's something I've been meaning to tell you. It's been on my mind a long time."

"You've got my attention for three seconds."

Morrison indulges in a pause, stricken with the acidhead's temptation to assign the heaviest profundity to the simplest of thoughts. After testing Maglieri's patience for longer than a sober person might deem wise, Morrison lays a trembling hand on his shoulder.

"I love you, Maurio," he says is a shaky half-whisper. "You're more of a father to me than my old man ever was."

It's impossible to tell if Maglieri is touched or repulsed by this addled declaration; he is a master of the effortless poker face. But he pats Morrison's shoulder in what could be construed as an affectionate manner.

"That's nice, kid. There's something I'd like to say to you, too."

Jim takes a step back, fearing he may not be able to absorb what he is sure will be a reciprocal expression of deep feeling and heretofore unspoken affirmation.

Maglieri pulls on his cigar only to find it has gone dead again. "This is this biggest night of your life, Jim, and I got a stake in it," he says slowly. "Don't fuck it up, or, so help me, you won't get a job chiseling skid marks off the shitters in this joint."

Deliriously amused, Morrison unleashes a hoarse cackle that the older man can't help liking for its childish lack of guile. Maglieri winks at the singer. "Okay, superstar. Knock 'em dead." Relighting his cigar, he watches as Morrison staggers out of the dressing room and into rock 'n' roll history.

At this moment, Maglieri cannot possibly comprehend the oracular precision of his warning. He has no way of knowing that, before another hour passes, he will shut off the stage lights and physically eject Morrison from the building in a hail of screamed curses and fierce kicks to the seat of those crusty bellbottoms with his shiny Italian loafers. Maglieri cannot foresee that tonight will be the last occasion the Doors ever play the Whisky, and at the same time a galvanizing moment in the intertwined histories of both the band and the club.

The New Face of the Whisky

With the indomitable success of the Whisky A Go-Go, the Sunset Strip was entering a new golden era. Though the old mainstays on the Strip—the Mocambo, Ciro's, the Trocadero—were in definite decline, new clubs, hoping to imitate and absorb the overflow of the Whisky's success, were on the rise. Focusing on rock 'n' roll and a much younger clientele, clubs such as the London Fog, Pandora's Box, the Sea Witch, and Sneaky Pete's started popping up on Sunset Boulevard. Even Bill Gazzarri had changed his Italian restaurant into a rock club and relocated it less than three blocks from the Whisky.

For Elmer Valentine, the success called for expansion. So he purchased another building on Sunset and turned it into a tiny but ultrachic rock club called the Trip. But managing the day-to-day operations of one of the most popular pieces of real estate in the U.S. was hardly Elmer's strength or desire.

To keep on top of the overwhelming volume of people and drinks and food being ushered in and out of the front and back doors of his clubs, Elmer called in the services of an old friend and fellow lawman from Chicago.

His name was Mario Maglieri.

Born in Campobasso, Italy, on February 7, 1924, and raised on the mean streets of Chicago, Mario first learned some of the skills necessary to run a successful nightclub while driving a beer truck for Al Capone at the age of sixteen.

After being drafted in World War II, his character was further strengthened by storming the beach in Normandy and taking a bullet to the leg and some shrapnel to the hand. Given a hero's welcome upon returning to Chicago after the war, Mario quickly became reacquainted with his former employer and landed a job as a court bailiff. He also followed the lead of his friend Elmer Valentine by earning extra money moonlighting as a nightclub manager. In fact, he did so well in these two jobs that at age

STRAIGHT WHISKY

twenty-one he was able to open his own club—Mario's Belmont Tap. The success of the Tap led to the opening of Mario's Lounge and, later, Mario's Steakhouse.

By the age of forty, Mario had stockpiled enough money to retire. Wanting to give his children a better life in the year-round sunshine of Southern California, Mario decided to sell his clubs, and, in 1964, move his family to Los Angeles.

But retirement didn't last long. His love of people and passion for the nightclub business made going back to work an easy decision when he received a desperate phone call from his old friend Elmer.

As Mario recalls:

"I was helping a friend of mine set up the Playboy Club down here on Sunset. You know, training bunnies how to dip and all that bullshit they got there. And then Elmer called me one day and said, 'You gotta help me, they're robbing me.' He didn't know how to run a club. So I say, no problem. I go down to the Whisky and I fire everyone in the place. That's how it all started. Suddenly, I was a rock 'n' roller."

Almost instantly, Mario became the new face of the Whisky. Rock historian Sue Schneider, who frequented the club nightly and later worked there, recalls the changing of the guard. "Elmer worked mostly during the day," she says. "He would come down at night and stand and watch what was going on, and then he'd leave. So the whole thing was left in Mario's hands."

Unlike Elmer, who was more interested in playing jovial host each night to the best party in town, Mario was a lovable bruiser who commanded respect with a simple smiling glance or warm hello. A sober family man, Mario patrolled the Whisky each night making sure the staff ran like a finely tuned clock.

The Doors' guitarist Robby Krieger reflects upon his first impression of Mario:

"He was kind of a scary guy, kind of the bouncer type, you know. Head honcho. But a nice guy, once you got to know him. He wasn't very old, but he had gray hair. That slicked-back, gray-hair look, very cool."

Mario was also undaunted by the growing use of marijuana and LSD by the younger generation and made sure the club was a safe haven where "the kids could have their fun":

"People smoke a joint, they relax, no big deal. But if you over-do it, I mean, how many joints can you smoke? One joint is not really gonna kill you. But people love to party. All they wanna do is party. If you say here in Hollywood that there's a party at John Doe's house, you won't get near it. They love to party, that's it, man. Party!"

As it turns out, Mario's brilliant blend of toughness and toler-ance would be the perfect combination to ensure the continued success of the Whisky.

The Doors

In the roughly forty-year history of the Whisky A Go-Go, count-less bands have performed at the club before going on to find fame and fortune on a global scale. Johnny Rivers, the Mamas and the Papas, Frank Zappa, Sonny and Cher, Van Halen, and Motley Crüe, to name a few, each give the club credit for having helped launch their careers. But only one band's name is truly synonymous with the Whisky A Go-Go.

That band is, of course, the Doors.

Formed in Venice, California, in 1965, the Doors were an embodiment of all of the mind-expanding trends of the era, mixing poetic, soul-searching lyrics with electrified jazz and blues explorations. "We were not folk rock," says Doors drummer John Densmore. "We were darker. We would scare people."

But the band's permanent linkage with the famous club is not without a bit of irony. When lead singer Jim Morrison and keyboardist Ray Manzarek met while students at UCLA in 1964, the Whisky A Go-Go with its Watusi-dancing crowd was the absolute last place they ever intended to play.

"The Whisky was for Hollywood swingers," remembers Manzarek. "At UCLA, it was the antithesis of everything artistic that you could imagine. It was slick and Hollywood—a rock 'n' roll version of the Rat Pack."

But, with the coming of the Byrds to the Strip and the counterculture revolution in full swing, the Doors' perspective quickly shifted. Soon they were competing with groups such as Buffalo Springfield, Love, the Young Rascals, and scores of other local bands for a chance to play in one of the Whisky's coveted house band slots.

Created by Elmer Valentine, the house slot was a way of promoting local bands by giving them a chance to warm up for the big-name acts that came through town. Often these house bands became headliners themselves. Two groups that started monumental careers from this humble platform were Buffalo Springfield and Fleetwood Mac.

At first, the Doors had no luck in their pursuit of the house slot and were relegated to grinding out their sets at a copycat bar next door to the Whisky called the London Fog. Although being a regular performer at the London Fog carried with it somewhat of a stigma, the Doors saw it as a way to hone their skills and loosen their inhibitions, so they continued to play there nightly.

"There were seven people total in the club," says Ray Manzarek with a laugh. "But Jesse the bartender kept telling us to play. 'No one will come in if you don't,' he'd say. We used to play four sets a night, which is when we began experimenting with the song structure. That was where we cut our performing teeth."

Eventually, their persistence paid off.

"Fortunately," recalls John Densmore, "an extremely sexy, pixie-voiced blonde named Ronnie Harran, who booked the Whisky, saw us. She had an ear for talent."

Smitten with Jim Morrison, the Doors' handsome frontman, and intrigued by the group's unique sound and lyrics, Harran lobbied her boss, Elmer Valentine, to give the band a shot.

Hesitant at first to allow the house band of the wannabe bar next door play his exclusive club, Elmer finally succumbed to his zealous employee.

"Ronnie said, 'You've gotta put this band in,'" reflects Elmer, "and she told her friends to call and ask for the Doors. Well, I got so many goddamned calls, I put them in!"

What happened next was pure magic. Some might even say black magic. The Doors' mesmerizing sound and poetic lyrics cast a spell on the Whisky's audience, and Jim Morrison's soulful voice and good looks kept the club packed with beautiful women. Within weeks, the Doors were being paid as the regular house band and opening for bands ranging from Van Morrison and the Animals to the Kinks and the Rolling Stones. But as the Doors' popularity grew, so did Morrison's affections for the bacchanalian lifestyle.

"I saw that guy Morrison two or three times a week," recalls Mario Maglieri. "He was always fucked up. Drugs and booze. He drank Jack Daniels like it was going out of style. You know, just a pathetic guy. But Jim was a good kid."

Morrison's belligerent antics became increasingly unpredictable. As Mario remembers:

"Well, I saw Jim Morrison pull his dick out onstage. Big deal, right?" Mario begins to laugh. "That son of a bitch. Too bad he's not alive, I'd give him a spanking. Anyway, he took his pants down to expose himself onstage. I said, 'What the fuck are you doing?'

"Another time I had a black act on," continues Mario, "and he was at the top of the stairs screaming, 'You fucking niggers! Jungle bunnies!' I said 'Jim, what are you doing?' They wanted to kill him. If I was black, I'd probably want to do the same thing. But the Doors, Jim Morrison, I always liked their music. It was like happy music, circus music."

Pamela Des Barres, author of the revealing groupie classic *I'm with the Band* and Morrison's ex-girlfriend, was a frequent witness to Mario and Jim's altercations.

She describes one incident involving Jim grabbing the microphone from the lead singer of another band while the guy was still onstage:

"Mario got on the loudspeaker and said, 'Jim, if you don't stop singing, I'm going to turn off the sound.' Well, at this point, Jim takes the microphone and puts it down the front of his pants, and Mario turns not only the sound but the lights off on this poor band."

She continues, "Mario had so much stuff to deal with like that. Jim was pretty much a major problem, but Mario loved him. He really dealt with Jim with love and fairness."

In a matter of months, however, on one fateful night in October 1966, the Doors' tenure at the Whisky would come to a screeching halt.

"It was a fun night," says Robby Krieger. "Well, actually it wasn't a fun night; it was a terrible night, 'cause Jim didn't show up for the first set."

Forced to play an hour-long instrumental set for a sold-out crowd, the band desperately went on a search for Morrison at their first break.

"In between sets, we found him at the hotel," Krieger remembers. "We kept knocking until he finally answered the door. Turns out he was on some sort of super acid trip and didn't want to come to work; he was too freaked out. But, when we got him to the Whisky, he finally calmed down and got into the idea of playing, so it was no problem."

Or so the band thought.

Hyped up on more than twenty-five hits of acid and unknown quantities of grass and booze, Morrison decided to take the musical set on a little detour.

At that time, it had been customary for the Doors to play their final set with renditions of "Break On Through," "Light My Fire," and other crowd pleasers and then close their show with a thundering version of their haunting ballad "The End."

However, less than twenty minutes into the set, Morrison felt the timing was right to jump straight into "The End"'s ominous first lines, "This is the end, beautiful friend, the end . . . ." What ensued was a thirty-minute glimpse into Morrison's delusional, psychedelic-driven mind that no one in the building was quite prepared for.

"When we started to do 'The End,'" says Krieger, "it was a whole different thing than we'd ever done. It started to grow longer and longer. Jim started to add this stuff about walking down the hall, and we'd never heard this."

As the legend goes, a deafening hush fell over the Whisky as Morrison wove the song into a somnambulistic journey through the twisted world of an insane Oedipus. The crowd at the club was transfixed and everything and everyone stood silent and mesmerized. The go-go girls stopped dancing. Even the waitresses and cooks in the kitchen stopped working.

"And then he got to those famous words," continues Krieger with a smile. "'Mother . . . I wanna fuck you, Mama, all night long!!!' It was as big a surprise to us as it was to the audience."

It turned out to be a big surprise to the Whisky's management as well. Too big of a surprise, in fact, because they stopped the show immediately and kicked Jim Morrison off the stage.

Despite the protests of fans, the Doors were never booked at the Whisky again.

But the incident only made the Doors even more famous as the sinister bad boys of the L.A. rock scene. Now that they had been publicly banned from the world-famous Whisky A Go-Go, it seemed the entire planet wanted to see what the band was all about.

Immediately snatched up by Elektra Records, the Doors watched their debut album hit number one in the U.S. in less than a year. The rest is left to history as the group continues to endure as one of the greatest rock bands of all time.

4

THE COSMIC G-SPOT

November 28, 1967

"Check it out, you can see a little bit of his left ball. See?"

Cynthia Albritton lifts her homemade plaster cast of Jimi Hendrix's penis so that it can absorb the feeble light of the dressing room's mirror. She holds it regally, her posture upright yet relaxed with the confidence of an artist showcasing an undisputed masterpiece. The Hendrix cast is her prize possession, the crown jewel in her burgeoning collection of handcrafted dick art. It's a beauty, in Cynthia's modest opinion, and she's happy to share it with the doe-eyed eighteen-year-old girl who's literally kneeling at her feet.

The girl, a redhead named Rhonda, listens intently to every word, but her gaze never strays from the cast.

"I wish we had a little more viewing light so you could appreciate the detail," Cynthia says. "Are they trying to save on electricity or what?"

The Whisky's dressing room is indeed much darker than usual tonight, since all but one of the light bulbs have been unscrewed from the mirror. But this wasn't the management's idea. The Who is set to take the stage in roughly two hours, and lead guitarist Pete

Townshend has recently insisted on cavelike lighting in whatever dressing room the band happens to be using. Mario Maglieri complied with Townshend's request with a shrug. He knows it's a prima donna move, but it's pretty innocuous compared to the shenanigans some other bands try to pull.

At the moment, Townshend isn't even around. He, bassist John Entwistle, and drummer Keith Moon are downstairs doing a sound check. Lead singer Roger Daltrey, who's suffering from a mild sore throat, has decided to stay in the dressing room and save all of his vocal capacity for the show.

Rather than simply sit and brood, Daltrey is using this down-time to put the room's infamous leather couch to its preferred use. He's sprawled across it lengthwise, with his pants jumbled at his ankles and his head propped against one arm. A kindhearted fan from Playa del Rey named Amber, who somehow talked her way into the club at this early hour, is sweetly soothing Daltrey's preshow jitters by using him as a pogo stick. With her miniskirt hiked high, Amber's bare ass bobs up and down in rhythm with the golden-haired singer's tuneful moans of gratitude. They are both having such a swell time, they pay no attention to the impromptu art exhibit that's taking place all of five feet away.

Even if he were not thus engaged, Daltrey probably still wouldn't show much interest in what Cynthia has to say. He's seen the Hendrix cast already. And he has already refused (some might suggest out of intimidation) Cynthia's request to add his member to her collection.

Doing her best to ignore the spectacle on the couch, Cynthia turns the cast around slowly, holding it at arm's length so that the kneeling Rhonda can get a closer look. But only so close. After a few heartbreaking mishaps involving excessive zeal or sheer clumsiness, Cynthia has learned to impose a strict look-but-don't-you-dare-touch policy with her pieces.

Cynthia asks Rhonda what she thinks.

"Wow," is the most detailed reply Rhonda is capable of producing. Her face is strained with the effort of visually consuming the cast like it's a genital equivalent of the Rosetta Stone.

"We needed a ratio of twenty-eight to twenty-eight," Cynthia says, not caring that her technical jargon is entirely lost on the girl. "I mean, that's huge. Way beyond the dimensions of our previous works. It was still barely big enough to hold him."

"What's this little crack here?" Rhonda asks, tracing her finger as close as she dares along a minor fault line running across the lower third of the shaft. "It looks like a scar."

"We had some problems extracting him."

Rhonda gasps. "You didn't hurt him, did you?"

Cynthia can't help rolling her eyes. These L.A. girls are sweet, but some of them are so dim it's a miracle they can make it through a single night in this predatory wonderland without ending up in a Tijuana white slavery auction.

"No, honey," she answers patiently. "That's a crack in the cast, not on his dick."

"Oh. How'd that happen?"

"He stayed hard too long. Usually they go limp after a minute or two and just slide out of the mold."

Cynthia thinks back to that cold February day back home in Chicago, just nine months ago. The day she emerged from anonymity by successfully preserving a detailed facsimile of Jimi Hendrix's manhood. It was pure luck that allowed her to get a shot at the rising guitar god before the release of his debut album, *Are You Experienced?* Almost, but not quite yet, a household word, Hendrix was more than willing to make a name for himself by any means necessary. Cynthia got her cast and virtually overnight was transformed from an unknown second-tier band chaser from the Midwest to a leading light of the growing cadre of A-list groupies.

She is now recognized as the founder of a tight-knit group of sexual artisans called the Chicago Plaster Casters, whose mission to preserve as many penises as possible has brought them instant national fame. Deservedly claiming the lion's share of credit for the CPC's notoriety, Cynthia nonetheless owes much of her success to a skilled Illinois fellatrix named Delores, whose hungry mouth propelled Hendrix to sufficient tumescence while Cynthia prepared the mold from a pliable substance called alginates. Under more common circumstances, this quick-drying paste is used to make dental molds.

"Jimi was so turned on," Cynthia continues, snapping out of her nipple-hardening reverie, "he wouldn't let us take the mold off. He wanted to ball it first."

"Wow. You must have been, like, so *flattered.*"

Cynthia shrugs, somewhat disingenuously. "My main concern is the artwork. In order to get a good clean cast, the guy needs to pull out before the mold starts to set. Jimi just wouldn't. So we got a slightly flawed, but still beautiful cast. I kind of dig the imperfection, actually. It's like the Penis di Milo."

Roger Daltrey chuckles midmoan. It seems he hasn't tuned out Cynthia completely.

"Jimi's lucky he didn't get hurt," Rhonda says reverently. As a quick afterthought, she adds, "We're all lucky."

"Well, he did lose some hair," Cynthia says. "But he was cool about it. I mean, it was his own fault. I kept them, about a dozen really nice pubes."

"Do you have them with you?" Rhonda asks in a voice made small by tremulous hope.

"Oh, Lord, no. They're in a locket back home. It's enough of a risk bringing this beauty all the way out here. But *so* many people were begging to see it," she says as she gingerly returns the cast to its form-fitted carrying case.

Rhonda is clearly sad to see it go. "So you're moving to L.A.?" she asks.

"That's the idea. Zappa tells me there are a lot more rock stars out here willing to stick their cocks in plaster. After visiting for a week, I'd have to say he's right." She lights a cigarette and shoots a mildly malicious look at the couch. "Notwithstanding certain wimps."

Daltrey doesn't hear the oblique insult, as his new friend Amber is noisily slipping and sliding toward orgasm. She invokes two-thirds of the holy trinity with operatic brio. "Oh, God, yes! Oh, Jesus, don't stop!!!"

Feeling left out of the overture, Daltrey chides her without losing the stroke. "Oy, wot's 'is, love?" he demands. "Forgettin' ol' Rog?"

Amber rectifies her error by chanting his name in an escalating whine, finally collapsing in a breathless heap on Daltrey's heaving chest. The singer looks just slightly less than satisfied.

Cynthia stubs out her cigarette and turns to face Rhonda. "Okay, down to business," she says. "What makes you think you're Plaster Caster material?"

Rhonda doesn't reply immediately. She knows it's a heavy question, one that demands a well-reasoned response.

Well," she says slowly, "I love music. It makes me happy. I want to make the people who make music happy."

Cynthia nods in approval. "Good answer. Most girls just say they can hoover guitar players till the cows come home."

"I can do that, too."

"Here's the scoop. I'm not really looking to expand my team. I have four girls back in Chicago, and I'd like to move them all out here. We have a pretty solid crew, and I don't see any advantage in taking on more staff."

Rhonda nods, her hopeful smile disintegrating a little with each word.

"But . . ." Cynthia continues, "there's no guarantee *all* my girls will make the trip. Or will want to stay if they do."

She lets Rhonda hold her breath for half a minute before resuming.

"You seem like a nice kid, so I'll keep you on my standby list. If there's an opening, you'll get a shot to prove yourself."

"'Old on there, Cynth. I've an idea." This comes from Daltrey, who has finally decided to pull up his pants, though his zipper remains at half-mast.

Cynthia regards him coolly. "I thought you weren't interested in what I have to offer, Rog. Having second thoughts?"

"Not exactly."

"Too bad. I'm sure Keith will be happy to oblige me."

Daltrey laughs. "I wouldn't bet on it. Only stick of Moonie's worth seein' is made of wood."

"Okay, what's your brilliant idea? As if I can't guess."

"Seems your young friend here . . ." Daltrey says, leaning forward. "Sorry, love, didn't catch the name."

"Rhonda."

"Brilliant. Seems Rhonda deserves a fair chance to demonstrate her capabilities. You, on the other hand, need to see what the girl can do before you consider taking 'er on."

"So you want her to blow you, but you still won't pose for a cast."

"About the size of it, yeah." He flashes his patented Mack the Knife grin at Rhonda. "That is, if you're game."

Amber, who has fallen into something of a postcoital trance, is promptly brought back to life by the whiff of competition. She nestles herself in Daltrey's lap and asks, "What's the matter, honey? Still got some jam in your joint?"

"Awake again, are we?" is the only answer Daltrey can manage as he casually tries to reposition himself.

Holding firm, Amber says, "I'm nowhere near done myself. Just taking a little breather."

"Right, great," chirps Daltrey. "It's just I think we oughta help young Rhonda with her career ambitions. Give an eager youth a little boost, ya know? Not meself I'm thinkin' of."

"Wait a minute," Amber says, the warmth of her tone dropping several degrees. "I hitchhiked all the way from Playa. You're gonna toss me over for some pimply schoolgirl?"

Rhonda rises to her feet for the first time in fifteen minutes, showing a hint of fire in her eyes. "I guess Mr. Daltrey is finished with you."

"Rog, love," Daltrey says with a wink. "Call me Rog."

Amber's eyes narrow to slits as she lights a cigarette. "Shouldn't you be in Home Ec, sweetie?"

"Shouldn't you be leaving?" Rhonda counters.

Cynthia sighs wearily. She's seen this exact conflict played out dozens of times over the past six months. It's always borne of the same utterly predictable reasons: the rock stars wanting to leave their stain on as many supplicants as they can, and the girls getting possessive over something that can't possibly be theirs exclusively.

Having to manage this jealous tension starts to weigh on Cynthia after a while. Doesn't everyone realize this is a game? People are being lynched in Birmingham, bombed to smithereens in Hanoi. That's the real world. This whole rock 'n' roll scene, whether it's the Whisky or the Fillmore or the Boston Tea Party . . . it's nothing but fantasy. So why does everyone forget so easily and act like this is something worth investing genuine emotions in?

For the next few minutes, the contest for bragging rights to Daltrey's next load only escalates. In spite of herself, Cynthia feels a twinge of admiration for the teenage girl's moxie in taking on an older, more experienced opponent in the contact sport of groupiedom. Rhonda shows absolutely no sign of backing down from Amber's increasingly venomous assault. Maybe the girl would make a useful addition to the relocated PCs after all.

For his part, Daltrey has cracked a beer and assumed the role of tough but fair moderator, letting each girl throw a few barbs across the room before cutting in to allow for a rebuttal. Things start getting out of hand when Rhonda makes a brutal reference to the miles on Amber's odometer, but before the contest upshifts from insults to blows, the dressing room door crashes open.

Keith Moon barrels through, performing some kind of warped cartwheel. He loses his balance and slams onto the floor so hard he upsets the cluttered coffee table, launching a small shower of stale beer and a cloud of cigarette ash into the air. Lying on his back with his hands cupped around his mouth, he fills the room with an aboriginal chant that contains no specific words, but rather a series of hoots and caterwauls and maniacal cackles. It's a standard entrance for Moon the Loon.

Daltrey is happy to see him. "Just the bloke we need!" he cries. "A sober voice of reason to 'elp us resolve this rather nasty dispute."

Moon pretends not to hear him. He starts rolling sideways across the floor toward the couch. His goal is Amber's bare left ankle, which he greedily takes into his mouth and starts chewing on like a mutton joint. She shrieks, but whether with horror or pleasure it's not immediately clear. Daltrey makes a few more attempts to get Moon's attention before giving up. All for the best anyway; the drummer's probably more useful distracting Amber. His sudden appearance has freed up Rhonda nicely.

"I believe we 'ave a winner," Daltrey whispers in the girl's ear as he ever so gently starts applying downward pressure on her shoulders.

Starting to feel left out, Cynthia thinks about leaving. Maybe she can catch a nap at Zappa's house before the night gets underway. Today has been a big letdown, as she had high hopes for adding Daltrey to her collection. Witnessing the mischief of the demented Moon, she rules out approaching him for a cast. He'd almost certainly comply, but the idea has fiasco written all over it. Better to cut bait. At least she still has the show to look forward to.

Just as it seems a full-blown four-way is starting to come together on the couch, Pete Townshend enters. As usual, the young songwriting genius resembles more than anything a wet rat retrieved from the nearest gutter. A cigarette dangles limply from his mouth, looking like an extension of his slack face. His shirt is drenched in sweat, thanks to his habit of ripping through sound checks with almost as much fury as the show itself. He doesn't appear particularly pleased with what's going on in the dressing room, but Townshend never appears particularly pleased.

"Rog," he mumbles in a customary monosyllabic greeting to his singer. 'Ow's a froat feelin'?"

"Much improved, thanks," Daltrey says, momentarily halting Rhonda's southward progress. "All's well onstage?"

Townshend nods sagely. "Fuckin' monster P.A. This place'll be a war zone tonight."

"Good news, mate."

"Me an' the Ox is goin' back the 'otel, grab a bite," Townshend says. "Wanna join?"

Daltrey pauses, considering. "Think I'll 'ang out," he answers. "Grab a slice next door maybe. Only two hours till curtain."

Townshend accepts this mild rejection as if he fully saw it coming. "Awright, 'en. C'mon, Keif."

Grabbing Moon by the collar, Townshend yanks him clumsily to his feet. It's clear he has no intention of being further rebuffed by his drummer, and Moon isn't apt to say no to Townshend under any circumstance. Moon blows a sloppy kiss at Amber as he stumbles to the door. She looks openly dismayed to see him leaving, so he invites her to accompany them back to the Continental Hyatt House. Her shoes are on in a heartbeat, and she leaves the room without so much as a parting glance at the fickle Daltrey.

For a moment, Pete Townshend lingers in the doorway. His eyes almost seem forlorn as he downs his pride and asks, "Sure you won't come?"

"Nah, 'ave a good bite," Daltrey says. "And prepare to rock your fuckin' nads off."

An awkward pause ensues, with Townshend still hovering. Across the room, Cynthia monitors this interaction closely, her intuition picking up the same vibes she was a few minutes ago, when Amber and Rhonda were quarreling over Daltrey. Townshend is clearly feeling jealous. His rigid posture and sad-sack tone of voice all but advertise it.

What Cynthia can't quite figure out is the *direction* of Townshend's feelings. Is he jealous of Daltrey for scoring a delectable morsel of fan flesh . . . or of Rhonda, who even now lies with her head blissfully cradled in Daltrey's lap?

Before Cynthia can contemplate this further, Townshend disappears. Suddenly she finds herself alone in a small room with two people who are within a hair of getting sexual. Seeing no reason to hang around and pretend not to notice for the second time in less than a half-hour, she picks up the carrying case and leaves the room, taking her plaster treasure with her.

Nineteen Sixty-Six

To historians, the year 1966 will forever mark a significant turning point in the evolution of American culture. For the first time, the rigid belief systems of the cold war–hardened establishment began to be widely challenged by the openly idealistic youth of America.

With President Johnson's administration obsessed with a paranoid need to control Southeast Asia, America's involvement in Vietnam was escalating nearly out of control. Forced to implement the draft to keep up with the faraway campaign, the U.S. went from fewer than two hundred thousand troops in Vietnam at the beginning of 1966 to nearly five hundred thousand by the end of the following year.

Suddenly and with very little input, America's young men were being forced to risk their lives for a cause they knew very little about. Even worse, the already tense race relations in the U.S. were being pushed to the limit by a biased draft that was sending young blacks to Vietnam much faster than it was sending their white counterparts.

All over the country, young Americans, black and white, were starting to speak out about what they saw as unnecessary warmongering by the federal government. And the civil rights movement that had been fractured by the death of President Kennedy was again back in full swing.

A revolution was beginning.

However, in contrast to those who'd fought in the bloody rebellions of the past, the soldiers of this cause called themselves flower children. They encouraged nonviolent protest and preached peace and love and unity for mankind. They spoke of liberating the mind and body through drugs and sex. Free love was their weapon. Music was their voice.

From Birmingham in the south to Chicago in the north, people "singing songs and carrying signs" were gathering. Peaceful protests called love-ins were being organized in Boston and New York City. But, over the next two years, nowhere in the United States was this revolution being fought harder and louder than in the Haight-Ashbury district of San Francisco and the Sunset Strip in Los Angeles.

Free Love: The New Golden Rule

On the surface, the summer of 1966 was playing itself out like an X-rated romp through Alice's psychedelic Wonderland.

Ken Kesey's acid tests were opening up strange, colorful new worlds for legions of willing hippies, and the Monkees' new hit TV series was sweeping the nation. Love beads and bell-bottom jeans were all the rage, and the Beach Boys' smash hit "Good Vibrations" was heard on every teenager's radio. In small towns everywhere, a simple hello was likely to be accompanied by a broad smile and a two-finger flash of the peace sign.

Flower power was in. But it was quickly becoming much more than a fad. To the flower children, it was a statement against what had come before. A bold rejection of the conservative, imperialistic ways of their parents.

Free love was the new golden rule, and soon it would be the only rule. It was time to burn the bra and "make love, not war," literally.

On the Sunset Strip, this liberation of minds and bodies was raging full steam ahead. With bands such as the Doors and the Rolling Stones pumping out heart-pounding, dark, tribal rhythms, sexual boundaries were falling just as fast as musical ones. Like sorcerers casting a carnal spell, these new rock groups were sending crowds of libidinous young women into frenzied heat.

Groupies

For the musicians in these rock groups, a performance at the Whisky A Go-Go or the Trip was sure to be followed by a veritable beggar's banquet of nubile young groupies hungrily awaiting them backstage. Performers had always been popular with the ladies, but these young rock stars had become more like pornographic pied pipers attracting hordes of female sexual prey. The loud music, wild shows, and exclusive parties surrounding the bands proved the ultimate aphrodisiac, and this new breed of groupies would do anything to be part of the scene.

As former groupie and rock historian Sue Schneider recalls, "We used to chase rock bands. We used to come from school. And when the Stones came to town, everyone started getting into it.

"It started as a game," she continues. "Like, how many bands could you meet? And chasing limos down the street. I guess if it were today we'd be called stalkers."

Coming in packs of fifteen or twenty at a time, these beautiful young women dressed in the most outlandish clothes and competed with each other for the opportunity to engage in a covert act of copulation with a band member or be part of a raucous orgy in the band's bus or hotel. It was a new brand of hedonism—one that combined rock music, sexual impulse, and drugs.

According to rocker Michael Des Barres of the band Silverhead, the intense explosion of the groupie scene was a phenomenon that could only have begun in Los Angeles:

"Los Angeles was the Babylon that we were looking for. We were looking for the playground, and it was here. There's a simple reason for that—the weather. You can't have a girl running around with two sequins on her tits and a Silverhead sticker on her pussy in twenty-below London! L.A. is the mecca, the holy grail for beauty. It's the magnet that attracts the cheekbones and great asses, and you put all that together with three chords and some pancake and you rock the fuck out, know what I mean?"

Leading the charge of the groupie brigade was a striking auburn-haired siren named Pamela whose list of conquests reads like a veritable "who's who" of classic rock legends. Having lost her virginity to Steppenwolf's Nick St. Nicholas, she was romantically linked to Jim Morrison, Mick Jagger, Frank Zappa, and Jimmy Page before marrying (and eventually divorcing) Michael Des Barres.

Rock 'n' roll had a powerful effect on Pamela from a young age. As she recalls, "The first record that I became aroused to where I actually masturbated to the music was the Stones' second record. I don't remember the title, but the words were 'Let me put it in, it feels all right.' I was like, 'Fuck, I don't believe he's saying that!' and it just made me want to get off.

"The girls and I spent a lot of time making lists of all the gorgeous boys in bands that we wouldn't kick out of bed. I kept my list in a little gold loose-leaf notebook in my purse. Mick Jagger was number one, written in flaming red."

She continues, "Oooooh! I loved the music! I lived for the music. I wanted to surround myself with it, get intimate with it and the glorious men who made it. I was so moved by it. Moved to tears, to orgasm. I wanted to make beautiful music with the musicians, and the fact that I never learned how to play an instrument never stopped me."

Miss Pamela, as she came to be known, became so popular that Frank Zappa put her in his movie *200 Motels* and later helped her and her groupie friends (Cynthia Plaster Caster among them) form a band of their own—Girls Together Outrageously, AKA the GTOs.

Though neither the movie nor the band achieved any real commercial or critical success, they gave Miss Pamela and the entire groupie phenomenon a measure of fame and ultimately helped her publish her bestselling memoir, *I'm with the Band*, in 1986.

Sue Schneider remembers the nonstop cavalcade of rockers who were both hunters and quarry in the ongoing game of carnal cat and mouse. "At the Whisky," she says, "you'd have Keith Moon back by the ticket booth, and you'd have Paul Kantner from Jefferson Airplane, and they'd stand there all night. Or you'd have one table full of Deep Purple. Or one table full of Led Zeppelin or the Hollies. Or Iggy Pop, who was the house act for a long time. And you'd have the girls there, the regular girls who were always at the Whisky. Sitting and talking to the bands, so the bands would buy drinks and spend more money."

Indeed, as Sue recalls, Mario Maglieri heartily encouraged the constant presence of groupies. "He was always like that, and he still is today," she says. "He likes having all the young girls at his clubs."

Michael Des Barres sums up his feelings about the groupies of the 1960s:

"I found them incredibly inspiring. They were as inspirational to me as Chuck Berry, 'cause they loved the scene and they nurtured it and they believed in it, and they made you believe in it more. Those girls created the ambience in which the lifestyle could be lived and the songs could be written and the music could be recorded. It was one fantastic sort of orgasmic organism."

The Sunset Strip Riots

By the winter of 1966, the once glamorous Strip, where movie stars such as Dean Martin and Frank Sinatra held court, had been completely transformed into a sea of young hippies, groupies, and wild rock bands raucously partying the night away. Jim Morrison and Mick Jagger were the new kings of Sunset Boulevard, and everywhere young women freely offered their bodies to the kingdom.

But, as the stream of coffins returning from Vietnam rapidly increased, the flower children's happy rebellion was turning into a full-blown fear of the government and authority. "Don't trust anyone over thirty" was the new unspoken attitude.

Meanwhile, along the Sunset Strip, the increasingly bizarre behavior and unruliness of the huge crowds were provoking the ire of local shop owners and law enforcement officials. More and more hippies were being harassed and jailed on trumped-up charges of vagrancy and disorderly conduct.

Something needed to change.

To try to quell the problem, the city of West Hollywood went into action. Pointing a quick finger at the Whisky A Go-Go, they made the club change its name to the Whisk, claiming the alcohol in the name was a bad influence on young people. They also saw fit to yank the Whisk's and other clubs' dance licenses to help drive away the crowds. On top of that, they implemented a no-cruising rule for cars on the Strip and imposed a 10:00 P.M. curfew for anyone who looked under the age of eighteen. But when authorities decided to further clear traffic by shutting down and bulldozing a popular new Sunset Strip dance club called Pandora's Box, the masses of young people said enough is enough.

What happened next was a now-legendary few nights of protest in November '66 known simply as the Sunset Strip riots.

There are conflicting reports as to what actually happened during these so-called riots, but what's known for sure is that, in contrast to the racially charged L.A. Watts riots of the year before, there were very few injuries, and, aside from a bus being overturned, very little vandalism.

The Monkees' Micky Dolenz, who was one of the protesters, claimed at the time that even calling them "riots" was perhaps a bit of an overstatement:

"There haven't really been riots. I was there. In actuality, they've been demonstrations. But I guess a lot of journalists don't know how to spell 'demonstration.'"

As the story goes, the night before Pandora's Box was to be

demolished, a massive crowd of demonstrators, including such notables as Sonny and Cher, David Crosby, Stephen Stills, Neil Young, and the Monkees, gathered in front of the doomed club to mount a peaceful vigil. Carrying signs, holding hands, and singing songs of peace, the crowd of several hundred spread out over Sunset Boulevard and effectively shut down all traffic.

It was a victory for flower power.

But then, in what was called by many a gross overreaction to the situation, an army of riot police bore down on the gathering in full draconian force. There, in plain view of the nation's press corps, hundreds of long-haired protesters were tackled, beaten, and thrown into paddy wagons or otherwise aggressively dispersed.

The media had a field day. The next morning, the scene on Sunset was the headline of every paper across the country. This only exacerbated the situation as news of the injustice caused flower children all across America to mount protests. For several more nights, it was a tense scene on Sunset and around the country as people held their breath in anticipation of more altercations.

But few altercations ever materialized. Instead, concessions were made by both sides. Though Pandora's Box was eventually bulldozed, local police agreed it was not their job to baby-sit the kids on the Strip nightly. As for the Whisky, Elmer Valentine successfully sued to get its name back, and dance licenses were returned to the clubs on Sunset.

But the vision of police dressed in riot gear struggling to force hundreds of hippies into paddy wagons was thoroughly ingrained in the American psyche. And, though interest in the issues out in Hollywood quickly gave way to concern over the more pressing issues of Vietnam, the riots proved to be a potent symbol of the deep rift suddenly dividing America.

As Bob Gibson, then manager of both the Byrds and the Mamas and the Papas, recalls:

"If you had to put your finger on an event that was a barometer of the tide turning, it would probably be the Sunset Strip riots."

The riots also inspired Stephen Stills to pen Buffalo Springfield's 1967 number-one hit "For What It's Worth (There's Something Happening Here)," which endures as one of the anthems for the anti-Vietnam movement.

Motown Meets the Strip

Though the riots on Sunset had come to an ultimately peaceful resolution, the local shops and law enforcement still harbored animosity toward the clubs. The intimacy of the whole scene was virtually undone by the increased police presence, and the hippies who had brought so much business to the area were looking elsewhere for the party.

What was worse, Elmer Valentine felt betrayed. His world-famous club, which had rejuvenated a long-fading area of Los Angeles, was blamed for having caused most of the problems. Elmer, who was a big fan of Motown, had already come under scrutiny for allowing black acts to perform at his clubs. That, he felt, was the main reason the Whisky had been singled out.

So, to get back at the local store owners and police, he decided to make the Whisky Hollywood's version of the Apollo Theater.

"It's fuckin' true!" explains Elmer, "It was out of spite, but also because I loved the music."

The complexion of the Strip changed overnight as vast crowds of black kids came to see their favorite Motown Acts. In a short span in mid-1967, some of the world's greatest black acts, including Marvin Gaye, the Miracles, Martha and the Vandellas, and the Four Tops, all played the Whisky. It was then that Otis Redding recorded his now legendary live album *In Person at the Whisky A Go-Go* and Jimi Hendrix had his first performance there.

As Pamela Des Barres recalls:

"Seeing [Jimi] play at the Whisky was beyond anything physical, like going to another planet. It took you to new realms, places you didn't know existed. The cosmic G-spot!"

Not only did Elmer's move rescue the Strip from what easily could have turned into a post-riots slump, but it also had the desired effect of making shop owners and law enforcement extremely nervous. Elmer thought it was all a great joke, but his point was made. Soon he reinstated a more integrated policy of booking the Whisky.

FROM MONTEREY TO L.A.

December 17, 1967

"Awww, come aaaaawwwwwwwwnnnnnnnnnn,
wontcha hold mmmmmeeeeeeeeeeeeeeeeeeeeeeeeee?"

Janis stretches out the last note. It seems to never end. This final note, a mournfully horny plea, reaches every corner of the room and fills it. Switching from tenor to contralto to soprano and then back again down the scale, it burns with life. At times, the sound of Janis's voice is not quite human. At others, it's all too painfully so. It demands the attention of everyone within its reach.

Janis Joplin is front and center on the stage of the Whisky A Go-Go, backed by her band Big Brother and the Holding Company. Her urge to command the room goes deeper than a typical performer's limelight lust. Her voice is much more than her vehicle to stardom. It is her source of validation, one that labors to be renewed with each and every performance. Anything less than the audience's total submission is a crushing failure for her.

She's got nothing to worry about tonight. Everyone in the Whisky is transfixed by this rather ungainly young woman in gypsy rags standing in the unwavering glare of a blinding spotlight. Many in the audience forget to sip the drinks in their hands. Neglected cigarettes grow stems of ash that fall in heaps on laps, only to sprout and be ignored again.

Even the go-go girls fail to catch anyone's interest. This causes them a fair amount of anxiety; after all, they're performers who thrive on the audience's attentions, too. And they face a sort of internecine competition the musicians usually don't have to deal with. As always, the Whisky features only two dancing girls a night. One dancer occupies the main cage above the stage, while the other is relegated to the hinterlands of the back loft, virtually invisible to the audience. Naturally, all the girls covet the pole position of cage number one, especially since rumors that scouts from *Playboy* are frequenting the club have spread like a brushfire after former go-go girl Cindy Waters appeared in this year's September issue.

It's hard enough for the dancers, ostensibly friends, to have to compete with one another. But it's harder still when they're vying for recognition next to an act like Big Brother and the Holding Company and its world-famous chanteuse. Over the past three nights, a few girls have given up in tears of rage and despair. They have waved the white flag in the face of a performer simply too powerful to challenge.

Not so the dancer in cage number one tonight, a twisting vision of sweat-sheened mocha flesh wrapped in two thin scraps of denim. She's a former stripper named Flo with no intention of fading gently into the scenery. As Janis's performance grows ever more incendiary, Flo reverts to the type of moves that earned her a hundred dollars a night in her previous career. Slipping a painted fingernail under the strap of her top, she starts to tug down gently like she's scratching an itch at the tawny cleft where her shoulder meets her chest.

It's a dicey tactical decision for Flo. The Whisky's policy regarding its caged performances is strict and unforgiving. By necessity. This is a legitimate live music venue, not a titty bar. Even the briefest unintentional glimpse of restricted flesh could shut the club down indefinitely. Mario Maglieri suspects the LAPD of planting moles in the Whisky's patronage in hopes of catching an errant flash of boob, or even better, a tuft of dewy down poking out from the skimpy confines of the dancers' outfits.

Mario can't afford a slip-up. He gives the girls one warning. One is enough, coming from him.

So to intentionally disrobe, even with the acme of finesse, is no minor matter. And yet so great is her need to be seen that Flo continues to tease away her top, keeping perfect time with the beat. With each provocative little tug, the fabric creeps down just a bit more, until the radiant round areola of her left breast starts to rise over the denim like the sun over the blue Atlantic.

This is brave new territory for the Whisky. But does she stop there? Not pioneer Flo. One more tug and her distended nipple, glistening and defiant, springs forth from its cloth cage and stands up to be counted in the glare of the spotlight.

And, still, nobody notices.

Poor Flo. Though she can't be blamed for thinking otherwise, the audience's lack of interest is no insult to her beauty. It's just that Janis is putting on what might be called a stunning performance. In fact, the term "performance" seems insufficient to describe what Janis is doing. This is more like Communion. Singer, song, and audience are one, melded together. Unity through music, an oft-expressed goal of the times, is truly being achieved tonight. Those in attendance are not apt to forget it, nor to keep the magic of this evening to themselves. First-hand accounts of Janis's greatness will circulate all across Southern California for months.

And then the song dies, and Janis seems depleted. She slumps. Hair hiding her face, matching dark crescents seep out from under her arms. Her knees are locked with the effort of staying upright. Spent.

The crowd lights an auditory bonfire in recognition of her sacrifice and her gift. Janis has won them over completely.

"Goddamn!" she howls into the mike, surprised as usual by the sheer power she and her band are capable of generating. "That was pretty good, wasn't it?"

For a few seconds, she disappears from view as she steps back to the drum riser, which serves as her personal sideboard. Grabbing a half-empty fifth of Southern Comfort, she reenters the revealing glare of spotlight in the middle of a long pull, the bottle held at a near ninety-degree angle to the floor. A few in the audience can't help but gasp at the sight of her sucking on a bottle of bourbon like a babe at her mother's breast.

Janis wipes the brown liquid from her lips with a smile and sets the bottle down at her feet.

"That last song was for my Irish drinking buddy out there. You know who you are!" she says, her voice colored with slightly crazed affection. She points a finger unsteadily into the crowd. "I see ya, you sumbitch. You can't hide from me."

Her finger cuts a wide swath in the direction of the booths in the back, undermining her claim of actually seeing whomever it is she's acknowledging. Many in the crowd wonder if any such person even exists. Is she really pointing to a friend, or has she simply lapsed into a brief bout with Southern-fried dementia? Or maybe it's all part of the act, a calculated bit of Janis's loopy stagecraft. Who can say?

Most of the people entertaining such thoughts would be floored to learn that the buddy to whom Janis is pointing is none other than Jim Morrison. Disguised in a ridiculous straw hat and wrap-around shades, Morrison has been in anonymous attendance for all four of Big Brother's shows. He's sitting in the far corner booth, cloaked in darkness. (Morrison snuffed out the tabletop candle when he sat down and snarled at a waitress who tried to relight it.) He's obviously in a private mood and probably doesn't appreciate Janis singling him out, even in tribute.

Why has the Lizard King come here four nights in a row? Is he inspired by Janis or intimidated by her? Does he see a kindred spirit or a pretender to his throne as reigning lost cause on the rock 'n' roll landscape?

If Morrison is troubled by such concerns, Janis soon seems to forget all about him, having moved on to a meandering, freeform exaltation of this Southern California crowd that has been so hospitable to her. She frequently loses her train of thought, only to restart on another parallel track.

"Well, fuck," she slurs. "We all wanna thank the shit outta you for giving us such a warm welcome." A long pause as her eyes glaze over.

"For a buncha Northern Cal hippies like us," she continues, "it's nice to see this city ain't the lowest pit a' hell, after all."

A few strained laughs from the crowd. People are starting to feel nervous. It's been such a wonderful performance. No one wants to see it marred by a bit of sad, drunken buffoonery. Just take a bow and exit stage left, Janis. Please.

"No, I mean it! Sincerely." Her voice crumbles into titters. "Y'all have been great. We'd love to come on back and get our rocks off with ya again sometime."

It seems that she has more to say, if only she could remember it. She stands in front of the mike, weaving slightly, trying to catch the thread of her thoughts. Then she gives up and blows a kiss to the crowd before shambling offstage. Waves of relief roll across the room and the Whisky's four walls reverberate with the chanting of her name.

Though in retrospect some will interpret her rambling tribute to Los Angeles as sarcastic, Janis was being sincere. She loves Southern California, much to her surprise. A stint in Venice Beach two years ago left a bad taste in her mouth, and she's been based in San Francisco ever since. But, returning as a bona fide star in the wake of her career-making performance at the Monterey Pop Festival, she has found Hollywood more than inviting. Its status as the planet's preeminent judgment-free zone really appeals to her. And she's been needing a change of scene.

So, for the past few months, Janis has been soaking up the sunshine and feeling more relaxed than she can remember. Bad influences and even worse habits were starting to get the best of her up north. Heroin, in particular. Everything came to a head at Monterey Pop. The adulation flooded in, but with it came pressure. Her need for the opiate release grew in direct relation to her ballooning fame.

Now she's looking better, eating regular meals, and getting a reasonable amount of sleep most nights. Her face is flushed with color, free of pastiness and the deep hollows that were beginning to form under her eyes. She's basically cut out the smack, a lifestyle change that has only strengthened her always formidable vocal range.

Yes, Janis is really enjoying herself down here. The climate is closer to that of her native Port Arthur, Texas, than the fog-shrouded Bay Area. And it's easy to get lost in a city like this. She has put a lot of preparation into her four-night stand at the Whisky, doing impromptu gigs at tiny hole-in-the-wall clubs all across the L.A. basin. It's a hit-and-run approach to performing. Just three or four songs, max. By the time word filters to the street that Janis Joplin is onstage, she's packed up her gear and disappeared out the back entrance. She truly doesn't seek attention during this training period. She just wants a warm place to prepare herself for what she knows is a crucial engagement at the most prominent club on the Sunset Strip.

When not singing or sleeping, Janis revels in what she frequently likes to tell people are her two favorite pastimes: drinking Southern Comfort and eating pussy. The latter takes up increasingly large portions of her time. Janis hasn't shared her loins with a man in almost six months, a record since losing her virginity in her teens. She's more than made up for that deficiency with a virtual daisy chain of ambrosial female lovers.

It's a matter of comfort as much as personal preference. Janis is at heart a sexually omnivorous creature. She certainly hasn't ruled out men in the long run. She just finds she feels more relaxed with women. Free to be herself, a shy girl from a small town in Texas, rather than Janis Joplin, superstar. And, oh, these Southern California girls. Nothing in Port Arthur, San Francisco, or any other part of the planet has prepared her for the legions of nubile sapphic sisters offered up every night on the Strip. Janis goes whole hog.

Quite a few of these sirens are milling around the dressing room after tonight's show as Janis and her Big Brother cohorts strip off their sweaty clothes and freshen up. Also in attendance is the camouflaged Jim Morrison, who sidles silently into the room and proceeds to plant himself in the least populated corner he can find.

Janis isn't willing to let him remain incognito. She runs over and drags the singer to his feet with a string of ribald oaths. They share a moment. Every eye in the room feeds on the spectacle of the king and queen of rock 'n' roll locked in a heated embrace.

An hour later they are holding hands in the backseat of Paul Rothchild's Mercedes as it speeds to a party in the Hills. Rothchild, who has produced all of the Doors' albums to date, occasionally serves as Morrison's personal assistant, a position only a true masochist would accept. His primary duty is to haul Morrison around the city at all hours of the day or night, from liquor store to sexual rendezvous to God-knows-where.

The Mercedes eventually arrives at the party and parks on the sloped front lawn, since the driveway is already filled with flashy, expensive rides. The house's front door is wide open. It's your standard five-bedroom affair owned by some executive or another from Elektra. Models and businessmen pose by the pool, tall drinks in hand. The glittering bowl of Los Angeles stretches to eternity at their feet. Someone lights a joint. Meaningless conversation is made.

Jim and Janis quickly disappear to a secluded corner of the living room, where they start demolishing a fresh bottle of SoCo. No one approaches them. Together, they project a kind of invisible buffer zone, keeping mere mortals from coming too close.

They have a lot in common, Janis and Jim. Both fat, unpopular kids who managed to get through their formative years by constructing a shell around themselves that let in oxygen and little else. Both knowing they possessed something inside that would propel them beyond the predictable mediocre trajectory the lives of their classmates would take. Neither expecting to live very long.

As the evening progresses and the bottle drains, Janis finds herself sharing more with this man than she would have thought possible. Jim is open, genuine, and sweet. He speaks softly and listens without interrupting. His hand strokes hers for almost an hour before rising to gently cup her breast. Janis likes it. She likes Jim. She's starting to entertain the possibility of ending her all-female streak of bedmates.

Then everything goes all to hell.

Across the room, Rothchild sees it happen first. Janis's head, which for a good twenty minutes has been propped up by Morrison's left shoulder, is now lying face-down in his lap. Morrison's right hand cradles the back of her neck, holding her in place. Wow, Rothchild thinks. Sexual exhibitionism isn't exactly new material for Morrison; in fact, it's held a high rank in his playbook for years. But he's never received public head from a star of Janis's magnitude. Especially not at a high-profile industry function like this one. It's a ballsy move, sure to further cement Jim's rep as Dionysus reborn.

For a brief second, Rothchild considers breaking it up. Except he knows how volatile Morrison can be when drunk, and the singer started on burgundy at about 4:30 before switching to the harder stuff. Maybe it's better to just let the scene play out and intervene only if it looks like it might get truly out of hand.

It's at roughly this point that Rothchild hears Janis scream. And then immediately notices that Morrison's right hand and forearm are tightly flexed. The son of a bitch is *forcing* her head into his crotch. Janis screams again, struggling with her entire body to break free of Morrison's one-handed headlock.

Rothchild bolts across the room to put an end to what is rapidly dissolving into a very ugly scene.

"Go, baby, go!" Morrison cackles. His goofy smile belies the seriousness of his intentions. But, if the look on his face is jocular, the steel grip on the back of Janis's neck is all business.

Rothchild manages to pull Janis from the pit of Morrison's crotch, but before he can calm her down, she breaks free and runs to the bathroom in hysterics.

Spewing a torrent of apologies in the general direction of the

FROM MONTEREY TO L.A.

host, Rothchild wrestles Morrison toward the front door. Jim has assumed his usual "who, me?" attitude of dumbstruck innocence in the face of the scene he has created. He looks genuinely stricken to be ejected from this classy party just as it was starting to get interesting.

Rothchild manipulates him through the front door and down the steep lawn to where the Mercedes waits. Shoving Jim into the passenger seat, he circles around the front of the car, wondering to himself for about the hundredth time this week, "Why do I put up with this maniac?"

Just as he turns the ignition and throws the car into reverse, Rothchild is startled by the cry of an enraged Texas banshee. Janis is barreling down the hill, bearing the empty SoCo bottle in her hand like a hatchet.

Ignoring Rothchild's frantic warnings, Morrison rolls down his window to have a word with her.

"Forget it, Jim!" Rothchild pleads. "Let's just roll."

"It's cool. I wanna talk to her for a minute."

"You can apologize tomorrow."

Jim does an unfeigned double take. "Apologize for what?"

The empty bottle in Janis's hand assumes a graceful downward arc, ending abruptly with a shattering collision against Morrison's left temple. Glass shards spray all over the dashboard, splattering it with blood. Rothchild screams. Janis uses her bare fists to pummel Morrison as hard as she can. Tears of rage pour down her contorted face.

Jim can't stop laughing. As always, he's fascinated by the sight of his own blood. Some brave soul grabs Janis from behind and pulls her away from the car. She's still cursing a blue streak and promising to kill Morrison if she ever sees him again. Rothchild thinks about jumping out and trying to work some diplomatic

damage control, then decides it's best to separate these two powder kegs as quickly as possible. Morrison is already fumbling with
the door handle, an endeavor that thankfully proves beyond the limited means of his present coordination.

Rothchild floors it and peels away. Morrison's crazed hooting
echoes up through the winding street as the Mercedes plunges into
Hollywood. Meanwhile, it takes the rest of the night and two
Quaaludes to bring Janis down to a semicomposed state. Most people leave, trying not to look at her. Hundreds of pieces of broken
glass will have to be carefully retrieved from the lawn when the sun
comes up.

Another pleasant evening, courtesy of Jim Morrison.

This incident, though widely dismissed as standard-issue rock
star misbehavior, proves deeply hurtful to Janis. She was finding
herself truly drawn to Morrison. And he seemed to share the depth
of her feelings. It looked for a small moment like maybe she had
found a man with whom she could connect on a profound level,
someone bearing the same scars of a lonely childhood. Someone
who might be able to reinstate her broken trust of the male of the
species and open up new possibilities for future relationships.

But, looking back on it, Janis goes hot with self-reproach for
entertaining such thoughts. How stupid she was. To have exposed
herself like that to Jim Morrison, of all people. Only to find he's no
better than any of the rest. Worse, in fact, because he pretended
to care. Whereas most of the men in Janis's life have been brutally
candid about what they really thought of her.

The humiliation stings and promises to be long-term. Not even
the sweet tangy kiss of Southern Comfort can take the edge off.
Janis soothes her wounds by spending most of the next three days
with her face planted between the dusky thighs of Flo, the fearless
go-go dancer whose brazen tit-flash garnered the attention of

absolutely no one in the Whisky A Go-Go.

Except, of course, Janis Joplin.

The Monterey Pop Festival

In the annals of rock history, a small handful of concerts have risen above the rest to achieve near-mythological proportions. Tales of their unprecedented all-star lineups and legendary performances leave classic-rock fans amazed that mere mortals were actually able to bear witness to such hallowed moments. There are, of course, Woodstock and Altamont, the legendary Rainbow Bridge, and perhaps the Beatles at Shea Stadium in 1965. But, in the past forty years, one concert reigns supreme in terms of its overall significance to rock 'n' roll. It was a concert that would reshape America's musical landscape and make events like all these others possible.

That concert was the Monterey Pop Festival.

The brainchild of Lou Adler and John Phillips of the Mamas and the Papas, Monterey Pop was in fact the first real rock festival ever held on American soil. Its unparalleled success as a well-planned, well-executed event made its format a blueprint for all subsequent music festivals.

As Lou Adler explains, it was a first-of-its-kind concert hatched from the ideals of bringing respect and legitimacy to rock music:

"It was me, John Phillips, Cass Elliot, and Paul McCartney, and we were all talking about the fact that rock 'n' roll—or what we called rock 'n' roll then—was not considered an art form, like jazz and the blues. When it was first invented, in the '50s, it was supposed to be this dumb thing that would be gone by the end of the summer, and here it was still thriving. So we were talking about ways to legitimize it, and one idea we had was to have a charitable event with all these different acts."

He continues, "John and I had both heard that in the late '30s, the series Jazz at the Philharmonic had validated jazz to people. So we thought putting rock music at the site of the already established Monterey Jazz Festival would validate rock."

Setting their sights on the best young pop music talent around, Adler and Phillips went about designing their own version of the Monterey Jazz Festival. They called it the Monterey International Pop Music Festival and set it for the weekend of June 16–18, 1967.

Billed as a weekend of "peace, love, and flowers," the official concert program carried the slogan: "Be happy, be free; wear flowers, bring bells—have a festival!" With the aid of million-aire promoter Alan Pariser, more than a hundred thousand orchids were to be flown in from Hawaii.

But booking the event turned out to be much more difficult than anticipated. Unlike the Los Angeles musicians who were per-sonal friends with Adler and Phillips, many of the prominent San Francisco bands were highly skeptical of an event promoted by slick L.A. hotshots.

"The San Francisco groups had a very bad taste in their mouths about L.A. commercialism," explains Adler. "And it's true that we were a business-minded industry. It wasn't a hobby. They called it slick, and I'd have to agree with them. We couldn't find the link. Every time John [Phillips] and I went up there, it was a fight—almost a physical fight on occasion. And that was right up to the opening day of the festival, with the Dead—the Ungrateful Dead, as we called them—threatening to do an alternate festival."

Fortunately, with the aid of respected Bay Area luminary Bill Graham and Beatles publicist Derek Taylor, many of the suspicions were eased. At last, by the summer of 1967, the stage was set. But Adler and Phillips could hardly have anticipated the cultural phenomenon that was about to occur.

Over the course of those three days in June, more than two hundred thousand people visited the beautiful Northern California coast to be a part of Monterey Pop. With television cameras from around the world watching, the concert showcased the first major American appearances of Jimi Hendrix and the Who and introduced an unknown Janis Joplin to a large audience.

"The media coverage was worldwide," says Adler, "and that had never happened before. We knew we had a lot of requests for media credentials, but it was still a shock on the morning of the festival to wake up and see all these TV crews from all over the world."

The concert also featured now legendary performances by Otis Redding, Jefferson Airplane, the Grateful Dead, the Byrds, the Mamas and the Papas, Ravi Shankar, and Buffalo Springfield.

For the musicians, the trappings of the event set a new standard of excellence.

"Artists were used to performing with a microphone and two small speakers," explains Adler. "We wanted them to have the best sound, the best facility, the best food backstage. We wanted it to be a utopia."

What they got were breakthrough performances by bands that brought the crowds to euphoric ovations and sent record executives scrambling for their checkbooks.

As one spectator at the festival recalls, "The action wasn't only on the stage; it was at the bar, where the record companies and the managers were in a heated bidding war."

Solely based upon their performances at Monterey Pop, several performers, including the Who, Jimi Hendrix, Janis Joplin, and the short-lived Electric Flag, received major record deals. Twenty-five-year-old Otis Redding's star also skyrocketed after Monterey. His classic "Sittin' On the Dock Of the Bay" reached number one less than six months later, just weeks after his tragic death in a plane crash.

The Monterey Pop Festival was an unprecedented smash. To the world, it proved that rock 'n' roll was an art form in its own right. To the music industry, it made evident just how big the business of rock music might become.

But the festival was not without its critics. Many suspiciously questioned the real motives of the organizers. The inaugural issue of *Rolling Stone,* published in November 1967, lampooned the event as "extravagant" and claimed that it was simply a "vehicle for Phillips' and Adler's self-glorification."

Another magazine called it "a combination trade show and shopping spree where [record company executives] might browse till they saw something they liked, then inquire about the price." And, in a review that was most likely balled up and eaten later, *Billboard* panned Jimi Hendrix's debut, reporting that "his chicken-choke handling of the guitar doesn't indicate a strong talent."

But as Lou Adler boasts:

"To this day, artists say it was one of the best events of its kind they were ever at. It really elevated promoters' outlooks on how to treat artists, and it made record companies conscious that the artist had power. After Monterey, artists really got more freedom to choose their album cover art, their producers, their songs ... It had a lot of ancillary effects on the industry."

Innocence Lost

In the aftermath of Monterey, it was plainly clear that if music was the voice of the counterculture movement, then the music festival was its body.

Monterey Pop had been a globally broadcast three-day peace-and-love party, and, as a symbol of unity, it gave flower children all over the world a reason to rejoice. Their time had finally arrived, and they were using it to declare a permanent Summer of Love.

For the record companies, the success of Monterey dictated a profound shift in the way they marketed their acts. Demand for live performances by rock bands, especially ones that took part in Monterey Pop, began to pour in from coast to coast.

Almost overnight, the intimate musical scene that had been cultivated in San Francisco was undone. One by one, the bands that had helped create the sense of idyllic anarchy in Monterey made their way to the record companies in Hollywood, where they were signed up and thrust onto big-money tours all over the world.

For his part, Lou Adler saw the ideological divide that had separated Northern and Southern California virtually disappear. In a gesture that must have greatly pleased Elmer Valentine, nearly all of the bands that performed in Monterey accepted Adler's invitation to come play the Whisky.

In fact, Jefferson Airplane, Country Joe and the Fish, Jimi Hendrix, Otis Redding, the Who, and Janis Joplin all played shows at the Whisky during this period before going onto superstardom shortly after.

As guitarist Mike Monarch, whose band Steppenwolf filled the Whisky's house slot for several months in late 1967, remembers:

"This was the Whisky's heyday. I mean, one week Jefferson Airplane played there. The next week the Who played there. Then it was Jimi Hendrix. Bands that would become the greatest bands of all time were coming to the famous Whisky A Go-Go."

Janis Joplin and her group Big Brother and the Holding Company, who received a huge record deal after Monterey, also became regulars at the Whisky.

Mario Maglieri fondly describes one night sitting at a booth with Janis:

"She was a great entertainer, but a raunchy chick. Dirty nails, stringy hair. Looked like she hadn't bathed in a month. And she had that raspy voice. Well, she was at the Whisky one night. I was sitting next to Janis, don't know what the hell we were talking about. The waitress came up to the table. Janis says to her, 'Gimme a drink.' So the girl brought over a Southern Comfort on the rocks. And what do you think Janis said? 'I want the whole fuckin' bottle!' That was Janis. I truly loved her musically and as a person. She was just a great chick, you know what I mean?"

In the starkest of terms, the Monterey Pop Festival marked the moment when the music industry officially grew up and became a business.

In the most idealistic of terms, D. A. Pennebaker, the man who filmed the festival, sums it up best:

"[Monterey Pop] was an extraordinary moment in American culture. There was a new sense of freedom in the air that was reflected in the music, in the drugs, in everything. You could feel it coming like a hurricane."

DOWN ON THE KILLING FLOOR

August 7, 1969

Traffic is murder on Sunset. Just a few minutes before six on a muggy Thursday afternoon, the sky is cloudless and dabbed an intense fusion of orange and purple. It's summertime in the City of Angels, and even the stone-cold crazy have enough sense not to stay inside. Here they all are, clogging every inch of the Strip. Moving east and west in equally imposing numbers, propelled by an array of smog-producing vehicles of both the two- and four-wheeled variety.

There's a potent tinge of desperation in the air. Everyone has the distinct impression something is happening nearby, right now. Something culturally significant. The problem is, no one knows exactly where or what it is. So they remain in limbo, nomads shuffling and cruising along Sunset with the increasingly dim hope that some benevolent gatekeeper will grant them entrance to whatever it is they're looking for. Or at least point them in the right direction.

Mario Maglieri suffers neither fools nor gridlock gladly. That's why he makes a point of leaving his home in Canoga Park to drive to the Whisky by no later than three in the afternoon. Or no earlier than eight in the evening. Those five hours in between gang up to form what is laughably called "rush hour" in Los Angeles—as if it's just sixty minutes long.

Mario avoids traffic like it's a social disease, so he's monumentally irked to find himself afflicted with it right now. His champagne Cadillac DeVille sits frozen about half a block east of the intersection of Sunset and La Cienega. The Whisky is less than a quarter-mile away, but at this rate it will take him another half-hour to get there.

He impatiently flicks the dial across the FM band, hoping to find something that will distract his attention from the simmering river of steel stretched out before him. He lands on a rock station playing the new Stones single, "Gimme Shelter." Mario has heard the song a few times before. He doesn't particularly care for it. But for some reason he stays tuned and finds himself listening to the muddy, heavily overdubbed chorus:

Rape,
Murder,
It's just a shot away,
It's just a shot away.

Mario shakes his head as he changes the station with a vicious clockwise twist of the dial. Now he's legitimately pissed, as much from the song as the traffic. What the hell gets into the minds of these rock 'n' rollers? Every goddamn song in the Top Forty these days is about crime, war, the breakdown of society, or some depressing bullshit like that. Isn't music supposed to make you feel *good?* Was there anything so wrong with short, upbeat tunes about hot rods and surfing and teenage beaver?

Suddenly a small pocket of traffic loosens up and the cars jolt forward like a pack of greyhounds released from the gate. Mario guns it, but has to slam on the brakes as a long-haired skeletal freak in tattered denim reels headlong into the street. The Caddy barely misses him. Burnt-rubber fumes rise from the baking asphalt as Mario unleashes a string of characteristically filthy oaths at the spaced-out freak.

Strangely, the guy doesn't move a muscle. He just leans against the Caddy's grille, eye-fucking Mario. There's an undeniable threat in his glare, like he's issuing a direct challenge: run me over if you've got the balls. Mario revs the engine twice, then lends his elbow to the horn, which he has expensively customized to achieve window-shattering volume. The sheer decibel overload startles the freak. Flipping Mario the finger, he shuffles into the lane of opposing traffic and comes within inches of getting creamed by a rainbow-colored microbus.

Pouring on the gas through the intersection, Mario thinks back to the song he just heard, the one that got under his skin. He grudgingly admits to himself that that little swish Jagger might actually be onto something. "Gimme Shelter" really does capture the mood of the U.S. in the summer of '69. These are strange days. The country no longer feels on firm footing. And, as usual, whatever is being experienced on a national scale gets amplified and distorted all the fuck out of whack on the Sunset Strip.

The near-collision with the street freak is a perfect example. A year ago, if some hippie wandered into traffic, he'd just smile sheepishly and flash the peace sign before walking on. But now there's an unmistakable undertone of confrontation, of violence begging for a reason to erupt. Like with all the fights in front of the Whisky. Why are the kids so fuckin' agitated, Mario wonders. In the early days—'64, '65—you'd have maybe three street-side brawls in an entire year, and they were like pillow fights compared to some of the shit he had to deal with back in Chicago. But this summer people are actually getting hurt, and it's changing the entire face of the Strip.

These thoughts trouble Mario Maglieri as he inches his way along Sunset. If he were where he should be right now, at home in front of a huge pile of his wife Scarlett's homemade linguini with clam sauce, he would undoubtedly be in a better mood instead of wondering how and why this once idyllic scene started to lose its way.

Forty minutes ago, Mario was just tucking his napkin into his collar when the phone rang. As soon as he heard his wife say, "He's eating, can't it wait an hour?", Mario knew it was a call from the club. And an emergency. (All his employees are on the strictest orders not to bother the manager at home unless the building is on fire; those are Mario's literal instructions.) After getting a semi-coherent briefing on the situation by a breathless cocktail waitress, Mario untucked his napkin and told Scarlett to put his dinner in the fridge.

As he was grabbing his car keys, their sixteen-year-old son, Mikeal, asked if he could come along. Mario thought about it for a few seconds before telling the boy to sit down and finish eating. Then he left, feeling a little guilty.

All summer, Mikeal has been working as a busboy/bar back/bathroom attendant/whatever at the Whisky, getting his first taste of nightclub management. It's experience that will prove invaluable over the coming decades. Mikeal likes his job so much, he volunteers to put in unpaid hours on his days off. The situation has created some tension between his parents. Scarlett would rather see him spend more time at home, or at least in the company of other teenagers rather than the increasingly seedy trade frequenting the Whisky.

Mario himself is of two minds on the issue. He feels strongly that a sixteen-year-old kid ought to have a job when he's not in school. Okay, not delivering hooch for Al Capone. Something a little steadier. It makes perfect sense to take the boy on at the club, where he can learn the family business while Mario keeps an eye on him. On the other hand, he can't help feeling that some decidedly undesirable influences are rubbing off on the lad, and Mario's managerial duties keep him so busy there's no way he can play chaperone all the time.

Thankfully, Mario doesn't have to brood over his son's upbringing any longer for the moment; the Caddy has finally arrived at the Whisky. He parks in his reserved spot behind the club and enters through the rear. The front door is propped wide open, letting in a blast of natural light that somehow seems highly unnatural in this place. As always, Mario is slightly shocked to see how shabbily unimpressive the Whisky looks in the unforgiving glare of California sunshine. It's like accidentally walking into the dressing room of a glorious stripper only to get an unwanted eyeful of crow's-feet and varicose veins. World-renowned courtesan by night, the Whisky shows herself to be a back-alley tramp under the scrutiny of God's flashlight.

As he walks across the empty dance floor toward the front office, Mario doesn't even notice the scrawny bearded kid hunched in the corner booth, scribbling in a tattered notepad. Completely absorbed in his work, the kid seems oblivious to Mario's entrance as well.

A small conference is underway by the cash register. Two young women, a cocktail waitress and a go-go dancer, are kneeling in front of a third girl who sits on the floor with her hands covering her face. Her tiny tanned shoulders heave with each sob that escapes her throat. The other two are trying to calm her, but to no avail.

"Okay, so I'm here," Mario says, breaking up the huddle. "What's the ruckus?"

The two kneeling girls start talking at the same time, while the crying one continues to bawl. Mario has to clap his hands together like a carnival barker to instill some sense of order.

"One at a time, for Chrissake! From the top, if you please."

Gradually, the story comes into focus. Tiffany, the seated cocktail waitress, arrived at 4:30 to start setting up the bar. Tonight's act, the Flying Burrito Brothers, didn't come by for a sound check, since it's the second show in a three-night stand and they're happy with the quality of the P.A. from their first performance. As she was setting up, Tiffany didn't even notice the short, skinny kid with the beard come in. She just happened to look up and there he was, sitting in the corner booth and writing.

Mario casually glances over his shoulder, noticing the kid for the first time. He is just as Tiffany described him. Mario's first irritable thought is, *that*'s the punk who brought me all the way down here? He doesn't look all that threatening, a pathetically scrawny specimen whose body mass seems to be at least half comprised of hair. A wild tangle of dark brown locks spills over a sloped forehead into an equally bushy beard that drools down onto shoulders a bird wouldn't want to claim. Can't weigh more than a buck-ten, dripping wet. And pale as death.

"So you told him to leave. And he wouldn't."

Tiffany nods, finally gaining control of her breath.

"What did he say to you?"

The question sends the girl spiraling into another fit of sobs. Mario is perplexed. Tiffany has been working at the Whisky for about three months now. In that time she's had to contend with more than her share of ass-grabbing and lewd propositions from the club's patronage. Though Mario cracks down on everything that comes to his attention, the female members of his staff tacitly understand that such misdeeds are part and parcel of working in this particular establishment. Thus far, Tiffany has borne it all with humor and grace. Mario sees in her the potential for that increasingly rare specimen, a long-term female employee of the Whisky. What could have possibly rattled her so?

"His eyes," she stammers in a soft, cracking voice. "I've never seen eyes like that. Dead like a doll's eyes. But crazy."

Mario gently helps her to her feet. The girl's own kohl-rimmed eyes are streaked black from her tears. She's a mess. "Go clean yourself up," he says with a semiplatonic pat on her ass. "I promise that motherfucker won't bother you no more."

Composing herself, Tiffany gives her boss a warm hug of gratitude, covering his swarthy cheek with kisses. He half-heartedly pushes her away and reminds himself to take a look in the mirror after dealing with this situation. For a family man working at the Whisky, lipstick on the collar is a constant occupational hazard.

He walks back to the darkened corner, consciously assuming a slow, unthreatening gait. Why play the hard-ass unless given no other option? Looming over the booth, his shadow falls across the table but garners no response from its occupant.

"Maybe you don't hear so good. We ain't open for another two hours," Mario says in a chummy, almost conspiratorial way.

Still no reply from the bearded kid, who seems totally consumed by the process of scribbling in his notepad. Looking closer, Mario sees that virtually every centimeter of the page is covered with indecipherable smudges.

Raising his voice, he says, "Ya hear what I said, pal? We're closed."

The grubby hand holding the pencil stops writing, then hovers in the air. Quaking just slightly.

Without making eye contact, the owner of the hand says, "That don't mean shit to me."

Huh. Some balls. Mario almost respects the little punk, in a way.

"What's your name?" he asks, still all smiles. "Ya got a name, right?"

The pencil resumes its mad scramble across the page. Just as Mario is about to repeat the question, the shaggy head turns an inch and whispers, "Charlie."

"Mario Maglieri," the manager says, extending his hand. An old-school sense of proprietorship compels him to offer every potential troublemaker the benefit of the doubt before applying fierce punitive measures. "Pleasure's mine, I'm sure."

The kid doesn't even acknowledge his hand, so Mario retracts it. He takes a seat in the booth without waiting for an invitation. "You like music, Charlie?"

"I like *my* music," the kid says quickly, seemingly engaged by the question. "Plus the Beatles got a few good songs."

"Ever hear a band outta Chicago called the Mellowtones? Great fuckin' act, I can't figure why they never made it big. Tough racket, huh?"

Charlie pivots his body to face Mario for the first time. The light coming through the front door is completely absorbed in his abnormally large, dark eyes. They seem to reflect nothing outward. Tiffany was right, Mario thinks. Like a doll's eyes.

"I'm making an album with Dennis Wilson," the kid says in a jittery voice that gains confidence with each word. "Hell, I'll be on that stage in six months' time, bringin' in more pussy 'n you ever seen, gramps."

Mario takes a seat across from the kid, absently examining his pinkie ring like he's got all the time in the world.

"Well, Charlie, you got two problems here. For starters, this club don't open for another two hours. Unless you work for me, or you're gonna be on that stage *tonight,* you don't belong here."

Mario cuts off the coming objection with a raised palm.

"The other problem you got is I don't like nobody hasslin' my waitresses. Not even friends of Dennis Fucking Wilson. Is that clear?"

"All I said was she'd look good with a glazed apple in her mouth."

"She took offense, if you can believe it. And I bet you had more to say to her than that."

The beard shivers with a derisive snort. "That chick belongs in a hog's wallow. Or a two-dollar cathouse."

"That's a matter of opinion, and yours ain't worth a pile of dry shit to me," Mario says, his patience spent. "*Nobody* gives my girls a hard time, not unless they want my foot in their ass."

The kid doesn't have anything to say to that, but whether his silence comes from intimidation or some other emotion is hard to tell.

Choosing to assume the former, Maglieri presses on. "I'm willing to forget what happened today, providing you do two things. Number one, you go over and apologize to her. And make it good. Name's Tiffany."

More silence from across the booth. It seems Charlie's attention has been reclaimed by the notepad.

"Number two, get your ass outta my sight, but quick. And don't come back for a few months, till I decide to forgive you for interrupting my dinner. Is that clear?"

The ink-pool eyes don't blink. Maglieri has the uneasy impression they haven't blinked since he sat down, but the hazy glare coming in from the open door makes it hard to tell.

For the first time during their conversation, Charlie allows some expression to steal over his face. He smiles, revealing an uneven line of brown teeth. It's a friendly smile, like he's amused by some private joke he's finally ready to share.

Maglieri returns it, thinking his point has been made and accepted. These fuckin' kids. All they're really looking for is an adult with the stones to do what their parents never got around to: bring down the whip and show 'em who's boss.

"I can have you killed, man," Charlie says in a dull monotone. "Anytime I feel like it."

A truck rumbles by the front door, its heavy tires rattling across the uneven pavement. For a long moment, their diminishing echo is the only sound heard inside the Whisky. Mario appears genuinely disappointed. He'd actually thought he could reason with this lad, an obviously misguided soul who probably wouldn't look much older than Mikeal if someone were to hold him down and shave that mangy mop from his face. Mario briefly considers doing it himself. It would be the biggest favor anyone ever did for the little shit.

Then he thinks, fuck it. I got enough problems already.

Leaning all the way across the table, so close he can smell the dirt and sweat, Mario cups his ear like he's hard of hearing.

"Come again, Charlie?"

"You heard me. I can kill you, fucker. I'm Jesus."

A two-second pause from Mario. "Is that right?" he drawls slowly. "Then I'm God. You lose."

Like a steel mousetrap, Mario's right hand comes down on the nape of Charlie's neck. Without stopping, it continues its downward curve, propelling the bearded face directly into the linoleum table-top. A crisp thud rings out in the club's musty air, loud enough to startle the girls by the register.

Yanking the kid's head back up, Mario extracts a few tufts of hair between his knuckles. He wipes them away with disgust, then quickly assesses the damage, hoping he didn't cause a concussion. Unbelievably, the kid is still smiling. His teeth are covered in blood and he couldn't look happier.

"Ya can't hurt me, you greasy old pig!"

Mario grabs another handful of hair and hauls the bleeding lunatic out of the booth. The kid reaches for the notepad, but Mario cuffs a hand behind his back and starts shoving him toward the front door.

"My songbook!" Charlie screeches, visibly upset for the first time.

"It's mine now, asshole. You just forfeited it."

Continuing toward the front door, Mario encourages their progress with a series of swift kicks to the seat of the kid's filthy jeans. As they pass the cash register, two of the girls watch the scene with relish.

One of them waves goodbye with mock sadness. Tiffany, however, keeps her eyes down. She can't bear to look at her tormentor even at the moment of his ejection.

In another two seconds, Mario and his cargo emerge through the front door and into the late afternoon sunlight. He throws the kid onto the crowded sidewalk with as much care as he'd show a sack of empty beer cans. A few passersby turn their heads, but most ignore the scene; this kind of thing is way too common on Sunset to draw much attention these days.

"I don't ever wanna see your face again, shithead. Best of luck with your career."

"You'll see it again, pig," Charlie says as he lurches to his feet. "I promise you that."

And then he's gone, swept up in the tide of humanity that flows nonstop along Sunset. Mario brushes his hands together briskly to remove any trace of the kid's filth, then re-enters the Whisky to pre-pare for another night of rock 'n' roll. Within five minutes, he's for-gotten about the whole thing.

A week later, flipping through the *Sunday Times* over breakfast, Mario will read about arrests made in connection with the horrific mass slaying that painted Benedict Canyon red on August 9, two days after he kicked the kid out of the club. Featured prominently on the front page will be a police blotter photograph of the alleged ringleader of assassins, who may or may not have been present at the time of the killings.

Mario will experience a brief jolt of recognition, followed by a queasy feeling of something like culpability that won't fully aban-don him for a long time to come. Staring at the black-and-white face of Charles Manson, Mario Maglieri won't be able to help think-ing, "I shoulda killed that little cocksucker while I had the chance."

The Changing Tide

By the beginning of 1968, the counterculture movement was surfing an unprecedented wave of momentum. Presidential front-runner Robert Kennedy was promising a quick end to Vietnam, while Martin Luther King Jr. was assuring that the awful reality of racism in America would not go unnoticed.

At the same time, a hurricane of creative and sexual energy was smashing headlong into America. Fueled by the skyrocketing popularity of psychedelic drugs and music festivals, bands such as Steppenwolf and Creedence Clearwater Revival were bursting out of America's suburbs into national prominence.

It was a period that inspired some of the greatest rock music ever produced. Crosby, Stills, Nash, and Young were becoming the first American supergroup, and the world was just beginning to appreciate the magnitude of the Beatles' masterpiece *Sgt. Pepper's Lonely Heart's Club Band.*

At last, it seemed, the tide was turning.

But all of this inertia came to a screeching halt when, on April 4, 1968, Martin Luther King Jr. was brutally gunned down while leaving his motel in Memphis, Tennessee. Then, only two months later, another devastating blow came when an assassin's bullet killed Robert Kennedy shortly after a speech in Los Angeles on June 5.

These two atrocious crimes would leave the psyche of the idealistic young hippie culture deeply rattled.

Helter Skelter

It was at this time that a thirty-two-year-old career criminal and con artist was released from a California state prison and given a one-way bus ticket to San Francisco.

His name was Charles Manson.

An aspiring singer/songwriter and self-proclaimed Beatles fanatic, "Charlie" quickly assimilated into the Haight-Ashbury drug culture and began experimenting with large amounts of LSD and methamphetamine. His penchant for fast-talking and self-aggrandizing tales soon made him a beacon for listless runaways looking for direction. Before long, he discovered just how vulnerable drugs made the mind and convinced a group of disillusioned young hippies high on acid that he was Jesus Christ.

Saying he was sent by God to save the Earth from "racial

Armageddon," Manson declared it was his mission to go to Los Angeles and become a rock star so the world could hear his message. Attracting a following of mostly drugged-out young women, Manson and his "family" stole an old school bus and headed south to the Sunset Strip.

Arriving in Los Angeles, Charlie found luck on his side. In a matter of days, he had befriended a young guitar teacher named Gary Hinman, who offered him a temporary place to stay. Hinman also happened to be a friend of the Beach Boys' Dennis Wilson, and soon Manson was introduced to the musical icon. Wilson was instantly struck with the oddly self-assured Manson and his horde of female followers and invited the crew out to his Malibu home. Wilson was even intrigued by Manson's huge portfolio of songs and allowed him to record a demo at his brother Brian's studio.

Almost overnight, Manson and his family were part of the hip L.A. set, spending their days lounging by Dennis Wilson's pool. It was as if destiny was completely taking over.

In fact, destiny *was* taking over. Because it was on one of these days lounging by the pool that Manson first met a young hippie transplant from Texas named Charles "Tex" Watson.

As Tex remembers, "I picked up Dennis Wilson hitchhiking on the Sunset Strip, took him home, and he introduced me to Manson."

Overwhelmed by Manson's force of character, Watson became an almost instant devotee.

"I did what a lot of kids did," explains Tex. "I dropped out of society, so to speak. Manson's philosophy took over my mind as the drugs made me gullible to his influence. Pretty soon his drugged, crazed philosophy became mine, although I did not totally understand it."

Shortly after they'd met, Watson introduced Manson to George Spahn, an old man with a large ranch just north of L.A. Wasting little time, Manson conned Spahn into letting him and his family move to the ranch by promising sexual favors from the family's young women.

At the ranch, Manson created his own little world over which he held complete dominion. Surviving by a combination of dealing drugs, stealing, and scavenging discarded food from supermarket dumpsters, Manson built a place of refuge where disenchanted hippies could drop out of society with relative ease. Every night, Manson and his family would take LSD, and he would preach about the coming of a racial war and Armageddon.

As evidence for this impending doom, he used the lyrics from "Helter Skelter," a track from the Beatles' new *White Album:*

Look out, helter skelter,
Helter skelter, helter skelter.
She's coming down fast,
Yes she is, yes she is.

According to one of Charlie's devotees, Helter Skelter, as the coming Armageddon was known, would begin "with the black man going into white people's homes and ripping off the white people, physically destroying them. A couple of spades from Watts would come up into the Bel Air and Beverly Hills district and just really wipe some people out, just cutting bodies up and smearing blood and writing things on the wall in blood. All kinds of super-atrocious crimes that would really make the white man mad. Until there was open revolution in the streets, until they finally won and took over. Then the black man would assume the white man's karma. He would then be the establishment.

"Charlie said that the family would survive this racial holocaust because they would be hiding in the desert, safe from the turmoil of the cities. He pulled from the Book of Revelations the concept of a 'bottomless pit,' the entrance of which, according to Charlie, was a cave underneath Death Valley that led down to a city of gold. This paradise was where Charlie and the family were going to wait out this war. Afterward, when the black man failed at keeping power, Charlie's family, which he estimated would have multiplied to 144,000 by that time, would then take over from the black man and rule the cities."

"It will be our world then," Charlie told his followers. "There would be no one else, except for us and the black servants."

Charlie forecasted that these events would occur no later than the summer of 1969.

But, aside from his preaching, Charlie still had his goal of becoming a rock star. Using his friendship with Dennis Wilson, he secured a meeting with Beach Boys and Byrds producer Terry Melcher.

That's where Charlie's luck began to run out.

Melcher came to see Manson perform several of his songs live and at first acted very impressed. However, after going to see Manson perform a second time, he told Manson his songs simply weren't marketable enough.

This infuriated Manson. Not only were his hopes dashed, but his music had been insulted. The next day, Manson unleashed a violent tirade at Wilson's house that got him and the family forever banned from the premises.

Undaunted, Manson made several more attempts to land a record deal over the next few months, but each time met with disappointment. Inwardly and outwardly, his rage began to intensify. And he was convinced that Melcher and Wilson were conspiring against him.

These suspicions were confirmed, at least in Charlie's mind, when the Beach Boys released their *20/20* LP in early 1969. On it, the track "Never Learn Not to Love" was musically almost an exact replica of a track from the demo he had recorded at Brian Wilson's studio just a few months before.

Going directly to Dennis Wilson's house, Manson demanded immediate compensation for his song. But Wilson refused. It was then that Manson gave a first glimpse of his potential for real violence. The story goes that Manson handed Wilson a bullet, smiled, then calmly walked away.

For several months after this event, it is reported that Manson's drug use and strange behavior dramatically increased. One of his favorite new activities was to take LSD, go down to Sunset Boulevard, and listen to bands rehearse at the Whisky.

As Tex Watson recalls :

"It was so laidback in those days that you could go by in the afternoon when they were not even open, walk in the door, and watch a rehearsal. One afternoon the Fifth Dimension was practicing, and we were welcomed to watch."

By August of 1969, a deeply embittered Manson had no record deal in sight, and it looked as though his forecast for Helter

Skelter Armageddon was going to be wrong. It was at this time, according to one of his followers, that Manson made the following declaration:

"The only thing Blackie knows is what Whitey has told him. I guess we're going to have to show him how to do it."

What happened next is one of the most chilling displays of brainwashing and mind control ever recorded.

Acting on Manson's orders, Tex Watson, Susan Atkins, Patricia Krenwinkel, Leslie Van Houten, and Linda Kasabian hitchhiked their way up to Terry Melcher's house in the Hollywood Hills. Though Melcher had recently moved out of the house, he was renting it to two major celebrities, director Roman Polanski and his very pregnant movie star wife, Sharon Tate. Polanski happened to be out of the country at the time, but Tate was home entertaining other members of the Hollywood upper crust— hairstylist Jay Sebring, coffee heiress Abigail Folger, and her lover, Voytek Frykowski. Another visitor, Steve Parent, had simply stopped by at exactly the wrong time to see a friend who lived in the backyard guesthouse.

Calmly entering the house, the Manson crew proceeded to systematically shoot, bludgeon, and stab their victims dozens of times. Tate was found with her hands bound by rope and hacked with a butcher knife in the stomach, chest, and back an estimated sixteen times. On the walls, the words "Pigs" and "Helter Skelter" were scrawled in the victims' blood.

After this unbelievable slaughter, the perpetrators simply hitchhiked back home to the Manson Family ranch.

The following night, they would break into another house and murder millionaire businessman Leno LaBianca and his wife,

Rose, in exactly the same way. Leno was stabbed an estimated twenty-six times and Rose an estimated forty-one times.

In the days after the murders, Armageddon never ensued, but the horrific Manson Family killing spree sent shockwaves through the world and brought Hollywood to its knees. The Manson Family was responsible for at least thirteen brutal murders in the L.A. area, but it would take investigators several nail-biting months to piece the crimes together and make arrests.

As Michelle Phillips of the Mamas and the Papas recalls:

"That was it. That's when our innocence was shattered. The social fabric was completely torn by the murders."

Elmer Valentine had been close friends with several of the victims and was personally devastated by the crimes, and Lou Adler had been an investor in Jay Sebring's salons. But the arrests of the bearded, long-haired Manson and his deranged hippie followers were what were most disturbing to the culture on Sunset Boulevard.

As Terry Melcher says, "It changed the tenor of the scene a lot. Because they looked like all the other runaway kids on the Strip. So there was an obvious loss of trust."

ASHES TO ASHES

January 11, 1971

"Well, well," mutters Steve Marriott in the trademark husky snarl that has helped him sell half a million albums over the past six months. "This is fucking *perfect*, innit?"

He lights a cigarette and curses impotently under his breath. There's little else he can do to address the catastrophe unfolding before his shell-shocked eyes.

Marriott, founder and frontman of rising supergroup Humble Pie, is standing on the sidewalk at the southwest corner of Sunset and San Vicente, directly across from the Whisky. It's a little before 1 A.M. on a drizzly midwinter's night. This has been one of the wettest Januarys in recent memory, and tonight hasn't seen a dry minute since sundown. But the rain isn't helping the situation. If anything, it seems to be mocking Marriott's predicament, staining his face like tears.

Humble Pie's lead guitarist Peter Frampton stands next to Marriott, looking sleepy and a little bored. He's a walking dictionary illustration of the ascendant rock star; every detail fills out the portrait, from the flowing hair to the diamond-studded leather boots. Frampton casually checks out the selection of tasty young things gathered around, trying to decide if any are worth squiring back to the Hyatt House. On a normal night, his painted-on satin pants would be drawing hoots and catcalls from the assembled late-night Strip crawlers. But there's nothing normal about tonight, and another stunning spectacle is consuming everyone's attention.

The Whisky is burning. Not a small contained fire, but a moving mosaic of smoke and flame. If not stopped soon, the fire could easily reduce the entire building to ashes. Flames have already licked away the purple and gold checkerboard pattern covering the front wall, exposing the ugly pockmarked cement underneath. "Holy shit!" seems to be the most common reaction among those gathered to watch. The Whisky is really burning. It's a horribly compelling scene that seems downright indecent, like the queen of England being ravaged by a gang of beggars in full public display. And there isn't a fireman in sight.

A few black-and-whites have recently arrived on the scene, mainly to keep the growing crowd contained to the south side of Sunset, where they can't get hurt. Some courageous and/or woefully stoned individuals have ventured across the street and put themselves within inches of the conflagration in order to rip priceless concert posters from display before they too are lost to the flames. One such adventurer found his fuzzy head of red curls ablaze and had to be covered by some good Samaritan's suede jacket before he became a human matchstick. It's hard to tell how much damage was done to the boy; he lies flat on the pavement with the jacket still swaddling his head, attended by a cop who's yelling into his handset for an ambulance.

No one can believe how much smoke there is. It belches and billows upward into the darkening sky. It seems thicker, more noxious than the typical carcinogen cloud produced by a small structure fire. It's as if not just mortar and brick are going up in smoke, but the immortal memories the club has generated are burning as well, dissipating in a mist of black soot high over the lights of Hollywood.

As Steve Marriott watches the building burn, he can't shake the feeling that he's witnessing an omen. Less than an hour ago, Humble Pie finished their first performance ever at the Whisky. It was a corker, three hours of power chord–driven mayhem and the closest thing to an all-out mêlée the club has seen since the Doors' last gig. Marriott and Frampton found themselves trading stunned smiles as the building took on a frenzied life of its own: walls swaying with the collective groove of three hundred–plus bodies, airborne clusters of freshly moistened and inscribed panties raining down at their feet, the entire front row slamming their heads toward the stage. Good fun, all around.

To someone standing in that pulsating crowd, it would seem clear that Humble Pie has definitely arrived. Already established in their native UK, the band has been slavering at the chance to conquer America for over two years. Their latest live LP, *Rockin' the Fillmore,* is starting to do things on the U.S. charts, and comparisons to the reigning heavyweight champ in the supergroup category, Led Zeppelin, are becoming more common in the stateside press. Marriott hardly allows himself to believe the growing hype. It's been a hard-fought battle for this blues-schooled quartet that just can't seem to buy any respect in the elite world of rock, even as their record sales continue to climb. But the proof keeps mounting: Humble Pie is for real. Tonight's gig seems sure to silence the naysayers once and for all. It's almost guaranteed glowing coverage in all the publications whose opinions count.

Cover of *Rolling Stone,* here we come! About bloody time. Can stadium gigs be far away? What happened to that blonde in the halter top? These are a few of the happily jumbled thoughts that raced through Steve Marriott's mind as he toweled off in the dressing room twenty minutes ago.

So to stand here now on this rain-swept street corner, ears still ringing, and watch the Whisky burn to the ground is almost more than Marriott can take. For a man given to a certain fatalistic frame of mind, it's a mercilessly ironic turn of events. If tonight were their last gig rather than their first, he could swallow the situation a bit more easily. No shame in leaving the place in ashes as you jump on a plane and head to the next stop on a scorched-earth campaign across North America. But the band had two more nights scheduled here, precious opportunities to strengthen their reputation at the premier venue on the West Coast. Now those opportunities have been irretrievably lost. It all seems too unfair. Marriott can already see the sarcastic headlines in tomorrow's trades: HUMBLE PIE SETS WHISKY ABLAZE—LITERALLY, BRITISH QUARTET TOO HOT TO HANDLE, PLANS FOR FUTURE GIGS UP IN SMOKE? PIE-MEN AVENGE BOSTON TEA PARTY ON THE WRONG COAST. And on and on.

Torturing Marriott more than anything else is a gut-wrenching tinge of intuition telling him that he may be personally responsible for this disaster. His head still in a bit of a haze, hindering his ability to tell fact from paranoia, the feeling just won't let him be. As he watches the first of three firetrucks make its noisy, belated appearance on the scene, Marriott tries to mentally re-create the scene in the dressing room after the curtain came down on the second set.

Still basking in wave after wave of ovations, the lads of Humble Pie repaired to the dressing room to perform their customary post-gig ritual of speed-chasing two six-packs of Watney's Ale tallboys. Tonight the twelve crushed cans fell to the floor faster than usual, as everyone was hugely amped on the riotous reaction from the crowd.

Removing his drenched shirt, Marriott accepted a snow cone–sized spliff from drummer Jerry Shirley. After taking two successive lung-busting hits, Marriott set the joint down on what he could have sworn was the ceramic death-head ashtray that has served as a sort of mascot during the most recent leg of the tour. Purchased by bassist Greg Ridley back in November in a Bourbon Street voodoo shop, the black-and-white carved skull features grooved teeth that serve as cigarette holders. When Ridley first showed it to the band, everyone thought it was a gas. Except Marriott, whose die-hard superstitious nature has kept him crossing streets to avoid black cats for years.

Still, over the past six weeks, Marriott has had to admit that Quincy, as the ashtray has affectionately been dubbed, has brought nothing but good luck. It was the show in New Orleans that really kicked the band into high gear, launching them on a blazing westward spree through the southern half of the nation culminating with this fresh triumph at the world-famous Whisky A Go-Go.

So tonight, when Marriott set down the smoldering joint, he felt certain it was safely held in Quincy's snaggletoothed embrace. And then he forgot about it completely as the band packed up their gear and filed out of the dressing room to the limo that waited outside. It was as they were exiting the front door that the first whiff of something burning started coming from the rear of the club. Within minutes, the entire empty dance floor was choked with smoke.

Humble Pie told their limo driver to pull around the corner and wait for them; the spectacle of the Whisky imploding in a ball of flames was too morbidly compelling to miss. Standing outside waiting for the firetrucks to arrive, Marriott turned to Jerry Shirley and said, "Fuckin' hell, glad we have good-luck Quincy with us. Might've met our deaths in there."

Shirley looked at him strangely. "What are you talking about? I lost Quincy two nights ago in Tucson. Dontcha remember? I almost missed the plane. Tore my hotel room apart lookin' for him."

The color in Marriott's cheeks faded just slightly. "Nah," he says. "Don't remember a bit of that. Thought the ol' boy was still with us."

"Nah. I think that chubby little groupie made off with him. Strange bird, what was her name?"

While Shirley tried in vain to recall the name of his Tucson road lay, Marriott slowly sank into a silent funk. If Quincy wasn't in the dressing room, on exactly what surface did he place the smoking joint? The truth is he didn't even really bother to look as he set it down on something that appeared vaguely round and black. It could easily have been a twelve-inch LP or God knows what other highly flammable object.

After another fifteen minutes, Marriott feels absolutely nauseous with guilt. Standing on the corner opposite the Whisky, he looks across the street and sees Mario Maglieri locked in an intense discussion with the fire chief. The leather-jacketed manager seems to be berating the chief for not sending his men through the front door to fight the blaze from inside. Apparently it's been determined that the building is doomed, and the best the fire department can do is contain the blaze from leaping to adjacent structures.

All of a sudden, Maglieri seems to be pointing across the street directly at the spot where Marriott stands. The singer freezes, momentarily paralyzed. A bus rumbles by, blocking Marriott's view for a few excruciating moments. When it's past, Maglieri and the chief are once again facing the burning building.

Marriott tries to relax, lightning another cigarette and gazing at the two-story inferno as if it were nothing more noteworthy than a parking meter. As casually as he can, he lets his eyes drift back to the spot where Maglieri is still debating with the fire chief.

There! He's doing it again! The old ball-buster is pointing directly at Marriott! The singer is flat-out convinced that Maglieri is telling the fire chief to question the band.

Frampton taps Marriott on the shoulder, jolting him. "Seen enough, then?"

"Too much, mate. Too bloody much."

"Ashes to ashes, so they say," Frampton says with a yawn. Frampton always looks at things with a slightly detached philosophical bent that can really start to bother Marriott after a while. Nothing gets to the golden-maned guitarist, not for long anyway. Right about now the only thing on his mind is room service back at the Riot House.

Marriott gestures toward the fire chief with as much nonchalance as he can muster. "S'pose he'll want a word with us?"

Frampton shrugs. "Why should he?"

"Well . . ." Marriott lets the thought trail off. "How d' you think it started?"

"Who knows? Probably an electrical short. Let the redcoats worry about it."

The normally oblivious Frampton slowly picks up on the fact that Marriott seems agitated. He chucks him on the shoulder and says, "Anyway, if he wants a word, let him find us at the hotel. Nothing we can do standing here in the rain. Right right?"

Marriott sighs heavily. "Right, right." He reluctantly follows Frampton to the limo that sits idling around the corner on San Vicente. As he climbs in, Marriott steals one last glance across the street. Mario Maglieri now has his back turned to the Strip, shoulders sagging, facing the collapsing carcass of his building. It's a wrenching image that Marriott wishes he hadn't seen. He climbs inside and pulls the door shut behind him.

As the limo creeps east along Sunset, Marriott's brain is ruthlessly hammered by the same two questions: "Did I do this?" and "What are the chances I'll get caught?" The latter question will lose its relevance within days, but the former will continue to eat at Marriott's peace of mind for a long time to come. And it will never be definitively answered.

Not until much later, after the initial shock wears off, does Mario Maglieri have time to consider the possibility that Humble Pie might have played some role in this debacle. It takes the better part of the night for the fire department to completely extinguish the blaze. The Whisky is rendered an ugly smoking shell, an eyesore on the glistening trail of the Strip.

In the end, Peter Frampton's hypothesis will prove correct: the fire at the Whisky A Go-Go is officially attributed to an electrical short. But no amount of official explanation will be able to snuff out the rumors:

"Humble Pie killed the Whisky in a backstage drug stupor!"

"Mario Maglieri deliberately torched the club to collect on the insurance!"

"It was all a plot to generate more interest in the new club opening up next year!"

"The mob did it!"

And on and on.

A Brief Respite

In the months leading up to the Manson murders, a deeply wounded nation was already struggling to come to terms with the senseless assassinations of Martin Luther King Jr. and Bobby Kennedy. Meanwhile, the continuous stream of bodies returning from Vietnam had sparked a dramatic increase in violent inci-

dents and riots. To most Americans, it seemed as though a rising wave of darkness was slowly enveloping the country.

So, when the largest, most decadent rock music festival ever
planned happened to be scheduled less than a week after the
Manson murders occurred, many people expected the worst. In
fact, some government and law enforcement officials made
attempts to put a stop to the concert, citing the looming potential
for disaster.

But, miraculously, the show was allowed to go on. For three
days in the summer of 1969, a nervous America watched and
listened as nearly a half-million flower children gathered peace-
fully and lovingly in upstate New York for perhaps the single
greatest musical event in history.

Woodstock

Woodstock stands alone as the grand crescendo of a counterculture movement that had taken years to mature. Its significance as a symbol of unity and hope during this dark period of
American history is unequalled. For the flower children, it was
a magnificent swan song that demonstrated the power of music
as a harbinger of peace and love.

Held on August 15–17, 1969, Woodstock was modeled directly
after the Monterey Pop Festival and took place at Max Yasgur's
farm near Bethel, New York. Like Monterey Pop, it featured
such names as the Grateful Dead, Jefferson Airplane, Jimi
Hendrix, the Who, and Janis Joplin, as well as some stunning
major debut performances—most notably that of Crosby, Stills,
Nash, and Young.

Far exceeding its expected turnout of two hundred thousand

people, more than 450,000 young hippies descended on the festival, at one point forcing a shutdown of the New Jersey State Turnpike.

But, despite gigantic crowds and a horrendous stretch of weather, Woodstock was the epitome of the peaceful ideals the counterculture movement stood for. In the three days of the festival, there were almost no arrests or violent incidents. Babies were born and babies were conceived. And psychedelic drugs and marijuana were celebrated as much as the music on the stage.

The concert was a triumph. A collective exhalation for an uptight nation begging for some relief.

But the good vibes of Woodstock failed to really change anything permanently. The festival had, unfortunately, been more like a small island that briefly surfaces only when the tide recedes. And the dark tide in America would not subside for long. Soon, the hellish events of another concert festival would sweep the optimism of Woodstock briskly away.

Altamont

For most cultural historians, the Rolling Stones' free concert at Altamont Speedway on December 6, 1969, marked the final nail in the coffin of the turbulent 1960s.

A disaster from its conception to its bloody completion, Altamont exposed a drug-induced moral decay that had slowly begun to invade the underbelly of the entire counterculture movement.

As Rolling Stones photographer Ethan Russell recalls:

"The frightening thing at Altamont, and everyone noticed it, was how much of the audience wasn't just high, they were gone. Their eyes were not entranced but vacant."

Coming at the end of the Stones' decadent North American tour, Altamont had been billed as "Woodstock West," its lineup including many of the same bands—the Grateful Dead, Jefferson Airplane, and Janis Joplin among them.

But hastily planned, Altamont was plagued from the very outset by massive logistic problems. Originally scheduled to be held in San Francisco's Golden Gate Park, the promoters were forced to find a new venue when it became clear just how massive the turnout would be. For weeks they scrambled to come up with a new location, and it wasn't until twenty-four hours before show-time that contracts were officially signed with the nearby Altamont Speedway. Almost overnight, the stage and sound equipment needed to be assembled and basic accommodations constructed for the estimated three hundred thousand fans venturing in from all over the country. It was a nightmare in the making.

The biggest issue looming for the panicked promoters was that of concert security. Since Altamont was nearly thirty miles outside of San Francisco's jurisdiction, they had to come up with a new security force to safeguard the performers. Acting on the advice and assurances of members of the Grateful Dead, the promoters arranged for the local Hell's Angels motorcycle gang to protect the stage.

When the day of the show finally arrived, the chaos was already in full swing. The previous night had seen two festival campers accidentally crushed to death by a truck as they slept in their sleeping bags. Then, just before showtime, another concertgoer drowned in a swimming hole.

The bad vibes rapidly increased with the announcement at the beginning of the show that bad acid and speed were being widely circulated. Compounding this unease was the fact that, unlike Woodstock's towering stage that everyone could see, Altamont's was only a foot tall and invisible to most of the crowd.

When the long-awaited Rolling Stones performance was beset by a lengthy delay, the crowd began to come unglued. Cold weather and a full day of heavy drug use and drinking had made the crowd increasingly unruly, and fights were beginning to break out near the stage. And partying as hard as anyone were the Hell's Angels. At one point, a young hippie fan accidentally fell backward into a Hell's Angel's motorcycle and was subsequently badly beaten by the gang with lead-weighted pool cues.

When the Rolling Stones did finally take the stage, the concert turned even more violent. Less than halfway into their set, as they banged out a loose rendition of "Under My Thumb," a young black man named Meredith Hunter appeared to wave a small handgun at "security" after they'd harassed him and his white girlfriend. Wasting no time, the Hell's Angels tackled him and brutally stabbed him to death in front of a horrified crowd.

Unaware of what had happened, Mick Jagger continued to sing, but was forced to implore the crowd over and over again to "please stop fighting and sit down."

The Stones went on to finish the concert, notably performing the first-ever live rendition of "Brown Sugar" before running for their lives to a helicopter and being whisked away.

The concert had literally and figuratively been a bloodbath. The press had a field day.

After achieving unbridled glory in the wake of Woodstock, the flower children now found themselves relentlessly vilified. For months after Altamont, the news was saturated with horrific stories and images of young hippies wildly doing drugs and getting violent. Matters were only made worse when the trial of the hippie-ish Manson Family began to grip the country.

But at Altamont, despite all of the horrors that were occurring all over the world, the flower children had no one to blame but themselves.

As Stanley Booth, the legendary Rolling Stones biographer, summed it up:

"The assassinations of the '60s had aged us . . . but they had been random, isolated events that didn't involve the rock 'n' roll generation. Altamont was nothing we could shrug off, and somehow we all lacked the will to rise above it."

The Music World Mourns

By the arrival of the 1970s, a deeply troubled counterculture movement was just barely getting by on life support. Its main symbol of strength, the major concert festival, was now looked at as too risky a venture, and distrust of the hippie culture was rapidly escalating. But things would get even worse. The Beatles had decided to split up, breaking hearts the world over and proving John Lennon's decree that "the dream is over." And soon, some of the music world's most powerful voices would be forever silenced.

The first major star to fall was Jimi Hendrix on September 18, 1970. After a career that lasted only three years, Hendrix died choking on his own vomit in London after taking a lethal combination of drugs. He was twenty-seven years old.

Less than three weeks later, on October 4, 1970, Janis Joplin was found dead of a heroin overdose in the Landmark Motor Hotel in Hollywood. She, too, was twenty-seven.

As Mario Maglieri's son Mikeal recalls:

"Janis Joplin was at the Whisky the night before she died. I thought I'd killed her for a while. I was serving drinks, and the next morning they said she'd died of alcohol poisoning. I was like, 'Oh, God, I killed Janis Joplin!' I had given her a case of Southern Comfort, but she never drank it. Thank God."

On July 3, 1971, Jim Morrison died of a heroin overdose while taking a bath in his Paris hotel room. Like Janis and Jimi, he was also only twenty-seven. Eerily, in an interview shortly before his death, Jim had made these uncannily prophetic comments:

"I see myself as a huge fiery comet, a shooting star. Everyone stops, points up, and gasps, 'Oh, look at that!' Then—whoosh, and I'm gone . . . and they'll never see anything like it ever again . . . and they won't be able to forget me—ever."

But, in some ways, the final and perhaps most symbolic blow to the counterculture movement came when the Whisky A Go-Go caught fire in 1971 after a wild Humble Pie concert. As a result of the blaze, the club was shut down for nearly six months before reopening again at the end of the year in a drastically stripped-down version.

Officially, the fire was blamed on an electrical short, but several sources felt the band had accidentally caused it. As the story goes, certain members of Humble Pie left several cigarettes and joints burning unattended in a makeshift ashtray while recklessly partying in the dressing room after their performance. When the carpet ignited, they all scrambled to get out of there without telling anyone.

When asked about the cause of the fire, Mario Maglieri has churned out various elliptical answers over the years. But during an interview with Sue Schneider in 1992, he finally put the issue to rest. Although he pointed to the band, he claimed not to hold a grudge:

"Nah, it was an accident. I remember that night they played. Of course, the dressing room was upstairs and the office downstairs in the back. I saw the lines going on the telephone. I thought, there's got to be a burglar up there or something. I figured there was no one else in the building. So I take a gun and I quietly go to the stairs to the middle door, and I open the door, and, all of a sudden, the smoke and the fire. So now I close the door, and I'm walking down the stairs going, 'Should I call the fire department? Was my insurance paid?' You know, things go through your mind. So I go straight to the ticket booth in front and call the fire department. Then I went to Europe for a while."

Ironically, Humble Pie's founder and singer, Steve Marriott, one of the men accused of causing the conflagration, died in a fire at his own house twenty years later.

When the Whisky A Go-Go reopened at the end of 1971, it was but a shadow of what it had been in the glory days of old. Gone were the elegant trappings of Elmer Valentine's vision of Paris in America. The new Whisky was little more than an empty open space with a bar up front and a stage in back. The name still carried weight, and music would continue to be played there, but, to many who had been present for the Whisky's glorious flowering, the dream truly was over.

It would take almost a decade for the club to rediscover its relevance in the midst of a new musical movement every bit as colorful and chaotic as that which had witnessed its birth.

HOUSES
OF THE
HOLY

At 9015 Sunset Boulevard, just two blocks west of the Whisky A Go-Go, stands a small, nondescript two-story building that, at first glance, looks like nothing more than a quaint Italian restaurant. It is an unpretentious-looking place where a cheeseburger special is scrawled on a chalkboard outside the front door and a generic sign on a window proudly boasts, "Voted the Best Steak and Lobster in L.A."

The inside has the look of any other Italian eatery. A large brick fireplace welcomes you into a dimly lit room filled with red leather booths and plain wood tables. On each table is only a small candle, neatly secured into the base of a simple wrought-iron pizza stand.

But upon closer examination, something very different about this place begins to emerge. It is a quality that almost defies explanation.

Covering nearly every inch of the walls and ceiling are priceless pieces of rock 'n' roll memorabilia that seem so at home that they go virtually unnoticed. And everywhere, lovingly framed or preserved inside glass cases, are countless photographs bearing witness to some of the world's biggest rock legends and movie stars in all stages of their careers, partying the night away. But they are not just partying anywhere. They are in this place, in these booths, on these tables.

In an instant, the restaurant's unassuming façade begins to melt away. A more in-depth tour reveals a veritable labyrinth of secret staircases and hallways leading to hidden bars, private alcoves, a dance floor, and even an old pirate ship's galley.

Indeed, this is no ordinary restaurant after all. This is a place that creaks and cracks with a spirit all its own.

This is the legendary Rainbow Bar and Grill—the home of rock 'n' roll.

THE GREATEST ROCK 'N' ROLL
JOINT IN THE WORLD

April 16, 1972

A full moon hangs fat and low in the sky tonight. Of course. What else could account for the incessant howling and baying that disturbs the hazy airspace over Hollywood on an otherwise normal Saturday evening?

Except those aren't wolves giving full-throated voice to their lunar mania. They are limousine drivers. And, rather than depend on their own God-given powers of oral expression, these prowling denizens of the night are relying on the high-decibel horns with which their sleek chariots are equipped. There must be a hundred of them blaring away right now, their synthetic cries overlapping and mingling. Just about every available limo in town is sitting on the Sunset Strip, and it's safe to speculate that most of them are carrying People of Importance.

In Los Angeles, People of Importance are used to waiting out long stretches of traffic in the cozy confines of stylish rented vehicles. That's what minibars and cocaine are for. What these folks cannot abide is being late for an Event of Importance. Fashionably late is one thing, but to delay your entrance too long is unacceptable. So the antsy passengers instruct their drivers to lean on the horn as a way of making their displeasure known. Naturally, the drivers comply. They are eager to oblige the whims of their clients, especially the ones known to tip lavishly.

Seen from the vantage point of the KABC traffic copter, the grid-lock along the Sunset Strip resembles a two-headed neon snake slinking east and west with something approaching symmetry. At least that's the image springing into the mind of KABC's "Eye in the Sky" traffic reporter as he looks down upon it from his aerial view-point. After signing off, the reporter spends a few minutes mar-veling at the serpentine trail of twinkling headlights, wondering what in God's name could be attracting all those limos to the same spot.

The snake's two heads meet in a short, narrow driveway a few blocks west of the closed Whisky A Go-Go. This driveway leads to a small parking lot behind an unimposing two-story building. It's nothing you'd be apt to notice while cruising the Strip, just a boxy brick-and-mortar structure with aged wooden paneling on the sec-ond floor that gives it a vague barnyard vibe. Stained-glass win-dows facing the sidewalk add a pleasantly surreal touch. A neon sign stretches high above the roof, spelling out the name of the place in vertical multicolored letters.

At long last, the Rainbow Bar and Grill is open for business. There goes the neighborhood.

Only one thing short of the Oscars could produce a limousine crush of this scale. After almost two years of hype, idle rumor, and wild speculation, everyone is dying to get a peek at what's been billed as the new crown jewel in the showcase of L.A. nightlife. If a small fraction of the promises prove accurate, the Rainbow will immediately be recognized as the gold standard of rock clubs worldwide.

And yet it all sounds rather implausible. Who ever heard of a rock club that doesn't feature any live music? According to a brief, elliptical press statement issued by majority owners Bob Gibson, Lou Adler, Mario Maglieri, and Elmer Valentine, the Rainbow will be a place for music industry heavies to just come and hang out. Food and cocktails, you bet. Live music, go somewhere else. And, yeah, there's still a cover, one that buys you two drink chits at the door in the 1950s tradition of Mario's Belmont Tap. Our place, our rules. You don't like it, no one's begging you to come here.

More than a few industry players greeted this announcement with raised brows. The arrogance of it. The sheer balls of opening a nightclub on the most expensive and desirable stretch of real estate in all of L.A. County, the throbbing heart of West Coast rock 'n' roll, right next to Bill Gazzarri's joint, which, by the way, features live performances seven nights a week. Who the fuck do these guys think they are? After the ignominious decline of the once-mighty Whisky, you'd think Maglieri and Valentine would be a little more prudent in their next venture. As for Gibson, he's just a public relations man. Though admittedly he's a good one, exactly how does that qualify him to run a club?

These and other outraged queries have been echoing through recording studios, executive boardrooms, guitar stores, head shops, and penthouse suites for months now. Curiosity has taken hold of a business that prides itself on being jaded. Which is why every top-tier player has come out to see for himself on opening night, whether invited or not. It's also why the Strip is such a jammed-up nightmare right now.

Of all the big names stuck in traffic, surely none is more irritated than Elton John. He sits in a rigid position in the back of his limo, refusing the complimentary champagne in favor of the heady buzz his rising sense of indignation delivers. His hair dyed roughly the shade Crayola uses for Burnt Orange, his compact frame packed into a white satin bodysuit with enough sequins to make a Vegas showgirl feel criminally deprived, Elton radiates stardom no matter how black his mood.

Tonight is supposed to be his night. Through a series of negotiations and closed-door meetings so complex as to make the Vietnam Peace Talks look like a handshake agreement, Elton's manager succeeded in booking the Rainbow's opening night, beating out competing offers from Rod Stewart and the Stones. It was a triumph of ruthless deal making. Elton rewarded everyone in his entourage with a new Rolex.

His satisfaction is now fading in light of the humiliating fact that he can't seem to get near his own bash. Looking out the limo's smoked glass windows, Elton hears a car door slam and spots a three-pack of golden-haired nymphs waltzing arm in arm toward the Rainbow, their laughter peppering the night in their wake.

"Finally lost hope," he mutters. "Who can blame them?"

It seems that quite a few people have decided to hop out in the middle of the street and finish their journey on foot. The sound of patent leather loafers and stiletto heels jogging across asphalt echoes through the dark as these resolute souls weave through the grid and eventually reach the sidewalk, sure they've made the sensible choice. But they are the exception. Most of the stalled passengers would rather sit it out till dawn than pull such a low-rent move. Emerging onto the red carpet while your driver holds the door for you is standard operating procedure for a gig like this, and the great majority of tonight's A-list invitees are damned if they're going to hoof it down the sidewalk like a fucking civilian.

Finally, Elton's limo creeps into the driveway. He steps out with the relaxed movements of a guy in no hurry at all. His smile awaits the exploding flashbulbs. He's made the scene.

Standing guard by the Rainbow's entrance is Mario Maglieri,

looking like the captain of an overloaded ship kept afloat by the sheer force of his personality. Elton crosses the carpeted driveway toward him, making a concerted effort to keep the grin on his face.

"There he is," Mario rumbles with a broad smile. "The guest of honor. We were getting worried."

"Lucky to make it at all," Elton says sharply. "Like trying to get out of Berlin in '44. Bloody nightmare."

"Take it as a compliment," Mario replies with good humor, ignoring the mild fuck-you attitude. "We've been gettin' calls all day from folks desperate for an invite. I'm talking about heavy hitters, not a buncha fuckin' nobodies. Although plenty of them, too, come to think of it."

It's barely 9:30, and the evening has already been complicated by more than its share of logistic hassles, but Mario couldn't look more calm. He stands casually with his weight settled back on his heels, waiting for Elton's four-person entourage to catch up with him. What a crew, not a straight-swinging dick among them. Feathers seem to be big with this gang. And mascara. In twenty-four years of marriage, Mario hasn't given Scarlett as much jewelry as he sees in front of him right now. Well, what the hell. Takes all kinds.

Elton is speaking rapidly into the ear of a trim bald fellow Mario recognizes as the singer's manager. Mario remembers the man clearly. He's the one who played an impressive game of hardball when it was time to book the club for tonight. That was back in early March. Mario was closely involved in the negotiations, as were Elmer, Bob Gibson, and the handful of other men with an ownership stake in the Rainbow.

The club was originally scheduled to open on the first of the month. April Fool's Day. What better occasion on which to launch this ship of fools? (The Rainbow's management team will soon come to be known and revered for their penchant for self-deprecation.) A series of last-minute problems delayed the opening for fifteen days. So be it, thought the owners. It'll just get everyone even more riled up.

Every major rock star in town wanted a shot at tying their fame to the Rainbow Bar and Grill on its very first night. Preliminary offers were meticulously screened to see who really wanted it badly enough. It eventually came down to a pissing contest between representatives from Elton's camp and the long-suffering management team of Rod Stewart. Both sides knew what a coup they were bargaining for. In the end, Elton's reps showed the sharpest teeth, making Swiss cheese of what the Stewart team insisted was their client's final bid. Shaking the winners' hands, Mario couldn't help smiling with admiration.

He's still smiling now, either because he's relieved the guest of honor has finally arrived or because he can't get over the dinner plate–sized, sapphire-encrusted glasses that frame Elton's face in a way Mario can't believe is supposed to be flattering. But what does he know? He's wearing the same suit he wore his first night at the Whisky. Even Mario would have to admit that, on the fashion timeline, 1964 and 1972 belong in different centuries.

As the star attraction and the rest of his entourage approach the entrance, formal introductions are made. Mario extends a hand and completely envelops Elton's with a knuckle-crushing shake. "Mario Maglieri. I'm a big fan, big fan."

"Pleasure's mine, I'm sure," Elton replies with a half-whimper as he retracts his throbbing right hand and gingerly massages it with his left. Christ, who *is* this silver-haired capo? Doesn't he bloody realize a piano player lives by his hands?

Elton's thoughts are interrupted as his shoulder is powerfully hooked by the same fleshy catcher's mitt and propelled toward the entrance. Mario holds open the door and gestures for Elton and his people to enter. Laughter and ribald exclamations ring out from the hazy darkness inside.

"Go ahead, killer," Mario says with a wink. "I think you've kept 'em waiting long enough."

With a curt nod, Elton and his posse pass through the wood-paneled door. And down the proverbial rabbit hole.

In fact, the place is sort of like a rabbit hole, with its warm, dark, slightly subterranean feel. But the liberal application of the color red helps keep everything looking lively. It's a very Italian kind of joint. Old world. The paneled walls, high-beamed ceiling, and oversized hearth seem to whisper tales of conquest and revelry that reach deep into the collective unconsciousness. The building feels far older than rock 'n' roll itself, yet breathes with a suitable spirit of wild abandon. This is a place made for partying. As such, it offers a variety of different environments in which to have good times both overt and covert.

The cavernous dining room is packed. Not a free seat to spare in any of the thirty-some booths, except for booth number one, which is reserved for the guest of honor. Restrained dinner-table conversation is not, nor will it ever be, part of the atmosphere here. Toasts are loud and frequent, laughter bubbles up from crowded booths and dark corners, and a cascading symphony of clinking glasses and silverware ebbs and swells but never fully dies. It's a good kind of clamor—the kind that belies the all-star clientele present tonight and says that *everyone* is welcome here. That sense of inclusion, which stems in large part from the come-one/come-all attitude of Mario Maglieri, will play a large part in the Rainbow's evergreen popularity throughout the next four decades.

Making a quick lap around the dining room, Elton accepts fealty from his subjects. It's phony, but everyone knows it, so it's okay. In a night or two, someone else will be in here getting the royal treat-ment, and someone else the week after that. Everyone under-stands. They may be bearing knives in their cummerbunds, waiting for a moment of weakness to strike, but for right now the music industry well-wishers genuinely wish Elton well. Blown kisses and insincere compliments rule.

Sashaying around the fireplace, which is thankfully dormant (there's enough body heat in the room to power the L.A. Coliseum), Elton is pleased to spy Bob Gibson greeting people at the entrance to the main downstairs bar. He has dealt with Gibson before and feels he has a bit of rapport with the man. No need to throw a fit, but it's only fair to give him a pinch of shit about the fiasco in the parking lot. I mean, really. It's embarrassing for everyone. Didn't they anticipate a huge turnout? This is a party for *Elton John,* isn't it?

The ever-shrewd Gibson has been briefed on his star attraction's frustration. He sees the sequined singer coming from all the way across the room and moves decisively into preemptive mode. Gibson wraps Elton in a warm hug and unleashes a voluble torrent of greetings and flattery while slyly motioning to the bartender. Before Elton can launch into a harangue about the parking backup, Gibson hands him a Long Island iced tea and offers a toast to the man of the hour. What the hell, Elton thinks. It's been a bloody long wait and the champagne in the limo was piss. There's always time for bitching later.

In fact, it never gets to that. Though Elton couldn't have known it at the time, the Rainbow's Long Island iced tea will come to achieve near-mythic status as the single most potent cocktail that can be (legally) purchased on the Sunset Strip. Whether Gibson has this in mind can't be said for certain, but his instincts are right on target; after inhaling his first Long Island and gladly receiving a second, Elton mellows notably.

The evening continues to unfurl with a kind of sloppy magnificence. By about eleven, pretty much all of the invited guests have arrived. Those still upset about the delay are quickly doused in the river of alcohol flowing from the three bars and pummeled by a nonstop barrage of complimentary hors d'oeuvres from the kitchen. Dozens of potential crashers are turned away at the front door by a pair of professional wrestlers moonlighting as bouncers. A few arrests are made. It's a party.

Bob Gibson relishes his role as host. Taking one Person of Importance after another on a guided tour, the PR man–turned-impresario swells like a proud papa handing out cigars. Or a mad scientist pleased with the monster he's created. Gibson starts the tour by introducing everyone to Tony Vescio, the pompadoured doorman brought over from the Whisky. Tony is the definition of a pro in this arena: slick without being oily, authoritative without coming on too strong. He sets the tone as soon as you walk in the door.

After a whirl through the star-studded dining room and a peek at the coed rugby scrum attacking the main bar, Gibson leads his guests into the merrily chaotic kitchen. The air itself seems edible, heavily laden with the aromas of ancient recipes from the Maglieri family cookbook. Everyone gets a chance to meet the head chef, Miguel Maurillo. Clutching a meat cleaver in one fist and wearing an apron splattered with marinara sauce, Miguel could easily be in the middle of a killing spree, but he's too busy managing this culinary chaos. Pizza dough spins woozily, salads are tossed with reckless abandon, large slabs of red meat sizzle in their fat. The stoves at the Rainbow keep firing until midnight, and there won't be a slow minute until then.

The tour moves from the kitchen to the back bar, which is

smaller and stocked strictly with the essentials. If you've got anything exotic in mind, you'll have to brave the crowd up front. But
back here the double-D-cups and dirty jokes of Antoinette the barmaid soon earn this little nook a crew of die-hard loyalists.

As the tour's closer, Gibson guides his guests up the purple-lit
stairway to the second floor. At the moment he's leading Linda
Ronstadt by her dainty hand, cautioning her to watch her high
heels on the narrow steps. Upstairs is where the bathrooms are, but
Gibson has another destination on his itinerary. He points to a
small platform on top of another truncated stairway that leads to a
double-bolted door. That's all there is to see, apparently. Linda is
starting to question Gibson's motives in dragging her up here.

"What do you think?" he asks.

"Wow," she says. "A door. What's behind it? The broom closet?"

Gibson goes deadpan. "You're warm. Guess again."

Linda tries to think of a clever answer for a few seconds before
she bores of the game. "I give up. What's back there?"

"Nothing. Yet." Gibson says with a sly, satisfied grin. "But in six
months' time, that door will let you into the most exclusive private
dance floor in the world."

"So there *will* be live music! I just won twenty bucks from
Amhet Ertegun."

"No live acts," Gibson explains with a patient wave of the hand.
"Just a juke."

"That's it? A juke?"

"The loudest juke you ever heard. Plus a full bar, an intimate
loft with candlelit booths, and best of all: total privacy. Only the
cream of the cream is gettin' in up here."

"So I'll be here opening night?" Linda asks, leaning in just a little bit closer.

"You're definitely in the running."

"You son of a bitch!" she says, shoving him away playfully. "What are you gonna call it? Bob's Backdoor Room?"

"Fuck that!"

"Oh, I guess you've got a better name?"

"Over the Rainbow," Gibson says, breaking into an infectious chuckle. "What else?"

Linda considers the name for a moment. "I like it," she admits.

Taking her hand, Gibson leads her back down into the maelstrom on the first floor. Mario Maglieri pulls him aside with a gracious bow to Linda and offers a quick update on the status of the evening. One waitress has already quit after receiving an obscene proposition by a bunch of drunk executives from BMI in booth number twenty-four. About a dozen glasses have shattered. A couple was discovered humping in the storeroom by a wide-eyed busboy. And the kitchen is fresh out of eggplant. All in all, it's been a pretty smooth ride. Gibson and Maglieri grab two glasses of champagne from a passing tray and toast their new venture.

And the party rages on.

As a strange footnote to the night, which is described in the trades as surpassing all expectations, many in attendance will wonder about the apparent absence of one of the Rainbow's high-profile owners. Throughout the following day, as various hangover cures are being applied all across the city, people will look at each other with bloodshot eyes and say, "What happened to Elmer last night?" There will be some argument as to whether he was there at all.

During the last year or so at the Whisky, Valentine has been getting sort of lost in the shadows. Everyone still recognizes him as a dominant force on the L.A. music scene; it's just that lately he's taken on a more low-key role. Some will suggest he's burned out, another casualty of the good life. Someone who couldn't hack the long haul. Others, claiming close personal ties, will say that Valentine has intentionally removed himself from the limelight. They say he has chosen to let Mario Maglieri take the up-front position, deferring to the man's effortless rapport with artists and patrons alike.

Rumors of increasingly strained relations between the two men have been gaining credence for some time. Some believe there's a lake of bad blood over the collapse of the Whisky—not just the fire, but the overall decline in clientele and musical offerings. But few within the Rainbow's establishment give the gossip much weight. With so much money to be made, how could two old friends let some petty feud come between them? The only way to survive is to look to the future. Plans are already being laid to reopen a streamlined incarnation of the Whisky that will offer a bare-bones, no-frills opportunity to catch the best emerging rock acts in Southern California. In the meantime, there's the Rainbow to focus on. The '70s are here, and once again it seems that the nightclub kings of the Sunset Strip will be setting the pace. Everyone else will have to be content with playing catch-up.

A Living Legacy

By 1972, the death knell had officially sounded for the counter-culture movement in the United States. Hippies had been systematically demonized in the press as America's version of the Viet Cong, and police were on alert to arrest recreational drug users faster than they could light up a joint. Federal officials classified rock 'n' roll as dangerous, and the musicians who created it were often tracked by the FBI. At one point, even John Lennon was forced to fight deportation, having been charged with attempting to subvert the U.S. government.

But all of this seemed only to stoke the flame burning inside America's youth. Idealism was quickly and defiantly replaced by hedonism, and the appetite for drugs and loose sex remained undaunted. And, more than ever, rock stars were worshipped like gods. All over the world, the popularity of their music was exploding, creating a demand even the well-oiled musical machinery of Los Angeles struggled to meet.

Sure, for all intents and purposes, the counterculture movement may have been dead. But, as the 1970s would soon prove, its legacy was just beginning to unfold.

Do What Thou Wilt

The incredible popularity of this "dangerous" rock 'n' roll worldwide meant that an unprecedented bounty of money was being dumped back into the record industry. It was a time when it seemed that every new band to hit the radio sold a million albums, and even bands that had faded in the '60s were return-ing to make a fortune. All of the people involved—the man-agers, the producers, and especially the musicians—were reaping untold riches beyond their wildest dreams.

In Hollywood, this rock 'n' roll culture of young nouveaux riches was steadily beginning to set the tone for the city. Openly consuming massive quantities of drugs and alcohol, they set a standard of decadence the likes of which the city had never seen. Insulated by the power their money brought them, they recklessly indulged their every whim, simply leaving behind blank checks to clean up their messes. It was as though, at least in their own minds, they existed in a world free of any personal responsibility. Even movie stars, who had long been members of the ostentatious new-money elite, found it difficult to relate.

But not everyone in Hollywood accepted the young rockers' blank checks. Frightened or put off by their brash arrogance and debauchery, many of Hollywood's old blue-blood restaurants and bars simply refused to provide service to this latest version of the hip crowd. They were content to cater only to the slightly less hip movie stars and studio executives.

So, when famed band manager and public relations guru Bob Gibson first conceived of dedicating a posh restaurant solely to the excesses of rock 'n' roll, he never attempted to conceal his motives.

"We were tired of getting fucked over by other places," declares Gibson, "and decided to fuck ourselves over instead. Back then, you were still hassled if you had long hair. You couldn't get service in a good French restaurant. This was going to be our revenge."

Gibson's plan was to make this new restaurant a shameless den of unbridled hedonism. A place where the record industry could throw lavish parties free from the judgmental glares of nervous maitre d's and without the hassle of dress and conduct codes. It would be completely exclusive, and it would be insulated—protected from the capricious discretion of local law enforcement to check for "fire code violations."

To pull the place off, Gibson solicited the help of his good friend Lou Adler and two other men who knew a few things about running a business—Elmer Valentine and Mario Maglieri.

The group was instantly intrigued by Gibson's idea and decided that with Maglieri and Valentine overseeing day-to-day operations, such a "restaurant" could become a reality.

For a location, they scouted out a dying restaurant/bar just up the street from the Whisky called the Windjammer. Partially owned by NBA superstar Wilt Chamberlain, the Windjammer was designed to resemble the interior of a pirate's ship, complete with wood planks, stained glass, a secret galley, and even a crow's nest. The place was also steeped in history. In a previous incarnation it had been the regal Villa Nova—a posh supper club best known for having hosted the first date between Marilyn Monroe and Joe DiMaggio and being the spot where Vincent Minelli proposed to Judy Garland.

It was perfect. Wasting little time, the group, along with several other music industry heavyweights, invested fifty-five thousand dollars to buy the Windjammer out. The stage was set.

In no time, news that the owners of the famous Whisky A Go-Go were going to open a dedicated rock 'n' roll restaurant spread like wildfire through the music world.

Requests for reservations from the biggest names in the record industry poured in from London to L.A. Everyone, it seemed, was anticipating that this restaurant was going to be something very special.

Welcome to the Rainbow

When the Rainbow Bar and Grill opened for business on April 16, 1972, it almost instantly became rock 'n' roll holy ground.

"It opened with a party for Elton John. He wanted to be first," recalls Gibson. "Then the next week we had a party for Rod Stewart, then the Stones, and suddenly we were on the map. Around the world, the Rainbow became the place to be."

As Mario Maglieri recalls:

"In 1972 we gave Mick Jagger his birthday party here. You couldn't get near it. They were on the roof trying to get in, there were so many people. And I remember him lying in the middle of the floor, all stretched out. You know, the rock star."

Right away, the Rainbow was the trendiest, hippest place in all of Los Angeles. And, without any pretenses, it more than lived up to everything Bob Gibson had dreamed of.

While sitting in the Rainbow's galley, Ozzy Osbourne reflects:

"You name anyone in the history of rock 'n' roll, they've all been in this club. It's incredible. We were like fucking vampires in this place, all gacked up and drunk. There were fights here—I mean, every possible fucking thing you can think of has gone on in this place."

He continues, "My wife used to come here before I married her, and I used to come here before I met my wife, but we never met each other here. I just hope they never tear it down."

Motörhead's Lemmy Kilmister, a loyal patron since 1973, describes the Rainbow this way:

"They don't treat you like shit and throw you out the minute the clock strikes. They're good people. Reasonable people. They have a sense of the absurd.

"But it's never really been a cultural center, as such. There's no books in here, you know? We weren't watching Eisenstein on small screens in the back. It's a place where you can pull birds, basically. It has a nice ambiance. I like all this wooden stuff. It's got nice paneling, a few nice masts to hang the women from— why not? If they put the plank back, we could walk the plank. Or if you've got a particularly stunning chick, you can take her here and make all the other guys sick, you know? It's that kind of place."

Although a few young actors like Dennis Hopper, Jack Nicholson, and Warren Beatty were able to cross over to the rock scene, most of the tamer movie crowd never even tried. In the early '70s, the Rainbow Bar and Grill was the exclusive turf of the rock 'n' roll elite, and everyone knew it.

Ambrosia

Adding to the Rainbow's burgeoning reputation for excess was the acclaim its food earned from critics. For years, the consensus was that the restaurant prepared some of the finest Italian dishes in all of Los Angeles. Even today, the Rainbow maintains a rabid fan base. "The best fucking pizza on the planet right here," exclaims Ozzy.

Another connoisseur of Rainbow cuisine is porn legend and part-time standup comic Ron Jeremy, who continues to dine at the restaurant on a weekly basis.

"The first time I came to the Rainbow twenty years ago I was actually skinny," recalls Jeremy. "I was posing for *Playgirl*. Now I get offers from *Field and Stream*. You can see the Rainbow here in my stomach."

He continues, "But the food here is incredible. Now that I'm in my forties, I think I look at the food in the Rainbow more than the beautiful women. You give me a choice between a beautiful blonde over here and a Rainbow steak and salad over there . . . I guess I'd still take the blonde. Wait until I'm fifty, then I'll take the steak."

The success of the food, according to Mikeal Maglieri, is that the recipes came straight from his mother Scarlett's kitchen.

"It was almost like a family atmosphere," says Mikeal. "The items on the menu weren't foods you couldn't pronounce. Half the recipes were my mother's, and that's family food."

To this day, Miguel Maurillo, the head chef who helped open the restaurant back in 1972, remains the number-one man in the kitchen, and Scarlett Maglieri, Mario's wife, still tests all the new dishes on the menu.

9

VALHALLA, I AM COMING

October 5, 1973

They are on their way. They'll be here before another hour passes. Why try to hide? You might as well try to hide from a tornado that's ripping across the dusty plains at a hundred miles an hour. Or two barrels of buckshot, fired point-blank.

This is roughly what Mario Maglieri is thinking. Mostly to amuse himself. He's not really worried, just a little excited by the news Tony Vescio whispered in his ear a few minutes ago. Led Zeppelin's private jet ("the Starship") is due to land at LAX twenty minutes from now. A caravan of limousines already awaits the band and its entourage on the tarmac. It will bring them directly here, to the Rainbow Bar and Grill, without stopping for fuel, food, or traffic signals, if possible. Their bags and equipment will be sent to the Riot House in separate vehicles. The band sees no need to waste precious time checking in and freshening up from the flight. They will be welcomed with open arms and thighs no matter how offensive their funk.

It's been almost a year since the Zep crew has paid a visit to the Rainbow, and they are almost pathologically eager to get back. Usually they announce their stopovers a week or two beforehand, allowing the staff sufficient time to buttress itself for the onslaught. But tonight Led Zeppelin's hulking manager, Peter Grant, only saw fit to provide advance notice of a few hours. He phoned Tony from the cocktail lounge in Terminal One at O'Hare as the Starship was refueling. Told him to clear their usual table and to have three cases of chilled Guinness set aside for their personal consumption during dinner. Then Grant hung up without saying goodbye, and Tony passed the information on to Mario.

The two old pros can't help but laugh. "So much for a quiet night, huh?" Tony says to his boss.

Mario sighs as he recalls the band's last social call. It was an orgy of food, drink, and semipublic group sex that basically turned the Rainbow into the West Coast's premier whorehouse for an unbelievable seventy-two-hour stretch. Mario loves these guys, but it's a love slightly tinged with dread. No other group of musicians has embraced the Rainbow with the kind of manic zeal as this British quartet credited with having invented heavy metal more or less on their own. The Rainbow is their well-marked turf whenever they're in town, a self-proclaimed home away from home. Other bands, even locals who have logged in many more hours here than Zeppelin, respect their claim on the place. Corner booth number twelve simply belongs to them whenever they deign to occupy it. Anyone else who sits there is just keeping it warm in their absence.

"Okay, look," Mario says. "Tell Cathy to go home. Call Tina or Dawn. One of 'em needs to pick up her shift."

Tony starts to ask why, then his mind flashes back to Zeppelin's last visit. There was some unpleasantness in the dining room involving the waitress Cathy and drummer John Bonham. Something involving the proposed use of a soupspoon as a sexual aid. Bonham had to be forcibly restrained, and the girl walked out on the spot. Mario shows a lot of latitude with his clientele, but there is a line, and when it's crossed, he becomes ferociously protective of his girls. Cathy is a top-notch waitress, and he can't afford to lose her. It cost him a 10 percent raise and solid week of sweet talk to woo her back last time.

"We gotta learn to cut that Bonzo off," Tony says. "Nice fella, but when he gets blind, there's no controllin' him."

"I'll handle the drummer. You deal with the waitresses."

The fact that Led Zeppelin is the single biggest band on the planet means little to Mario. What impresses him, even moves him, is their almost canine sense of loyalty to his establishment. It's flattering, and it's rare. But loyalty, like everything else in the full-throttle world of Led Zeppelin, comes with a hefty price tag. When they storm through the door, it guarantees a major disruption of whatever passes for peace and quiet around here. Their very presence is combustible, and few get close without a healthy share of battle scars. But they're good kids, deep down. So Mario stands outside the club and waits, smoking a cigar and anticipating their appearance.

Even in the best of spirits, celebrating a freshly conquered arena or another report of staggeringly high record sales, the lads of Led Zep can be a bit hard to handle. But, when they are in a black mood, when things haven't been going to their satisfaction, they can become truly dangerous. And things have not being going well for the band of late. Mario knows this, of course. He keeps tabs on a handful of artists with whom he's established a meaningful bond over the years. Even a casual perusal of the music industry trades reveals that the '73 tour has been a rough one for Zeppelin. So, when a somewhat frantic Tony informed him that they would be making an unscheduled visit tonight, Mario knew it was time to batten down the hatches and brace for heavy weather. The guys in the band promise enough trouble, but the frenzied flocks of mostly teenaged fans and groupies who follow their every move can really cause headaches. And Mario is quite sure this feverish multitude has already gotten wind of what's going down.

He's right. Word is spreading across Hollywood like an especially virulent outbreak of the clap: Led Zeppelin is in town. Tonight. If you've got a teenage daughter, lock her up. If you *are* someone's teenage daughter, steal a key or gnaw away the lock with your teeth if you have to. Slip into the highest heels and the tightest pair of hot pants you can find, paint your face, and get your ass over to the Rainbow, where it can be properly ravished. A Zep visitation only occurs once every few years and is usually anticipated by months of fanfare. An unannounced one like this has never happened before. It immediately qualifies tonight's appearance as the biggest event of the '73 L.A. groupie season, and every girl who's remotely in the loop finds out about it before the band even enters the Pacific time zone.

Less than four hours ago, Jimmy Page, Robert Plant, John Paul Jones, and John Bonham were two thousand miles away. Wrapping up a three-night stand at a sold-out Chicago Stadium on their eighth carpet-bombing raid across the U.S. in the past four years. As everyone knows, this hasn't been a blue-ribbon tour so far. But only those intimately involved realize how much of a stone-cold bummer it's been from the get-go.

Before the band even left their homes in England, lead guitarist Page fell into a heroin nod and managed to get his left hand stuck in a train door at Victoria Station, fairly well mangling his ring finger. It was far too late in the game to consider postponing the thirty-eight-city tour. Peter Grant's philosophy, a winning one thus far, is that once the wheels of a monster endeavor such as this get rolling, there's no choice but to carry on in the face of any adversity short of a band member dying. And one death might not even do it.

So the show goes on. From the moment of touchdown in New York, the tour seemed to take on the farcical air of a Murphy's Law Road Show. Everything that could possibly go wrong most surely did, at precisely the most damaging moment. Technical failures, strange illnesses, thieving roadies, traffic jams, you name it. These and other mishaps keep springing up at every bend in the road. Even the usually unshakable Robert Plant has been heard to use terminology like "curse" and "bad mojo" in his rambling postshow hotel-room discourses.

Jimmy's hand is an ongoing concern. Everyone in the band is inspired by the wounded guitarist's stoicism, but it isn't enough to lift them out of their malaise. And, in truth, Jimmy has found it nec-essary to call on more than the force of his considerable will in order to maintain his composure. He has instituted a strict self-prescribed medicinal regimen involving copious doses of Jack Daniels, China White, and, according to some of the tour's more salacious rumor-mongers, the vaginal juices of young virgins. Whatever he's doing, it seems to be working well enough to get him onstage every night. But his level of playing has ebbed from a preternaturally gifted virtuoso to merely a highly skilled craftsman. This drop-off pains no one more than Jimmy, who keeps upping the dosages of his varied remedies in hopes of a breakthrough. It's yet to come.

The three consecutive ho-hum gigs in Chicago only seem to add an exclamation point to the negative energy surrounding the tour. Robert's voice, usually capable of overwhelming a fleet of fire engines, is shredded from overuse and the chilly Midwest air. And an unsettling trend started in Minnesota that has dogged the band at each subsequent venue: fans throwing lit firecrackers onto the stage. Plant almost loses a toe one night. It leaves the entire band feeling edgy and unfocused during their three-plus-hour shows.

So they are hardly in peak form in Chicago. Plus the P.A. sucks, placing way too much emphasis on the intricate fingering of bassist John Paul Jones (though, in retrospect, this is viewed as a small miracle, since Jonesy is the only musician in the band playing up to par). Everyone is in a shitty mood, dreading the remaining thirteen weeks of the tour, wondering what fresh calamity awaits. For the first time in Zep's illustrious career, the wheels are truly threatening to come off.

Which is why Peter Grant abruptly decides to make an unscheduled visit to Los Angeles. The boys need a break, in his view. Chance to blow off a bit of steam. The seasoned manager is a masterful reader of people, or at least of the musicians under his charge. During his tenure he has accumulated a detailed understanding of the temperament of his four superstars, and he knows which role to play in the face of any given crisis. The tour badly needs a change of energy, an unscripted detour that will shake off the nagging cloud of gloom.

What better diversion than a quick, one-night pillaging of the Sunset Strip? The members of Led Zeppelin reserve a special place in their hearts for the world's most famous stretch of rock 'n' roll paradise. It was at the Whisky A Go-Go that they played one of their first gigs on U.S. soil, back in January '69. And, three years later, they first laid their claim on the Rainbow. The band feels safe on the Strip. They are among their own, and pretty much anything they do is tolerated, if not wholly understood.

So be it. Within moments of having his brainstorm (while taking a customary six-minute piss in one of O'Hare's sulphurous men's rooms) Grant mentally rubber-stamps it and goes in search of the nearest pay phone. He instructs road manager Richard Cole to make the necessary switches in travel arrangements and not to tell the boys until they are in the air. Meanwhile, Grant gets on the horn and calls an irate booker in Wichita, where Zep is scheduled to play tomorrow night.

"No, sorry, pal. We can't make it. Try to reschedule for the end of the tour. Sure, you got obligations. So do I, to my band. They're worn out. In absolutely no condition to perform out in the middle of fucking Dogpatch tomorrow night! Fine! Fuck you, too!"

Grant slams the phone down after an impressive volley of obscene oaths. This could prove to be an expensive change in the itinerary. Who cares, they can afford to eat the loss. Kansas in late fall? Forget it. Who needs the subpolar temperature and horsy chicks, anyway? They can resume the tour as scheduled on Thursday with three nights in Dallas. Rejuvenated. Ready to burn through the next thirteen weeks in the manner to which both the band and their fans are accustomed.

As soon as the Starship loses contact with the runway, Grant tells everyone to shut up and listen. He's barely able to finish his surprise announcement before the plane explodes with rowdy cheers. Brilliant idea! The Sunset Strip, in-bloody-deed! Everyone tells Grant what a genius he is. Plant and Bonham start a rollicking sing-along of "For He's a Jolly Good Fellow" that's so loud the captain has to kick open the cockpit door and scream for some relative quiet.

Only as his limousine navigates the L.A. traffic does Grant start to feel some qualms about the wisdom of his decision. The monster has clearly been let out of the box. Most of the boys can be counted on to keep their behavior within an acceptable range of misdemeanors. Jones is sure to tip a few jars and quietly call it a night—that's about as wild as he gets. Page will probably disappear late in the evening when no one's looking, retreat to his hotel suite, and not be seen again until tomorrow afternoon. What he does behind locked doors is anyone's guess. Plant is so single-mindedly focused on sex and such an inherently mellow guy that Grant never has to worry about him making a scene.

The only question mark, as always, is Bonham. A truly divided man, Bonzo can mutate from teddy bear to enraged grizzly within the space of two drinks. And you can never really see it coming, no matter how many times it happens. He's especially prone to violent outbursts during prolonged periods of separation from his wife, Pat. While the band burns across the globe, she and the other Zep spouses wait out the spring thaw back home, trying not to expend too much emotional capital praying for the phone to ring or an illegibly scribbled postcard to arrive from some exotic port of call. Of course, the idea of bringing the wives on tour is laughably inane. In fact, no one's ever been daft enough to bring it up, despite the fact that in Bonham's case there's a good argument for making an exception.

Well, fuck it, Peter Grant thinks. If the drummer gets out of hand, I'll just have to club him on the back of the head and lock him in the toilet. Better that than to let things get out of hand like last time. The fact that Mario became personally involved in Bonham's confrontation with the waitress still bothers Grant. He has great respect for the club owner, not to mention a considerable stake in his own reputation as a manager who can keep his band of barbarians in line. If Grant hadn't been distracted by those two bikini models making out by the fireplace, he could have broken up the confrontation before it got ugly. He'll have to be more vigilant tonight.

Just as Grant makes this resolution, Zeppelin's armada of limousines pulls into the Rainbow's driveway. The lads emerge gracefully, one by one, every bit the triumphant band of marauding million-aires in the mood for some good, dirty fun. John Paul Jones looks particularly dapper: ultraflared velvet bellbottoms over maroon

leather boots, an open-necked double-knit shirt with spangles running down the sleeves and what appear to be miniature radishes
sewn around the collar. Very sharp indeed. Jones seems to be the
only one who showered after the Chicago gig. The others still wear
their painted-on performance togs. Their sweat is dry, but its olfac-
tory remnant is still very much with them. The scent permeates the
air, sending out pheremonal messages of virility that are not lost
on the assemblage of female noses.

Mario greets them at the entrance. He seems genuinely glad to
see them, amused as always by the fanatical zeal with which these
guys embrace their star status. All the bandmates embrace him
warmly. Except Bonham, who hangs back sheepishly until Mario
busts his balls in a way that makes it clear all is forgiven.

"What, too big to say hello to me, Bonzo?" A long pause while
the drummer stammers, not sure if he's being rebuffed or just
teased. Then Mario laughs and says, "Come here and give me a
hug, you crazy sonuvabitch." Bonham grips him and holds on for
dear life. He's never stopped feeling guilty for his boorish behavior,
and he was worried that Mario might hold a grudge. Everyone
laughs gently at his misty-eyed relief.

The entourage enters the dining room like a blast of shrapnel.
Heads turn, but not for long. It isn't in anyone's interest to be
caught staring in horror or wonder at the unruly spectacle of Led
Zeppelin. The steely eyed Richard Cole has been known to dislodge
the teeth of more than a few gawkers with what he modestly likes
to call "a flick of the ol' foot." He parts the crowd of onlookers with
no more than a glare and clears a path toward the reserved booth
number twelve.

Robert Plant lifts the velvet rope cordoning off the booth and
gallantly holds it aside to let two young ladies pass through. Plant
vaguely thinks he might remember them from his last Rainbow

mission. Sisters, he seems to recall. There's a definite resemblance in the arched brows and bee-stung lips. Whatever their relation to each other, the girls definitely remember Robert. They immediately buttonhole him at the door with matching French kisses and offer themselves as his dinner companions.

Once in the booth, Plant situates himself between them and decides not to bother with their names just now. Memorizing names is his Achilles' heel, and besides, there's plenty of time for that later. Or not. His only real concern is whether he should eat the tall one as an appetizer and save the short one for dessert, or vice versa. Hard decisions make Plant uptight. After a few minutes of fretting, he asks the girl on his left if she'd mind sticking a straw in his can of Guinness and guiding it into his mouth. He's unable to perform this simple task himself, as both hands are occupied with the process of sneaking into the skirts on either side underneath the table. Plant decides that the first girl to go wet at his touch will be the first to climb onto his face.

Alas, it's a dead heat. Dear, dear. What's to be done? Robert gets a headache trying to sort it out, so he decides to just settle back and let the universe flow according to its own whims. Who made him the boss, anyway? He's just a weary traveler in a strange land, happy to be here.

Meanwhile, Peter Grant tries to elbow John Bonham into the booth, a maneuver that resembles a bull elephant digging in and using all its primeval force to shove a slightly smaller rhino into a tar pit. The intensely claustrophobic Bonham wants to sit at the end of the booth, but Grant won't have it. Keeping Bonzo pinned in the center with Grant on one side and Richard Cole on the other is the safest way to avert another debacle.

Bonham finally takes his place with a great show of indignity. He promptly starts to sulk, muttering a string of curses and half-threats in Grant's general direction.

"Shut the fuck up and drink, ya fat cunt," Grant says, sliding three tall cans of Guinness toward the drummer.

Bonzo looks hurt for about half a second before ripping into the closest can. Grant is the only human being on the planet, with the possible exception of his wife, who can get away with talking to him like that. But Pat's seven thousand miles away at the moment, raising their infant son, Jason. So it's up to Grant to play a combination of prison warden and wet nurse to the volatile, highly emotional John Henry Bonham.

Thankfully, Grant's foresight pays off, and the drummer behaves himself. He's so tired from all the traveling and performing that after a paltry nine beers he passes out face first into a steaming bowl of chowder. Without interrupting an intense conversation with Bob Gibson, Grant extracts Bonzo's clammy face from the bowl before he can drown.

Amazingly, it is the quiet, reserved, almost hermitic Jimmy Page who is responsible for the only public outburst of the evening. It's a mild one, by Zep standards, the genesis of which unfolds entirely out of the band's sight. Back at the rear bar, away from the revelry in the dining room, the striking Miss Pamela sits by herself on the corner stool. Entirely by herself. A single woman drinking alone at the Rainbow, whether attractive or not, is sure to receive some attention. But no one approaches Miss Pamela. She's supposed to be the property of Jimmy Page, after all.

Her famed cover-girl features don't reveal it, but Pamela is in the grip of intense despair. She's been snubbed, either intentionally or by oversight. No one told her about Zep's last-minute stopover in L.A. She had to hear about it from Sable Star, Pamela's main rival as reigning queen of the L.A. groupies. It was so humiliating to get the news over the phone like that. Sable clearly knew Pamela hadn't been notified. The satisfaction in her voice as she dropped the bomb was riper than the schoolgirls trying to get into the Rainbow with fake IDs tonight.

Even though she's been his unofficial "road wife" for the past two years, Pamela didn't expect Jimmy to personally contact her. That's not his style. Particularly during *this* tour; it's been communicated to her through indirect channels that, in light of the ongoing difficulties, it would be best if she didn't travel with the band. Pamela obediently agreed to stay in L.A., where she hoped for an extended stay with Page in January as he recuperated from the completion of the tour.

So it's no big deal not to get a personal call from her lover informing her of his plans. But *somebody,* some lowly roadie or gopher or guitar tech should have received explicit instructions to invite Miss Pamela to meet Page at the Rainbow. No such invitation came. It cost her a great deal of hard-earned pride to get into her red Camaro ("the Thrasher") and drive to the Rainbow by herself, but she was convinced this had to be a slip-up. The other possibility, that she has been deliberately cut out, is too devastating to consider.

For most of the evening, Miss Pamela holds her post at the back bar in silence. Antoinette treats her gently, refilling her drinks before being asked and basically leaving her alone. Pamela's volition is formidable, which is one of the qualities that attracted Jimmy to her in the first place. She *will not* enter the dining room like a beggar with a cup in her hand, no way. She's Miss Pamela, not some sixteen-year-old runaway from the Valley. She will wait here until Jimmy shows her the respect she's due by coming in and asking her to join him. Or at least sends Richard Cole to do it in his stead. That's the more likely scenario, and a perfectly acceptable one to Pamela. But she won't move a muscle until it happens. Not even to get up and powder her nose, for fear it will look like she's given up hope. Besides, she's secretly afraid of what she might see if she passes by the dining room.

After another half-hour, her resolve crumbles. She feels the urgent need for some fresh air. The cramped back bar, so close to the frenetic kitchen, can become suffocating after a while. She instructs Antoinette to hold her stool and to tell Jimmy or anyone else who might come looking for her that she'll be back in a few minutes. Antoinette nods, her wide, generous features betraying her sadness. It's crystal clear to the salty barmaid what's going on here. Girls get thrown over for fresher competition every night at the Rainbow. It's just a little heartbreaking to see it happen to a bona fide member of rock royalty like Miss Pamela.

Pamela walks out through the front entrance and takes a few deep breaths. It's a dismal, wet night, but the air feels good. Her composure gradually returns. Confidence creeps back into her pores. Then she happens to glance across the driveway and gets the shock of her life.

Her long-time paramour Jimmy Page is escorting a young female to a waiting limousine. Very young. Pamela immediately recognizes the girl as Lori Mattix, the underage fashion model who made such a splash recently on the cover of *Star* magazine, a publication known for dressing up barely pubescent girls to look like sex-crazed groupies. It's a big seller on the rock circuit.

Page's right hand is holding the limo's door open for the girl. His injured left lies on her bare shoulder in a way that looks both protective and lascivious. Even at this distance, in the middle of a drizzly mid-October night, Miss Pamela can't help but notice the wrenchingly perfect silk-and-butter texture of young Lori's skin.

Why shouldn't her skin be buttery?, she thinks to herself, already shaking with tremors of indignant fury. The little slut's only thirteen.

In the interest of fairness, it should be noted that Lori Mattix celebrated her fourteenth birthday about six months ago. She marked that milestone at Disneyland, stopping for burgers and malts at Johnny Rocket's on the way home after a thrill-filled day inside the Magic Kingdom. Her "chaperone" was none other than Jimmy Page, who got the nod for the job when he approached Lori's mother and snowballed her with his impeccable British decorum and clipped aristocratic accent. Mrs. Mattix was totally charmed and practically offered up her daughter's (supposed) virginity on the spot. She told all her scandalized suburban friends how polite that Mr. Jimmy Page was. Such a classy gentleman couldn't really be into devil worship and whipping women with straps of rawhide, could he?

Naturally, Pamela wasn't informed of Page's L.A. visit six months ago. Nor of the two secret trips he's made since to see his new girlfriend.

A long moment expands outside the Rainbow. At least it seems long to Pamela, and even longer to Page. They stare at one another across the driveway. Former lovers, top-tier representatives of rock 'n' roll the world over, and, amazingly enough, true good friends. What a way to end it. Not that Pamela thought it would last forever, but she thought she could count on a certain measure of dignity when Jimmy decided to call it off. He owes her that much.

The look in Jimmy's eyes seems to communicate this understanding, and for a fleeting instant, Pamela allows herself to think that he is simply sending young Lori home. Then Jimmy ducks into the backseat and slams the door behind him. The limo inches out onto Sunset Boulevard, dragging Miss Pamela's heart behind it like a cheap tin can strung to the bumper of a newlywed couple's car.

Standing a few feet behind her by the doorway, Mario has been observing this scene while puffing on a fresh cigar. Sometimes he feels like Zeus, detached though not uncaring, watching over the ongoing sexually charged tragicomedy of impetuous gods and goddesses. (The fact that he owns a sprawling mansion on Mount Olympus Drive, high over the lights of Hollywood, only reinforces the feeling.)

He walks up behind Miss Pamela and wraps an arm around her shoulder. Recognizing his beefy touch, she collapses against him without turning around. Mario gives her a minute or two to let her wounded outrage flow, then tries to soothe her. Before the tears have dried, her overriding emotion morphs from grief to anger.

"That fucking son of a bitch! Who the fuck does he think he is?! I should call the cops and have him arrested for child molesting!"

"Ay, take it easy now," Mario says. "You know the rules of this game. Hell, you wrote half of 'em."

"That's right! There are rules! Like when it's time to end something, you have a little fucking respect for the woman you've been with for two years. Bastard!"

Mario chuckles. He likes Pamela's fire. "Come on inside, sweetie."

She starts to pull away halfheartedly. "Are you insane? I can't face them now. I'm sure Sable's laughing her cheap little ass off."

"Just come hang out in the kitchen. I'll get you a nice bowl of soup."

"I couldn't eat anything. I feel sick from the sight of that underage whore."

"I'm talking about the secret Maglieri recipe for minestrone. Not available anywhere outside of southern Italy, except right here. Prepared by yours truly."

Pamela's resistance softens just a bit. She fumbles for a cigarette but can't get it lit and just throws it away. "I guess I'd be stupid to turn down an offer like that, huh?"

"Fuckin'-A right, you would. Come on."

He offers his arm and she takes it gratefully. Mario guides her into the kitchen through the staff entrance, sparing her the possibility of being spotted by someone she knows. She slides into a seat in the warm clinch of the kitchen, drawing amused comfort from the maniacal screams of Miguel as he prods his staff to keep the food production in high gear.

Mario takes off his jacket and hangs it on the chair next to Pamela's. Shooting her a wink, he rolls up his sleeves and shoves one of the assistant chefs aside so he can personally fix her bowl of soup.

The Mighty Zep

In the world of 1970s rock 'n' roll, Led Zeppelin sat like a dark overlord wielding absolute power over their vast minions of fans.

From 1969 to 1978, they ruled the rock landscape like no band before them, smashing sales and concert attendance records with every new album they released. With their eardrum-crushing blend of pounding rhythms and instrumental virtuosity, the band garnered fame and wealth that brought record executives (and thousands of young women) to their knees.

But, more than anything, Led Zeppelin had mystique. Rumors of lead guitarist Jimmy Page's obsession with infamous cult leader Aleister Crowley left the band cloaked in a mysterious shroud of black magic and mysticism. And Led Zeppelin did little to dispel this image. Doggedly shunning publicity and very rarely giving interviews, the band shamelessly steamrolled through city after city, leaving behind only a trail of wrecked hotel rooms and heartbroken groupies to do their talking.

Holding Court

When the powerful Zeppelin train rolled into L.A., they had only one destination in mind: the Rainbow Bar and Grill. At the Rainbow, they indisputably held court.

"Led Zeppelin used to party here in this joint night after night," says Mario Maglieri. "When they were in town, they never left it. You'd have maybe five guys sitting at a table and three broads under the table giving 'em head, ya understand? Page, Plant . . . they were just young guys partying. If I was young, I'd probably do the same."

It was a warm, almost familial, relationship between the Rainbow's owners and Led Zeppelin, one that started well before the restaurant opened its doors. In the past, Zeppelin had performed some of the most intense shows the Whisky A Go-Go had ever seen—most notably in 1969, when they allowed a young, unsigned Alice Cooper to open for them.

And Led Zeppelin wasn't afraid to stretch their loving bond with Maglieri and company to its limits.

"One night, one of the guys from the band fell off the end of the booth, went down on his knees, crawled across the floor, and bit a waitress on the leg. Hard," recalls Mikeal Maglieri. "I looked at the cashier and I said, 'That's it! Find my father, I quit! Tell him I got his keys. I can't take it anymore!'"

Even the band's crew got in on the shenanigans. As Lemmy Kilmister recalls, "The first time I ever came into the Rainbow, one of Led Zeppelin's roadies was screwing some chick on the table downstairs. When they finished, everyone stood up and gave him a standing O. Fucking brilliant!"

Another night at the Rainbow, Zep drummer John Bonham lit into a violent rage after consuming more than twenty Black Russians, his favorite vodka concoction.

Mario reluctantly recalls the scene:

"That particular night, Bonham was screwed up, as usual, and he punched his chauffeur, punched a few customers, and took a swing at me. I was waiting for it—I had to take care of myself. And he wound up with thirteen stitches in his head. I didn't mean to do that; I really loved the guy. The next day I went to Ritchie Blackmore's house after we closed the Rainbow, and who's sitting in the corner? John Bonham. I said to myself, 'Do you have to fight this guy again?' Then he started crying like a little baby. 'Oh, I'm sorry, I love you,' this and that. But he meant it. He wanted me to stay at his house in England. He was really a great guy. It's just too bad that had to happen, but if I hadn't stopped him, he would have hurt himself or someone else real bad."

Unfortunately, that's exactly what happened soon thereafter, when a belligerent Bonham picked a fight with a small, unassuming karate master working as a bouncer at the front door. Bonham was sent to the emergency room shortly after the altercation.

Whole Lotta Love

To this day, Led Zeppelin is as much mythologized for their once insatiable appetite for young groupies as they are for their music. Legendary stories linking the band's sexual exploits to live sharks and bathtubs full of baked beans are as much a part of the band's identity as "Stairway to Heaven." In their heyday, Zeppelin attracted an absolutely massive following of young women, each bent on performing the most desperate and degrading acts imaginable for a chance to get close to the band.

Though the wildest Led Zeppelin stories may never be publicly revealed, it is widely reported that Jimmy Page enjoyed golden showers and traveled with his own whip locker. One report claims John Paul Jones was once caught in bed with a drag queen by Richard Cole. And another unspecified member of the band supposedly had an unquenchable penchant for bestiality (especially with dogs and, believe it or not, octopi).

But it was Jimmy Page's fetish for young virgins that was best known among the groupies. To satisfy this desire, Page often picked out his future conquests from teen model pages in magazines and had the band's managers arrange a meeting.

The beautiful Lori Mattix was one of these conquests. Though she was only fourteen at the time, she had lost her virginity the year before to David Bowie. But Page didn't seem to mind, and the two developed a steamy two-year relationship.

"I was modeling for *Star* magazine," explains Mattix. "That sort of catapulted me into this Hollywood nightlife. And then my first boyfriend, Jimmy Page, read the magazine and fell in love with me and decided he was going to find me and have me. And that's what he did."

The very next time Led Zeppelin was in Los Angeles, Page arranged to have Lori meet them at the Rainbow.

"I'd gone to the Rainbow with an infamous groupie named Sable

Star," says Mattix. "This is a girl I used to model with, and she just lived to fuck famous rock stars. That was never my approach, but it was hers."

Mattix was apparently uninterested in Jimmy Page during this first encounter. Page, however, was up to the challenge. The next night, according to Mattix, Page had her kidnapped and brought to his room at the Continental Hyatt House.

"The room was dimly lit by candles," recalls Mattix, "and Jimmy was just sitting there in a corner, wearing this hat slouched over his eyes and holding a cane. It was really mysterious and weird. He looked just like a gangster. It was magnificent."

Apparently, Page's spell was cast, and, for the better part of two years, Lori traveled with the band on tour.

Melody Maker Breaker

Ultimately, it was Led Zeppelin's mind-blowing decadence with their groupies that got them into trouble at the Rainbow. But the trouble was not from the Rainbow's management. It was from the band members' wives back in England.

As the story goes, after playing a sold-out show at the Forum in L.A., the band went back to the Rainbow to party. Paparazzi photographers witnessed Jimmy Page (the only unmarried member of the group) being met outside by renowned groupie Bebe Buell. Bebe proceeded to throw a fit, chastising Jimmy for being so cruel to "poor little Lori Mattix."

Taking the argument into the Rainbow, Page and Buell sat down with the rest of the band. But apparently the argument was within earshot of a nearby drunk patron who decided to try to impress his girlfriend. Walking up to the Zep table, he began to hassle Page.

Within seconds, Zep road manager Richard Cole placed a karate kick to the man's head, shattering his jaw and sending teeth to the floor in front of the table. Unbeknownst to Led Zeppelin's entourage, a photographer had witnessed the scene and taken a picture of their entire table, groupies and all.

Within weeks, England's popular *Melody Maker* filed the story, complete with the photos of the band surrounded by groupies. A copy of the story quickly circulated to all of the band members' wives, instantly creating transatlantic marital mayhem that no one in Led Zeppelin was too happy about.

Peter Grant, Zep's notoriously imposing manager, placed a furious call to the band's publicist in an effort to find out how the story reached the English press. The publicist reportedly replied, "If Led Zeppelin wants privacy, they shouldn't hang out in notorious groupie saloons like the Rainbow."

It goes without saying that cameras inside the Rainbow were always taboo. However, ever since the Zeppelin debacle, Mario has permanently insisted that any camera on the premises has to first be cleared by him.

MIDNIGHT MADNESS

March 23, 1974

"No, seriously. What's his name?"

"I told you," says Lou Adler. "Twice."

"Okay. What's his real name?"

"Marvin. But, Jesus, don't call him that. He's rattled enough already."

Mario Maglieri shrugs. "I won't talk to him at all if I can help it. Not after that hissy fit he threw yesterday."

"Rehearsals can be tense. You came at a bad time."

"My ears are still ringing. Dear God, what a pair of lungs."

"It wasn't a shining hour for him," Adler concedes.

"No shit. I used to think Cher was a handful."

Adler and Maglieri are standing at the front entrance of their most recent venture, the Roxy Theatre. Stretching some thirty feet above their heads is a pole topped by a red neon circle, inside of which an illuminated *R* flashes with mesmerizing aggression. It's a logo that has already achieved notoriety along Sunset and will soon be famous across the world. Occupying a plot of ground that shares a common driveway with the Rainbow, a mere bottle's throw away, the Roxy has been open for about six months now. In that brief span, a string of the biggest names in rock, pop, and soul

have graced the stage, and the new nightclub has earned a reputation that rivals and even threatens to eclipse that of the now-
fallen Whisky.

Like the bar and grill next door, the Roxy is actually a renovat-
ed version of an aged building with its own fabled niche in the history of Los Angeles nightlife. "Why rebuild when you can refur-
bish?" seems to be the mantra of the owners. The Rainbow has
more than disproved the need to start from scratch when there is
already a solid foundation to work from. The same formula of keeping what's of value and discarding the rest was applied during the
creation of the Roxy, with equally positive results.

It's a little past seven o'clock on a Tuesday night and the Strip
is asleep, more or less. This is the kind of night Mario keenly appre-
ciates. Just a quiet evening where a guy can stand outside and
watch the world pass by. But it won't stay like this for long. Within
an hour, there will be a line two blocks long waiting to get through
the Roxy's double glass doors. Mario plans to be long gone by
then. Tonight belongs to Lou, anyway.

"Well, can't blame the kid for being a little high-strung," Mario
says, returning to the conversation. "Sure he can handle the glare
of the spotlight?"

Lou looks him in the eye, seeking common ground. These men
are partners whose careers are by now inextricably linked. They
already share healthy slices of the Rainbow. Four years from now,
Adler will officially buy into the Whisky, and, though Maglieri will
never play an ownership role in the Roxy, he will be intimately
involved with running the club for the next three decades. Working
closely with a handful of other music industry heavyweights, these
two men have effectively devoured a large chunk of Sunset
Boulevard with fairly brutal dispatch, but on a personal level, they
approach the business from completely different directions. Adler,

for all his razor-sharp negotiating acumen, essentially aligns himself with the talent. He thinks of himself as a creator rather than a deal-maker. Maglieri, on the other hand, is a businessman through and through. He can hang with the rock stars, even enjoy their company most nights, but he never forgets his role in the equation.

Art versus commerce, once again. Never the twain shall meet, but Adler takes a stab at it anyway. "I admit he's a little tempera-mental. The guy's a performer, okay? I've got absolutely no doubt he'll be huge."

"You mean more so?" Mario asks with a look of exaggerated surprise. "Jeez, we already had to widen the doorway half a foot just to let him through."

Lou isn't in the mood to play along. "Take your cheap shots while you can. This kid is going places."

"I'm sure you're right," answers Mario equitably as he produces a Rainbow waitress ticket from his pocket. "He's already knows how to order like a rock star."

"What's that?"

Mario puts on his reading glasses and surveys the ticket. "Three ham sandwiches. Fried calamari, large. Two sides of potato salad and macaroni apiece. Large house salad, extra dressing. Bag of chips and a banana split. And a twelver of Pabst." He tucks his glasses back into his pocket. "As you know, we don't stock Pabst, but your performer insisted. I had to send someone up the block to Gil Turner's."

"Jesus," Adler mutters, grabbing the ticket from Mario's hand so he can examine it himself.

"He told Cathy to sneak it in through the back," Mario contin-ues. "Even gave her a secret knock to the dressing room."

Lou shakes his head. He's got too much to worry about for one night. The curtain rises in exactly ninety minutes. He hands the ticket back to Mario and says, "I'd better make sure he's still conscious. Just bill it to the production."

"You said you wanted everything line-itemed. I need a name."

"His name's Meat Loaf. Like I told you."

"I don't know, Lou," says Mario dubiously. "Billing a ham sandwich to Meat Loaf sounds tricky. Next thing I know, there'll be some guy callin' himself Eggplant asking for a 'me parmigiana.' Could get a little confusing, know what I mean?"

Maglieri's eyes are twinkling brighter than the Roxy's neon marquee. He's having a hell of a time busting Lou's balls.

"Then bill it to me," Adler says as he turns away and walks into the theater.

"Ay, lighten up, pal," Mario says with a laugh to his back. "I'm only trying to take your mind off the opening-night jitters."

But Lou is already inside and doesn't hear him. Lighting a fresh Romeo and Julieta, Mario rips up the ticket and strolls back to the Rainbow. He never had any intention of charging his partner's production for the food.

Lou Adler can be excused for being slightly on edge. Tonight marks the North American debut of his latest entertainment venture, *The Rocky Horror Show*. In many ways this is the biggest gamble of his career. Though the musical extravaganza is already a sensation on London's West End, there's hardly any guarantee it will find a stateside audience. The history of live theater is riddled with the smoking husks of highly ballyhooed shows that didn't survive transatlantic translation.

So Adler is making a bold move. Especially by choosing to open the show out here rather than in New York. "Who the hell goes to see legitimate theater in L.A.?" his investors asked. "Wait and see," he replied.

As with all of Adler's risks, this one is well calculated and based on his tendency to think two or three steps ahead of every move he makes. He plans to convert the play into a slick, big-budget movie, and he wants to start the process sooner rather than later. Instead of trying to lure the studio chiefs to Manhattan for a ruinous weekend of wining and dining, Adler has opted to bring *The Rocky Horror Show* directly to their backyard. And the beauty of this scheme is that he doesn't have to shell out big dollars to some shifty club owner for the venue.

Lou has a friendly wager for an undisclosed amount with his good buddy Jack Nicholson that he'll sell the film rights within a month of the show's opening. Ever since seeing the original stage production in London, he knew this campy mélange of horror movie clichés, show tunes, and sexual boundary breaking had major potential for the big screen. He secured the American rights promptly and booked the Roxy for a running engagement. Lou acts fast when he sees something he wants. (In the end, Jack will have to pay up before two weeks are out, after Twentieth Century Fox wins a bidding war with two other studios. And Lou Adler's street cred as the sharpest producer in the intersecting worlds of music and film will be further burnished.)

But right now he's way too wrapped up in pre–curtain call mania to think about any of that. He performs a quick check of the seating layout and sightlines, sitting in a half-dozen different spots around the club and looking for any movable obstructions. It's the third QC check he's made since lunch. Telling himself everything's fine, he ducks backstage to check in with the cast.

The majority of this motley assemblage is loitering around, smoking cigarettes, running lines, exercising their vocal chords, and making small talk. It's an electric, convivial atmosphere. Most people seem to be keyed up but not panicked. There's undoubtedly a bit of nerve-settling blow making the rounds, but Adler doesn't look for it and doesn't particularly want to know. As long as his people are feeling loose and ready to perform, he's happy.

His star attraction doesn't seem to be the least bit bothered by opening-night nerves. Tim Curry, resplendent in fishnet stockings and high heels, leans against a wall at the back of the theater smoking a Pall Mall out of a provocatively long cigarette holder. He's a study in gaudy nonchalance, so relaxed he probably wouldn't draw any notice at all if it weren't for his outfit, which is complemented by heavy pancake makeup, wet ruby lipstick, and a soaring fright wig of jet-black curls.

Curry has embraced with almost religious zeal the persona of Dr. Frank N. Furter, the gregarious Transylvanian transvestite who is the show's lead character and mascot. The depth to which Curry immerses himself in the role can be a little unsettling to those who don't know him very well. Adler, like most people closely involved with the production, thinks it's a hoot. He walks over to chat amiably with Dr. Frank for a few minutes.

Curry stuns Adler by momentarily popping out of character to inquire whether *Daily Variety* columnist Army Archerd will be in the audience tonight. For some reason, it's been a constant concern of his since the troupe began rehearsals last month. Adler tells him that the invitations have been sent, but they won't know for sure until showtime. Curry inserts a fresh cigarette into the holder like a daisy into a bayonet's sheath and waits impetuously for Adler to light it. Lou obliges him and walks away with a few well-chosen words of encouragement. Curry blows him a theatrical kiss through a perfectly symmetrical smoke ring.

There's so much leathered-and-laced flesh on display, Adler feels like he's in an Old West bordello conceived by Federico Fellini. But what strikes him the most is the potent whiff of cockiness circulating about the theater. Everyone seems quite sure of knocking this jaded Hollywood crowd flat on its ass. For his part, the producer keeps his hands in his pockets with his fingers tightly crossed.

Only one cast member has sequestered himself from the randy frenzy backstage. This would be Meat Loaf, performing double duty in the key roles of Eddie and Dr. Scott tonight. Born Marvin Lee Aday, this oversized crooner from Texas earned his nickname in high school when he accidentally lumbered onto his football coach's foot and broke two of the man's toes. He began his career with small roles on Broadway and has been knocking around the L.A. music scene for the last few years without breaking through to a mass audience. Despite opening for name acts like Iggy Pop and the Stooges and Ted Nugent, the Loaf has yet to establish himself as a star in his own right. There's no denying his talent. He has genuine stage presence and can hit the high notes with the ease of a castrato. And his doughy, moonfaced charm seems to really connect with the preview audiences.

But, Lord, is he a handful! Nothing meets his satisfaction during rehearsals. One of the key lights is shining directly in his eyes, or a member of the chorus is blocking his meticulous choreography, or he's just not happy with the book. His voice is as formidable in complaint as in song, and he puts it to use liberally.

"What exactly is this kid's problem?" Adler can't help but wonder at times. Here he is, floundering for a career, flirting dangerously with the twin devils of obesity and obscurity, and he's landed *not one but two roles* in the most anticipated show to ever debut on the West Coast! You'd think he'd be kissing strangers on the street, not needling everyone around him. Some frustrated cast members have quietly suggested changing the lyrics of one of the show's more popular tunes from "Damnit, Janet!" to "Cork it, Porky!" Nonetheless, the entire production has gelled under Adler's careful supervision, and all the major players, including Meat Loaf, have honed their performances to perfection.

Adler has never confronted the temperamental heavyweight directly. That kind of approach would be woefully counterproductive. With some artists, an iron fist is the best (indeed, the only) way to coax out a performance. It's what they're looking for, having been deprived that kind of tough love from their parents, acting coaches, bedmates, whomever. But Meat Loaf is not of this masochistic ilk. He's a hothouse flower, albeit an enormous one. Rub him too roughly and he'll fall apart completely. His rages stem from insecurity, naturally, and the closer opening night has come the thinner his skin has become. Which is why he's locked in what is supposed to be a communal dressing room right now while the rest of the cast flits about backstage.

Adler knocks on the door softly. "Marv . . . Meat Loaf? You in there, buddy?"

No response. Leaning against the door, Adler can just barely hear some operatic moaning from the other side. This is not a good sign. The kid should be saving his voice. Lou knocks harder and gets a reply just as he's ready to put his shoulder to the door.

"It's open." Not much louder than a whisper.

Adler enters the dressing room gingerly. The banquet of assorted Rainbow fare Mario itemized sits untouched on three folding stands. The forgotten twelve-pack of Pabst warms on the floor. Meat Loaf slumps in an unfortunate director's chair that creaks and wheezes under his girth. He's already in full costume and makeup, thank God. There's one battle that no longer needs to be fought. But his mind seems far away from what's about to happen.

Adler pushes aside a tray of uneaten food and casually takes a seat in an empty sofa. "Ready to knock 'em dead, kid?"

Meat Loaf doesn't seem to hear the question. He gazes into the oversized mirror, the intense crush of light bulbs shining into his face and streaking his makeup with sweat. Those operatic strains he heard through the door, Lou notes with relief, aren't coming from his performer's vocal chords. A phonograph on the floor is playing an LP by Meat Loaf's hero, Enrico Caruso, who belts out a wafting aria of passion and remorse. Lou has to admit it adds a nice melodramatic touch to the proceedings.

"Almost magic hour," he says. "You look like a million bucks. How about going outside and mixing with the cast? It's a goddamn zoo out there, a lotta fun."

Meat Loaf takes an extended moment to consider an answer. He's staring at his own reflection with the apex of either narcissism or self-loathing, it's hard to say which. Lou's patience wanes. Finally, the singer opens his mouth and out springs a complaint.

"My last scene in the first act really doesn't work, Lou. It makes absolutely *no sense* for Dr. Scott to . . . "

Adler cuts him off. "Enough, okay? Enough. We've got a real tight show here, and I promise you . . . Hey, are you listening? I promise this gig is gonna make you a star."

Meat Loaf shrugs, unconvinced. Adler presses on. "You don't believe me? How about this: if you don't land a recording contract within the next two years, and I mean with one of the majors . . ."

Meat Loaf pretends not to be hanging on every word.

" . . . if that doesn't happen," Adler continues, "I'll personally buy you a brand-new Rolls Corniche. Whaddaya say?"

This almost proves too much for the Loaf's delicate sensibilities. He rolls his eyes with an excess of theatricality that would shame Tim Curry and actually groans in despair. Maybe the ultra-shrewd Adler has pushed the wrong button for the first time in his career.

But, then again, maybe not. All of a sudden Meat Loaf is on his feet, releasing a creak of gratitude from the wobbly chair. He looms over the still-seated Adler, eyes alight with self-righteous fire and brimstone.

"Mr. Adler," he booms with the same diaphragm-deep baritone he uses onstage, "the artist cannot be bought. He seeks not the dirty lucre that drives the man of business. The sole obligation of the artist is to his craft—and to those few non-Philistines in the public who have the taste to recognize quality when they see it."

What? Now it's Adler's turn to roll his eyes. Why exactly does he align himself with these creative types, again? There's something to be said for Mario's Maglieri's approach of always making the bottom line the top priority.

With a thundering crash, the door flies open and a dozen crazed members of the cast pour into the dressing room. They latch onto Meat Loaf by whatever appendage they can get a handle on and start hauling him out with a great cacophony of vulgar hoots and catcalls. He feigns resistance, loving every second of it. Now *this* is the kind of star treatment he deserves: literally being dragged onto the stage by his fellow thespians, who can't bear to face the crowd without their fleshy anchor. It's an oddly wondrous spectacle, straight out of a loony bin carnival, and it confirms Fellini as the patron saint of the evening. Sitting on the sofa, Adler can't help but laugh with delight. He's truly in a great line of work.

There's a bit of difficulty getting Meat Loaf through the door-frame, and someone's fingers get mashed in the process. Eventually he squeezes through, but doesn't quite have the nerve to look Lou in the eye as he says, "I'm taking you up on that proposition, by the way. About the Rolls."

"You got it, big man," Adler replies. "Break a leg."

Thankfully, Meat Loaf doesn't break his leg or anyone else's during the show, but he and the rest of the troupe do succeed in slaying the crowd. Big laughs at all the right times, lots of energetic toe-tapping. The sing-along finale brings down the house, generating wave after wave of ovations. *Rocky Horror* conquers L.A. without even trying all that hard.

And, best of all, Adler never has to honor his commitment to Meat Loaf. Almost exactly two years after the West Coast premiere of *Rocky Horror,* the singer signs a contract with Epic. The first fruit of this deal is a thick little slice of '70s rock opera called *Bat Out of Hell* that will go on to sell millions of copies and spawn three Top Forty singles.

Lou Adler knows a star when he sees one.

The Whisky in Decline

By the beginning of 1973, the enormous buzz surrounding the Rainbow had yet to give way to any kind of hangover. The place had firmly established itself as the real deal to everyone in the music industry, and Lou Adler, Elmer Valentine, and Mario Maglieri were once again the kings of the Sunset Strip.

But, in many ways, the success of the Rainbow had come at the expense of that of the Whisky A Go-Go, which had struggled to regain form after it burned down in 1971.

As Mikeal Maglieri recalls, "They opened up the Rainbow, and it was like my dad's interest went up the street, and I was really disappointed. I was like, 'How can he leave the Whisky? The Whisky is it!'"

Before long, the Whisky's extended closure, combined with the owners' waning interest, had opened the door for a new club to step up and assume the title of L.A.'s premier live music venue. That club was the Troubadour.

Located just a couple of blocks south of the Strip on Santa Monica Boulevard, the Troubadour was slightly bigger than the Whisky and had been designed specifically for rock 'n' roll. Able to accommodate 350 people, the Troubadour also featured a much larger stage with facilities far better equipped to deal with the demands of rock bands. So, with the Whisky in serious decline, the Troubadour quickly built a strong support base and became the new home for such young, burgeoning acts as the Eagles, Fleetwood Mac, and Dan Fogelberg.

But, unlike Mario Maglieri and his favorite-uncle managerial style, Troubadour owner Doug Weston was far less tolerant of the rockers' antics. He was also well aware that his club's genuine lack of competition would be fleeting and thus made every effort to lock his best acts into restrictive long-term contracts. It was an aggressive style that offended many of the up-and-coming bands, but a lack of good alternatives forced most to submit to Weston's demands.

Fortunately for the music world, Lou Adler recognized what was going on and did something about it.

The Roxy

Almost from the moment the Rainbow opened for business in 1972, Lou Adler's eyes began to stray toward the seedy strip club located right next door. The club, called Largo, was set up like an old-fashioned burlesque theater. It had a seating capacity of nearly five hundred, excellent acoustics, and even a perfect space for a cozy bar on its top floor.

Determined to give the Troubadour the competition it deserved, Adler decided to purchase Largo. His plan was to turn it into a plush, state-of-the-art concert venue that, in the spirit of the

Rainbow, would eliminate many of the hassles that artists complained about in other clubs—for instance, there would be large, carpeted dressing rooms with showers and the finest sound system money could buy. Adler also figured this larger, well-conceived venue could lure major acts for the occasional intimate engagement.

Putting together an investment team that included music industry titans David Geffen, Bill Graham, Elliott Roberts, and Elmer Valentine, Lou Adler bought Largo in the spring of 1973 and began preparations for what would shortly be the next great rock venue on Sunset.

He called it the Roxy.

When rumors began to surface that Lou Adler and a team of rock 'n' roll heavyweights were going to open an elaborate first-class concert hall, the music world's focus almost immediately shifted from what was currently going on at the Rainbow to what might possibly happen next door at the Roxy.

The public was given their first hint when it was announced that Neil Young would be opening the club with two shows per night for four consecutive nights. Predictably, the response was incredible, and the new owners of the club were besieged with more ticket requests than they could handle.

Just hours before the club opened, David Geffen quipped, "Well, I made more enemies today than in my whole life."

As Graham said at the time:

"In L.A., everyone is a quote 'star.' Guys all day have been calling up saying, 'Billy, baby, this is Harry. I need six tickets for tonight.' Harry, Harry, who in the hell is Harry? Then he tells me he's the vice president of Bugaloo Records or something and that he would consider it a personal favor. If I'm in a good mood I tell him I'll try to find him some standing room in the kitchen."

Opening Night

When the Roxy finally opened its doors on the evening of September 20, 1973, after its $250,000 facelift, it was abundantly clear that Doug Weston and his Troubadour would have all of the competition they could handle.

Like the Rainbow's debut the year before, the Roxy's opening night was a parade of the music industry's biggest and brightest stars. Among the first customers to march through the front door were Bob Dylan, Elton John, Alice Cooper, Jackson Browne, Helen Reddy, Carole King, Herb Alpert, and members of the Allman Brothers Band. Even Elvis Presley was in the building at one point in the evening. And the show they were treated to was more than worthy of the audience.

The night kicked off with the stoner comedy duo of Cheech and Chong delivering a barrage of their trademark zingers:

"How about that Billie Jean King beating Bobby Riggs? Well, it wasn't the first time a man got licked by a girl."

The comedy routine segued into Graham Nash performing a rare solo set, followed by a DJ spinning records for the beautiful *Soul Train* girls dancing through the excited crowd.

Finally, after the stage was arranged with his customary wooden Indian, spindly tree, and grand piano, Neil Young greeted the crowd: "Welcome to Miami Beach!"

Wearing dark sunglasses and a white sport coat, Young proceeded to belt out a powerful two-hour set, only taking a break every few songs to methodically roll and smoke a joint onstage in front of the enthralled audience. Neil closed the show by performing the first-ever live rendition of his classic "Tonight's the Night," which he'd written only weeks before about former CSN&Y roadie Bruce Berry, who had recently died of a heroin overdose.

After the show, the party raged on next door at the Rainbow and continued nonstop through the weekend, with each of Neil Young's remaining three nights posting sellout crowds.

For the next several months, in fact, the Roxy was a perpetual sellout as some of rock's biggest acts (accustomed to playing ten-thousand- to fifteen-thousand-seat arenas) booked themselves at the intimate Roxy.

Once again, the title the Whisky had lost to the Troubadour was back on the Sunset Strip. This time it was the Roxy's turn to wear the crown.

The Rocky Horror Show

By the winter of 1973, Lou Adler had undoubtedly proven that he possessed the Midas touch. In a career that had spanned almost fifteen years, he'd managed to make millions on just about every "risky" venture he'd ever undertaken—from Monterey Pop to the Rainbow to the Roxy. And his new label, Ode Records, was rapidly becoming one of the most successful harvesters of experimental new talent in the music industry. His instincts were impeccable, and everyone knew it.

So, when his girlfriend, model Britt Ekland, took him to a tiny

London theater to see a new musical about an alien transvestite from planet Transsexual, Adler didn't second-guess himself when he thought it could be a hit. Acting on impulse, he met backstage with the show's producer, Michael White, and thirty-six hours later had secured the play's American theatrical rights.

Already, Adler was planning to debut this little stage play, oddly titled *The Rocky Horror Show*, at his new club back in the United States.

"Don't Dream It, Be It"

These five words are the resounding mantra of *Rocky Horror*'s final triumphant chorus. Contrasted with the play's intentionally B-grade horror-flick feel, the words seem to resonate with an unexpected depth that leaves the audience both inspired and uplifted. The result, as evidenced by the play's meteoric rise after its very first London performance, was a cult-like following of fans that came back to watch the play over and over again.

Described by creator Richard O'Brien as "something any ten-year-old can enjoy," *Rocky Horror* first opened on June 16, 1973, under the meagerest of circumstances. "It played for sixty-three people a night for five weeks," remembers O'Brien, "on a budget of two thousand pounds."

But, after this brief run at the tiny London theater, the show's tremendous response and return patronage allowed it to move into a five-hundred-seat theater in a much nicer section of the city.

By the end of 1973, shortly before most of the primary cast moved out to Los Angeles on Lou Adler's dime, *The Rocky Horror Show* was bestowed the honor of Best Musical of the Year by the prestigious *London Evening Standard's* annual poll of drama critics.

In fact, so popular was the play that even Mick Jagger was unable to get a ticket for its final London performance. A few months later, however, when *Rocky Horror* opened up at the Roxy, there was Mick sitting in the front row right next to John Lennon and other members of the rock 'n' roll royalty.

Rocky Horror *Becomes a Picture Show*

Once in Los Angeles, the legend of *Rocky Horror* continued to grow. With a cast that included the venerable Tim Curry as the androgynous lead character, Dr. Frank N. Furter and hefty rocker Meat Loaf as the leather-clad rebel, Eddie, Lou Adler's experiment of turning the Roxy into a playhouse was an instant smash success.

As Meat Loaf recalls, "When we did the show at the Roxy, every night there was somebody different here. I mean, people like Carole King would come dressed up as one of the characters, and anytime Keith Moon was in the audience, there would be nine bottles of champagne lined up. He was there several times. It was just 'the thing,' you know? Raquel Welch came, Elvis came. I mean, that's why I met Elvis Presley. It was an amazing thing. He held court. He invited Tim Curry and me to meet him after the show, and I tell you that was worth it forever."

Even the critics took to it—one reviewer called it "a delicious assault on Mom and Dad and Apple Pie guaranteed to seduce anyone under the age of twenty-five away from the straight and narrow."

Another critic described the play as "Glam met rock, cross-dressed it, slept with it, and taught the audience all the tunes."

Once again, Adler's indomitable instincts had been dead on. *Rocky Horror* seemed to tap right into the pulse of the sexually omnivorous, hard-rocking 1970s.

But Adler had a vision of *Rocky Horror* that transcended the stage. In his mind, the play was much better suited to the silver screen. So, relentlessly promoting the project to a team of Twentieth Century Fox executives, he soon convinced them, and he and *Rocky Horror* veteran Michael White were chosen to produce the project.

A little more than six months later, in October 1974, filming of *The Rocky Horror Picture Show* officially began at an old English castle just outside of London.

The Rocky Box-Office Horror Show

When filming wrapped in December 1974, the air of anticipation surrounding the film was enormous. Most of the original cast had reprised their roles in the film, and Adler had added established actors Barry Bostwick and Susan Sarandon to take on the leading roles of newlywed couple Brad and Janet.

To promote the movie, Adler brought the stage version to Broadway for a planned extended engagement before the movie's scheduled premiere in late 1975.

But, amazingly, the play absolutely bombed. Though it featured the entire cast from the L.A. performances, *Rocky Horror* inexplicably failed to inspire the New York crowds. Less than six weeks later, after much negative press, the Broadway run was canceled.

To make matters worse, when *The Rocky Horror Picture Show* finally limped to the box office, it completely tanked—on both coasts of the United States.

After an incredible eighteen months of going from an experimental production in a small London theater to a smash international stage hit to a major motion picture, it at last seemed that *Rocky Horror*'s luck (and Lou Adler's Midas touch) may have run out.

A Cult Movie Phenomenon

Then Adler heard that a few devotees of the film (in New York of all places) had persuaded a movie theater owner to show the film at midnight on the weekends. Apparently, the film was consistently drawing huge crowds of young people dressing up like the characters on screen and mouthing the dialogue.

The second he heard that, Adler knew where *Rocky Horror*'s fortunes would lie.

News of the movie's midnight madness quickly spread to theater owners all across the country, and soon many were willing to give *Rocky Horror* another shot—in that very specific time slot.

Remarkably, the phenomenon that had happened in New York began occurring all over the U.S. and, within a year, had spread all over the world. *The Rocky Horror Picture Show* was a hit and defined a whole new trend in film—the midnight movie.

In 1977, there would even be a sequel to *Rocky Horror* called *Shock Treatment*. Today, *The Rocky Horror Picture Show* remains undeniably the most successful cult-classic film of all time. All over the world, it continues to be a weekly midnight phenomenon.

Even the stage version has endured, with celebrities such as Russell Crowe, Tracey Ulmann, and Jerry Springer all having lent their talents to its lead roles. In October 2000, *Rocky Horror* made a triumphant return to Broadway, this time meeting with critical acclaim and lasting until January 2002.

As Lou Adler reflects, "The success of *Rocky Horror* came out of the failure of *Rocky Horror.* I think if *Rocky Horror* [the movie] had come out and been even moderately successful, it might be gone today. The fact that it failed and we had to look for an alternative way of exhibiting it was what made it a phenomenon."

Indeed, King Midas still had his touch.

THE BOOGIE NIGHTS

September 6, 1974

Suddenly, in the midst of all the screaming and sickening thuds of fists and wood against flesh, a curtain of confusion parts within the recesses of David Bowie's brain, allowing a badly needed ray of clarity to shine through. What a relief. Or is it? Out of nowhere, Bowie remembers an ancient Chinese prophecy he either read in a dime novel during his youth or saw in an old Charlie Chan movie on TV the other night:

You will live in interesting times.

Hmm. Bowie notes to himself how these cryptic words could easily be interpreted as a curse. Curses seem easier to believe in than blessings these days; so many of them are being realized with appalling regularity on the nightly news. No subscriber to fortune cookie wisdom, Bowie nonetheless has little choice but to recognize a basic truth in the prophecy. Whether it portends sweet salvation or impending doom, he truly *is* living in interesting times. More so every minute.

Bowie is partially hiding behind the kaleidoscopic jukebox in

Over the Rainbow, Bob Gibson's small, private club located on the second floor of the world-famous Rainbow Bar and Grill. Even in wounded retreat, the rock star cuts a striking figure with his finely hewn features, long thin limbs, and orange feathered hair.

As Bowie watches a beefy, baton-wielding phalanx of West Hollywood sheriff's deputies beat the living daylights out of a crazed man wearing the trademark white cotton uniform of a martial artist, everything around him slows to a crawl. He feels like he's been granted a surfeit of time to linger on an assortment of tiny, unassociated details: shards of broken glass littering the bar, a small pool of blood on the dance floor reflecting an overhead neon Budweiser sign with mirrorlike fidelity, the facial expressions of other people standing nearby (which run the gamut from delirious amusement to incredulity to outright horror).

These details don't add up to anything that makes sense, but they are rather interesting to mentally catalog. Bowie makes a game of it. Much more pleasant than listening to the unbearable cries of the man in the karate uniform as the nonstop barrage of batons inflicts damage on every inch of his body.

"They shouldn't hit him so hard," Bowie half-whispers. "He's just confused, I think."

Bowie, on the other hand, is feeling sharper now than he has in some time. The dark rum cocktails he's been consuming since lunch have instantly evaporated in his bloodstream. His head is clear, his eyes calmly focused. He is able to watch this violent, improbable scene unfold as if he were a detached observer rather than a battered participant.

Bowie doesn't even feel the swell of the baseball-sized bruise on his left cheek or taste the twin trails of blood that flow from both nostrils into his mouth. He's in the grip of a mild case of shock resulting from a highly traumatic encounter, but that's not how it feels to him. It feels like he's watching a particularly engrossing TV show and is free to comment on the action without fear of being directly affected in any way. He will get quite a jolt tomorrow morning when he realizes just how close to death he came tonight.

In the two years this private club has been open for business, this is the first time the police have had to break up a brawl in the cozy confines of Over the Rainbow. They are making up for the lost time with a stunning display of force.

"I think he's been sufficiently subdued," Bowie says, a crack of genuine alarm creeping into his voice.

If anyone hears him, they pay no mind. The half-dozen deputies continue to pound on the prone man until he's unquestionably lost touch with consciousness. His white uniform is speckled with blood—mostly his own, though some of it Bowie's. The man's eyes are both swollen shut, and one arm dangles in a bent position that looks painfully unnatural. Wiping their wide sweaty brows, two of the deputies drag the inert body to an upright position and haul it off the dance floor. The man's lifeless legs drag behind him. One foot is bare, its shoe lying unnoticed on the floor. The officers can't be accused of taking an excess of caution in keeping the man's head from smacking into the wall as they carry him down the narrow stairway to the ground floor.

"Okay, folks, show's over," barks the lead deputy to the slack-jawed crowd of onlookers. The appearance of this commanding enforcer of the law incorporates a wide range of members of the animal kingdom: torso of an ox, bucktoothed-beaver smile, walrus mustache, dull cow eyes . . . . Bowie counts how many different creatures he can spot in the deputy but has trouble keeping the tally clear in his head. The sense of calm focus that Bowie has been clinging to for the past few minutes is rapidly dissolving into hysteria.

"We'll need to talk to a few of you, one at a time," the lead officer tells the crowd. "Everyone else should just relax. The situation has been taken care of. Go back about your . . . business," he says hesitantly, not really wanting to know what the business of these people might be.

It's clear he and his colleagues are eager to split. If the assembled denizens of the Strip packed into Over the Rainbow are uncomfortable with the presence of lawmen in their rules-free alcove, the officers seem to share some feelings of trepidation. There's undoubtedly such a mother lode of controlled substances in the room it would take until dawn to make all the appropriate arrests. It would be like trying to round up every hooker on Sunset Boulevard at the same time—a logistic migraine. This has already been a draining night, and the last thing these deputies want is to spend the rest of it dealing with dozens of collars for petty possession. So they try to quickly clean up the scene and disappear before someone does something so egregiously drug induced that pretending not to notice fails to be an option.

Gradually, a measure of normalcy returns to Over the Rainbow. The music comes back on, drinks are bought and quaffed, and pretty soon most people are recounting the bizarre incident instead of reacting to it. David Bowie is having a more difficult time bouncing back. He looks ready to faint at any moment. His bodyguard, a man named Julian with roughly the dimensions of the meat locker downstairs, wraps an enormous arm around Bowie's shoulders and guides him back to the private table in the loft where they were enjoying the evening until all hell broke loose.

At approximately quarter to nine, about two hours ago, Karate Kurt was sitting in the downstairs bar, sipping glass after glass of ice water and trying to keep his ever-present feelings of indignant rage in check. He made no attempt at conversation, just sat brooding in the morass of his own concerns. No one paid much attention to Kurt. The Rainbow has become known as something of a fashion safety zone. Whether it's a faux-silk boa, crotchless panties stretched tight over black leather chaps, or just a shiny coat of body paint, pretty much anything goes around here, clothing-wise.

So no one looked twice at Kurt, decked out in the traditional karate uniform known as a *gi* and a pair of woven mat shoes of the variety favored by Chinese short-order cooks. A red headband emblazoned with two interlocked gold dragons kept his sandy blow-dried mane in check.

Last month, on his maiden voyage to the Rainbow, Kurt showed up in bare feet, as befits any self-respecting martial artist. Tony the doorman turned him away with barely suppressed chuckles of derision. While the Rainbow dress code may bring new meaning to the word "lax," Tony still insists that all patrons show up sporting some semblance of footwear. Making his dejected retreat to the parking lot, Kurt could still hear Tony's bitterly sarcastic words stinging his ears: "Blow a few bucks on some Hush Puppies and come back anytime, pal!" Kurt had to stay up all night whaling on the punching bag in his cramped studio apartment before he'd beaten the humiliating memory from his consciousness.

What makes Kurt such an angry man? Nothing so insipid as unfulfilled longing for money, sex, or fame. No, his anguish stems from the curse of being born in the wrong era, on the wrong side of the planet. A New Jersey native of Polish/Italian descent, Kurt is convinced he has been cosmically misplaced. His soul belongs in sixteenth-century feudal Japan. He is a samurai whose noble role is to walk the Earth in search of wrongs to right. That is his destiny, he's quite sure. So why is he a thirty-six-year-old white guy work-ing at a gas station on the ass end of Hollywood? Clearly, some-thing has gone very wrong in the grand scheme.

Kurt has tried to fashion every aspect of his life to bring real-ity closer to his perception of how things should be. It's an ongo-ing exercise in futility. Though he moved out to California eight years ago to be near the Pacific, makes origami in his spare time, eats raw fish and seaweed (virtually unheard of in '70s Caucasian culture), and practices karate six days a week, he's nowhere near reconciling his cosmic predicament. In fact, his efforts seem laugh-ably inadequate to heal the perceived breach in space/time that is the bane of his wretched existence.

Feelings of impotent rage are nothing new for Kurt. He's been grappling with them for going on a decade, with varying success. But, over the course of the past year, it seems that his passion has made him the butt of a hideous joke being played on him by the entire nation, because in the autumn of 1974, Oriental culture has become ubiquitous in America. Coast to coast, the trendsetters and hipsters are seeking wisdom, or at least a good pickup line, in the arcane traditions of the East. Bruce Lee's recent death and subsequent martyrdom has pushed him past Clint Eastwood to assume the mantle of the silver screen's top badass. Pizza, that perennial takeout favorite, is overshadowed in popularity by dish-es with exotic names like chow mein and moo goo gai pan. Music fans cannot make it across the FM dial without stumbling upon Carl Douglas's maddeningly catchy single, "Kung-Fu Fighting." Dilettantes in every major metropolis are planning life changes based on the whims of the *I Ching*. And so on.

What a sham, like everything else in this spiritually bankrupt society. Kurt sees the current American interest in the Far East for exactly what it is: a fad. As meaningless as the pet rock or the hula-hoop. There's no true connection with the fundamental beauty of Asian culture, nor even the pretense of a desire for one. It's just a momentary infatuation that will soon grow tiresome and be forgotten. Discarded, along with the piles of uneaten food these overstuffed Americans leave on their plates.

Like that big fat guy who was sitting in a booth across the bar from Kurt, flanked by a pair of vapid young models. The man, probably a record exec, shoved aside a platter of ravioli he'd barely bothered to taste. The waitress asked if he'd like her to wrap up the food and was treated to a contemptuous sneer in return. As if a man of his worth would deign to doggy-bag an entrée rather than throw it in the trash without a nanosecond's consideration of his wastefulness. Kurt's grip on his ice water tightened as he watched the tubby executive struggle to rise from the booth, assisted by the two bosomy airheads who will no doubt be luxuriating in his fluids before the night's done.

The whole disgusting tableau seemed a perfect metaphor for America at large and its insultingly shallow preoccupation with everything that matters to Kurt. Who knows, he thought, next year Eskimo culture will probably be all the rage: fashion trends will be dominated by pullover fur-lined coats and nose rubbing will surpass oral sex as standard-issue foreplay. For a few months, anyway. And then it will be on to something else. Nothing is real in this plastic, disposable wasteland, and none of it lasts, so it really shouldn't matter.

Except it does. It matters a lot.

This is what Kurt was thinking at exactly 9:00, when David Bowie walked in the front door of the Rainbow Bar and Grill. Surrounded by a glittery entourage that included the multitalented Brian Eno and what looked like an entire horn section of Puerto Rican boys, the ethereal superstar bypassed the dining room and headed directly through the bar for the stairway to the second floor. Over the Rainbow has one of the strictest door policies on either coast, but a name of Bowie's magnitude is sure to gain admittance whether he calls ahead of time or not.

As he sashayed past the stool where Kurt sat, Bowie allowed his languid gaze to brush over the anguished karate man for a second or two. Dumbstruck, Kurt got the unmistakable feeling that Bowie was laughing at him. The corners of the singer's mouth curled in just a bit of a snicker as he checked out Kurt's *gi*. Before Kurt could determine if this impression was accurate or just another manifestation of his chronic paranoia, Bowie disappeared up the stairs.

Kurt sat there for a few more minutes, trying to regain his composure. What were the chances? David Bowie, of all people, walking in here tonight, looking Kurt directly in the eye, and making fun of him. Almost impossible. And yet the more Kurt considered it, the surer he felt it *did* happen. After swallowing the remaining ice cubes in his glass, he decided to go upstairs and remove all doubt.

Unbelievably, he was able to talk his way into Over the Rainbow. If this were a normally busy night, he'd have had the proverbial snowball's chance of getting past the doorman. But tonight was a bit slow, the after-dinner crush had yet to set in, and the doorman took pity on Kurt.

He walked into the dark, beery embrace of the private club and made his way to the bar, where he could anchor himself with some more ice water. The bartender served it to him with one of those ridiculous loop-the-loop straws that seem to define the form-over-function mentality of the mid-'70s design aesthetic. Kurt threw the straw to the floor impatiently and surveyed the room. So this is where the fattest of the swine come to wallow, he thought to

THE Whisky a Go Go

Presents For Six Nights...

THE BYRDS

& Special Guests...

THE DOORS

JUST ADDED!

BUFFALO SPRINGFIELD • May 16th Thru May 21st, 1967

ON THE SUNSET STRIP

The Whisky a Go Go

Presents On The 14th Thru 17th Of December, 1967

BIG BROTHER AND THE HOLDING COMPANY

WITH
Sweetwater

& JERRY ABRAMS' HEADLIGHTS
On The Sunset Strip

The Whisky a Go Go

Presents

The Jimi Hendrix Experience

On July 2nd, 1967

On The Sunset Strip

The Whisky a Go Go

PRESENTS ON JANUARY 2ND THRU THE 5TH, 1969

LED ZEPPELIN

WITH ALICE COOPER

ON THE SUNSET STRIP

THE WHISKY-A-GO-GO

Presents From England On May 4th Thru The 8th, 1971

HUMBLE PIE

Coming On May 9th, 1971
The Mothers Of Invention
& Coming May 12th: Sweathog
ON THE SUNSET STRIP

THE WHISKY-A-GO-GO NAME IS A REGISTERED TRADEMARK & IS USED BY PERMISSION OF W.A.G.G. INC. • POSTER DESIGN & ILLUSTRATION © 1999 BY DENNIS LOREN • PUBLISHED BY ELECTRIC POSTERS

THE WHISKY-A-GO-GO

PRESENTS

IGGY POP

& THE STOOGES

SEPTEMBER 15 THRU 17, 1973

ON THE SUNSET STRIP

THE WHISKY-A-GO-GO

PRESENTS

VAN HALEN

LAST CLUB SHOW

BEFORE THE FIRST WORLD TOUR

FEBRUARY 25, 1978

ON THE SUNSET STRIP

LOU ADLER, ISS
MARIO MAGLIE

ELMER VALENT
RAINBOW WILL

D **JOHNNY RIVERS**

c.1964

Photo Courtesy Michael Ochs Archives

A ROOM-ROCKING

OF CHUCK BERRY'S

K-STRING CLASSIC

OVER BEETHOVEN"

BY CHANGING THE
NAME TO THE BYR
ROGER McGUINN

c.1965

Photo Courtesy Michael Ochs Archives

THE BAND WITH A
DRUMMER, MICHA
PRINCE VALIANT (

P ON THE STAGE,

THE BYRDS CRANK

Photo Courtesy Michael Ochs Archives

c.1965

HROUGH A MIND-
NDING VERSION

!TRIP

THE BYRDS

BYRDS

SOUND OF THE 7TH SON

c.1965

THE TRIP. SO HE P

BUILDING ON SUI

S BY NOW, GOING
HE SPRING OF '66
THE DOORS HAVE

EXIT

c.1965

Photo Courtesy Michael Ochs Archives

AYED THE WHISKY
Y FORTY OR FIFTY

THE HOLDING CO
JANIS JOPLIN IS F

c.1967

Photo Courtesy Michael Ochs Archives

AND CENTER ON T
OF THE WHISKY A
BY HER BAND BIG

V LEGENDARY FEW
GHTS OF PROTEST

Photo Courtesy Michael Ochs Archives

c.1966

I NOV '66 KNOWN
LY AS THE **SUNSET**
NSET **STRIP RIOTS**

NO ONE APPROA

MISS PAMELA. SI
SUPPOSED TO BI
THE PROPERTY C

c.1973

Photo Courtesy Michael Ochs Archives

OF JIMMY PAGE,
AFTER ALL. NO O
APPROACHES MI

TEENAGE GROUPIE **LORI MATTIX** WAS ~~UGHT~~ **ZEP DRUMMER** ~~ER~~ **JOHN BONHAM**

c.1973

Photo Courtesy Michael Ochs Archives

~~TO~~ **A VIOLENT RAGE** ~~C~~**ONSUMING MORE BLACK RUSSIANS, FAVORITE VODKA**

SECOND-GUESS HI

WHEN HE THOUGH

LOU ADLER'S GIRL

BRITT EKLAND, TO

c.1973

Photo Courtesy Michael Ochs Archives

TINY LONDON TH

TO SEE A NEW MU

ABOUT AN ALIEN

TRANSSEXUAL, HE

NIGHT MARKS THE
CAN DEBUT OF HIS
T ENTERTAINMENT
'EST VENTURE, THE

c.1974

Photo Courtesy Michael Ochs Archives

E **ROCKY HORROR**
R **SHOW,** OPENING
HE ROXY THEATRE.
ERICAN DEBUT OF

WEEK WERE ASTR[O]

FIGURES FOR THO[SE]

CAROLE KING WA[S]

OFFICIALLY A SUP[ER]

c.1971

Photo Courtesy Michael Ochs Archives

AND **LOU ADLER'[S]**

ODE RECORDS WA[S]

QUICKLY BECOMI[NG]

A HEAVYWEIGHT.

c.1971

Photo Courtesy Michael Ochs Archives

D TOMMY CHONG

ARES THE TASK OF

...LY GUIDING THE...

THIS IS WHAT RO[...]
WAS THINKING A[...]
EXACTLY 9:00, WH[...]
DAVID BOWIE WA[...]

c.1974

Photo Courtesy Michael Ochs Archives

IN THE FRONT DO[...]
OF THE RAINBOW[...]
BAR AND GRILL. [...]

Photo Courtesy Michael Ochs Archives

SABLE STAR. MACKENZIE PHILLIPS. RODNEY BINGENHEIMER.

FOR A SUICIDAL S
DARBY CRASH HA

c.1977

A LOT OF THE SAM
IMAGE-CONSCIOU
CHARACTERISTIC
AS YOUR STANDA

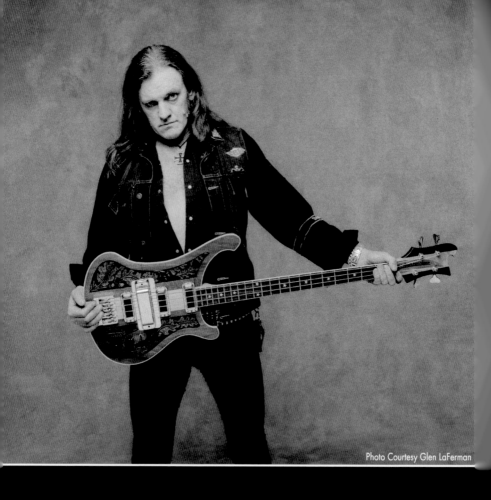

Photo Courtesy Glen LaFerman

Photo Courtesy Glen LaFerman

TO US AT ALL," SA

W.A.S.P. GUITARIS

CHRIS HOLMES. "A

OUR FIRST COUPL

c.1983

Photo Courtesy Glen LaFerman

OF VIDEOS, THEY

UP BANNING US I

THEY SAID WE WE

DEMEANING TO W

RE WHAT I CALLED

REET GLAM," SAYS

'S **BRET MICHAELS**

Photo Courtesy Glen LaFerman

E WERE LIVING IN

OOR AREA OF L.A

...h and legendary record producer Rick Rubin

Axl Rose and friend enjoying drinks

John Belushi just outside the Rainbow and Roxy shortly before his death.

Best friends, Sam Kinison and Ron Jeremy

Hugh Hefner at the Rainbow

Rainbow manager Mike Weber and Jimmy P...

Gazzarri with two lovely Rainbow patrons.

Lemmy upstairs at Over The Rainbow

Vince Neil, Ron Jeremy, and Bill Gazzarri

John Bonham celebrating his birthday at the Rainbow

David Lee Roth at the Rainbow

Sam Kinison with Bill Gazzarri

Bret Michaels and Pamela Anderson enjoying drinks at the Rainbow

Scarlett and Miguel in the Rainbow's kitchen

John Bonham with walking stick

Axl, Elvira, and friend partying late night at the Rainbow

Robert Plant and friend

Paul Stanley and friend atop the Whisky

John Entwistle at the Rainbow

CC Deville and Sam Kinison at the Rainbow

AT THE WHISKY AND
RAINBOW, **MARIO** K
A TIGHT REIN, ALTH

c.2002

Photo Courtesy Glen LaFerman

SON **MIKEAL** SERVE
AS PRESIDENT AND
GRANDSON **MIKE J**

himself. He recognized a few faces, though most of them he was unable to place.

Platinum porn queen Seka was standing at the end of the bar, drinking a daiquiri in a way that almost deserved a triple-X rating. Kurt pegged her instantly, having spent more than his share of time in the Pussy Kat Theatre on Santa Monica Boulevard. (It's his one vice; how can anyone live in this contemporary Gomorrah without becoming just a little bit corrupted?) The Pussy Kat runs a rotation of sixteen-millimeter peepshow strips packaged under the banner of "Swedish erotica," even though all the performers involved seem to be American. That's where Seka made her mass-audience debut before moving on to headline in adult features and becoming the most highly recognized woman in pornography (with the possible exception of Linda Lovelace). Kurt read recently in a local scandal sheet that many denizens of porn have claimed the Rainbow as their preferred stomping ground over the past few months, but that didn't prepare him for a personal encounter with a starlet of Seka's caliber tonight. As she stood there, laughing and radiating carnal license, Kurt had to forcibly pull his eyes away. Her face and figure dredged up too many shameful associations.

Recovering from his mild shock, Kurt spotted the Bowie group. They'd taken over a table in the low-lit loft that hangs directly above the dance floor. Kurt relaxed against the wooden rail and allowed himself to watch and wait.

Across the room, his surveillance went unnoticed at first. Bowie lit a cigarette and laughed at a ribald limerick freshly delivered from the mouth of Brian Eno. Bowie only heard the last half of Eno's rhyme, but he could feel the weight of expectant glances as the table awaited his response. He treated his fawning coterie to a contrived courtesy chuckle that fooled everyone except for Julian Helms, Bowie's longtime bodyguard, roadie, personal assistant, procurer of bedmates and contraband, and overall Man Friday.

"Very clever, Brian," Bowie said coolly. "Pick that up on the wall of a public loo, did we?"

"Why not?" Eno fired back. "Isn't that where you get most of your lyrics?"

"Touché."

Bowie is no stranger to the Rainbow. He first came in 1972 on the heels of his enormously successful Ziggy Stardust tour. That overwrought extravaganza signaled his farewell to the alien persona that had launched his career as glam's preeminent weird genius. Since then, Bowie has undergone more than a few self-induced reincarnations, each of them further removed from the general population of planet Earth than the last. His fan base has grown in direct proportion to the aloof disaffection of each new identity. He is now untouchable, a card-carrying member of the cultural elite. Needless to say, he always gets a warm welcome around here.

Bowie's latest inscrutable guise is that of a heavily made-up, possibly rabid "Diamond Dog." Never more than a wisp of a man, with this new look he seems determined to push the envelope of anorexic rock star chic, to see just *how* thin and white this duke can become without the regular presence of a respirator at his side. Some of his critics claim Bowie is dangerously close to evaporating in the haze of his own androgynous persona.

Of course, his fragility is exactly what makes him an icon. But it's also what makes him a target for those lost souls in the crowd who gaze into Bowie's dark mirror and see reflections of themselves they'd rather not look at head-on.

Karate Kurt is one of these unfortunates. Though he shuns Western culture in almost all its forms, finding it tacky and without subtlety, he's been obsessed with David Bowie since the summer of 1971. Ever since he flipped through an issue of *Rolling Stone* and read an interview in which Bowie casually said he planned to conquer Japan the way the Beatles conquered America in '64. The blithe arrogance of that pronouncement made Kurt's knuckles go white.

Ever since, he has kept the walls of his fifty-five-dollar-a-month studio plastered with images of Bowie ripped from magazines, album covers, and anywhere else he can find them. He listens to Bowie's records incessantly and has memorized most of the lyrics. A casual visitor to Kurt's pad may wonder why anyone would turn their meager living space into a shrine to the very person they claim to most despise. Kurt doesn't linger on this kind of contradiction. His worldview matches his outfit: black belt, white shirt and pants. No grays to be found.

Though Kurt was scoping out Bowie's table in what he felt confident was a surreptitious manner, the singer became keenly aware of his stalker's presence. Bowie leaned close into Julian's broad-beamed shoulders, his pointed chin resting snugly in the cavernous crook of the bodyguard's neck. Using his burning cigarette to point, Bowie casually indicated the wiry man in the white open-topped getup leaning against the bar.

"See that bloke?" Bowie whispered. "He's been staring at me like mad."

Bowie could feel Julian smile by the constriction of the cable-thick muscles in his neck. "It's called fame, David," he said. "I'd have thought you'd be used to it by now."

"I am," Bowie replied, immediately embarrassed by the haughty reproach in his voice. (In fact, Bowie has already started writing the lyrics to his preterdisco hit "Fame," which will go to number one on the U.S. charts nine months from now.)

He retracted his head from Julian's shoulder. "But that cat's starting to freak me out. He looks over here real slyly, then turns his head like a whip every time I glance back. And what's that he's *wearing?*"

Brian Eno had been flagrantly eavesdropping on this private exchange. He cast a look over his shoulder at Kurt, who seemed to be absorbed by the process of furiously spinning his index finger around the interior of his empty glass.

"That's a *karate* outfit, darling," Eno drawled, plainly delighted to be in possession of a prime bit of pop culture before Bowie got his hands on it.

Bowie had had about enough of Eno tonight, so he didn't bother to reply that he knew what it was, he just couldn't imagine why anyone would be wearing one in a posh Hollywood nightclub.

Karate Kurt, for his part, couldn't hold back any longer. He needed some kind of closure with his quarry—at the very least, an honest confession that Bowie had been mocking him downstairs. Kurt set his empty glass down and made a move toward the loft, but his path was immediately blocked by a brawny guy in leather pants dancing with a slender young thing in a Catholic schoolgirl's uniform. The lass's legs were wrapped all the way around his waist, and he seemed to be supporting her weight entirely with his crotch as they swayed to the blaring power chords of "All the Young Dudes" piped in from the overhead speakers.

For a moment Kurt was trapped, unable to progress toward Bowie's table or retreat to his space at the bar, now occupied by a pair of spectral groupies who'd remained on the shelf far past their respective sell-by dates. Kurt felt a small shiver of claustrophobia tiptoe up his spine, but, after employing some meditative breathing techniques, he managed to keep his cool. Finally another space opened up at the bar and he lunged for it, taking a moment to collect his thoughts and try to figure out a fresh approach.

All of a sudden, that need was taken away. Bowie stood up, disentangled himself from the rest of the group at his table, and started walking across the floor, making a beeline in Kurt's general direction. Kurt could hardly believe it. His martial arts training had taught him to react to any and all scenarios, no matter how unlikely. But this was almost too good to hope for. After a few more steps it became clear that Bowie was trying to navigate his way toward the restroom.

Perfect.

Kurt watched as the men's room door swung closed behind Bowie. He waited what he felt was a discreet length of time (six seconds) before following in hot pursuit.

Kurt opened the door slowly, not wanting to forfeit the element of surprise. The men's room was empty except for Bowie, who stood at a urinal taking care of business. Kurt noted with revulsion that he pissed with both his hands on his hips and his elbows bent, like Superman. What a phony.

Kurt took up residence at the urinal directly to Bowie's left. He could just barely sense the singer stiffen with unease, even though he was careful to make no abrupt movements.

Bowie stayed face forward, making a concerted effort to avoid any eye contact. After what must have felt like an eternity to both men, Bowie shook and zipped up, not bothering to flush. He carefully tried to pass by Kurt, leaving as wide a berth between them as possible. The karate man made no movement to stop him. Bowie decided to pause at the sink to wash his hands, thinking he was in the clear and even beginning to chide himself for being so paranoid. Julian was right; he should be more comfortable with being gawked at by now.

Then Kurt hooked his right arm savagely into the crook of Bowie's left elbow and clamped down hard. He spun Bowie around with an aggressive jerk, a little thrown off by how light the singer was.

For an instant, Bowie was too shocked to react. Kurt had him pushed up against the sink, the edge of which dug painfully into Bowie's lower back. Leaning in close enough to plant a kiss, Kurt started screeching at him in a low-pitched, rapid-fire monotone. "You caught yourself a trick down on Sunset and Vine, but since he pinned you, baby, you're a porcupine!"

Bowie blinked a few times, slowly. His body didn't seem capable of responding to the monosyllabic message ("RUN!") rocketing from one clouded synapse to another.

"I'm sorry?" was all Bowie could think to say. Maybe if he acted polite the guy would just let him go. Maybe all he wanted was an autograph.

But Kurt barreled on with his nonsensical rant, gaining momentum as he went. "You sold me illusions for a sack full of checks," he warbled, his whole body shuddering with some sort of internal combustion. "But you've made a bad connection 'cause I just want your sex!"

Now Bowie was in a full panic. He was so startled by this jabbering apparition he didn't even recognize the words being hurled in his face as the lyrics from his own song, "Cracked Actor," released last year.

"Ain't that right, gay boy?!" Kurt spit in his face, shaking him by the lapels. "Huh? Ain't that right?!"

Seeing his all-too-short career flash before his eyes, Bowie desperately tried again to extract his arm from this maniac's vice-like grip. To his immense surprise, he felt himself slip loose. The soapy water on his hands had provided just enough lubrication.

Without a word Bowie spun on his heels and lunged for the door.

Running out onto the dance floor, he lost his footing and twisted an ankle painfully. He got up and started to limp toward his table, waving his hands wildly to get Julian's attention. But the bodyguard was caught up in a heavy conversation with one of the Puerto Rican hornblowers and took no notice.

Even over the thundering music, Bowie could hear the men's room door crash open. He turned just in time to see Kurt launch himself from the floor with a perfectly executed flying side kick. Bowie didn't have much of an opportunity to admire the martial artist's beautiful technique before Kurt's size-nine mat shoe slammed into his chest. Bowie fell to the floor like a house of cards in a high wind, and Kurt landed on his chest with both knees.

"Cocksucker!" he screamed. "Goddamn it, you're nothing but a flaming old faggot! Go home, man! Go home!!!"

Kurt wasn't really aware of what he was saying. The words surprised him. He'd never had a beef with Bowie's widely advertised bisexuality. At least not that he was aware of. It was the Japan comment that made him so mad, right? Wasn't that the start of it all? Kurt honestly couldn't remember such details in the midst of combat. So he stopped trying. With brutal precision, he hammered his fists into Bowie's gaping face, left right left right left . . . .

And then Julian's oversized hands were lifting Kurt up and slamming him into the bar hard enough to knock all the wind from his chest. The bodyguard's intense concern for Bowie was quite possibly the only thing that saved Kurt's life. If he hadn't been busy tending to the bleeding singer, Julian would most certainly have tried to rip Kurt limb from limb. It would have been a hell of a fight.

Meanwhile, one of the waitresses had put in a call to the

police from the phone in the coat-check room. Kurt was backed into a corner by a jeering mob of wasted onlookers. The outsider, once again. He was pinned there until the heat arrived, which turned out to be amazingly quickly. No one was really sure what had happened, so there were no attempts at retribution on Bowie's behalf. Besides, everyone was so cooked, it was little more than a brief diversion in the course of another long and winding evening.

Apparently the waitress had been a little hysterical in her description of the brawl, because a full deployment of six sheriff's deputies came tramping up the stairs and into the club. Hearing their heavy footsteps and seeing all those uniforms, more than a few people impulsively swallowed whatever was in their pockets without looking too closely at what it was.

Kurt actually had a chance to get out of the whole thing with a minor drunken assault charge, which he could have probably pled down with decent legal counsel. But, when one of the deputies made a joke about his *gi* and Kurt responded with a palm strike to the officer's throat, the karate man pretty much sealed his own fate. That the six deputies didn't actually *kill* him was a small miracle, though after they put their bloodied batons away and dragged his carcass from the floor, some in the room thought he might have been better off dead. One thing was for sure: he certainly gave the clientele at Over the Rainbow a full night's entertainment. And David Bowie the scare of his life.

Almost a decade after this decidedly odd evening on the Sunset Strip, Bowie will pen a catchy tune drawn heavily from traditional Asian riffs called "China Girl." It will prove to be one of three Top Ten hits that qualifies his 1983 LP *Let's Dance* as a powerful comeback onto the pop charts after a prolonged slump. Whether Bowie had the night of September 6, 1974, in mind when writing the song, no one can say for sure.

Just as no one can say whatever happened to Karate Kurt, because he was never seen in the Rainbow again.

Just Push Play

On August 9, 1974, exactly five years to the day after the Manson family murdered Sharon Tate and four of her friends, Richard Millhouse Nixon officially resigned from the office of president of the United States.

Though the events were in no way connected, both symbolized the end of significant ideologically extreme movements in America. One had been an attempt at a free-love utopia based on music and nonviolence, the other an attempt at an Orwellian police state kept in line by paranoia and perpetual war.

However, both movements colored the American cultural landscape and ultimately helped create the listless, gas-guzzling, pleasure-based society of the mid to late 1970s. In the words of Aldous Huxley, America had become nothing more than a spiritually detached, industrial behemoth bent on "amusing itself to death."

Entertainment was big business, and the deregulated corporate machines that Nixon had created were willing to strip-mine the distant corners of the Earth to give Americans what they wanted.

It was at this time that a Japanese company proudly announced that it was about to be first to market with an electronic product they promised would lead the powerful entertainment industry to new heights.

Incredibly, this lofty marketing claim turned out to be an understatement. When executives of the Sony Corporation popped a small cassette into their new SL-6300 VCR and pressed play, they launched a revolution.

With this single invention, Sony changed the way people watched TV, the way they looked at movies, and even the way they scheduled their evening hours. Suddenly, every home was its own theater, and people could watch any movie whenever they wanted to and in complete privacy. Personal entertainment would never be the same. More dramatically, Hollywood would never be the same. Almost overnight, every movie that had ever been made had a powerful new distribution channel that ensured a brand-new bounty of untold profits.

The possibilities for new wealth appeared almost unlimited. Like the music industry only a few short years before, the film industry seemed to be staring into the face of an unprecedented boom.

Straight to Video

When Sony's first-edition Betamax VCR officially hit stores in May 1975, it generated a renaissance in filmmaking not seen since the advent of movie sound technology.

With the intense competition for theater space no longer a factor, a preponderance of low-budget mainstream films aimed strictly at the video market rapidly began to emerge. But soon the straight-to-video filmmakers realized that making a profit that way was not as guaranteed as they'd anticipated. It was still far too easy for their films to get lost in the shuffle between the classics and the new theatrical releases that everyone recognized.

Children's movies instantly did well in stores, and documentaries certainly gained momentum. But it was another type of low-budget film that seemed to fare best against Hollywood's star-studded, big-budget features. This was, of course, porn.

At best a niche industry before the arrival of the VCR, the adult film industry was by far the biggest beneficiary of the VCR's promise of privacy. No longer was the average Lonesome Larry relegated to a nickelodeon behind a curtain in the back of an adult bookstore. This ingenious technology had answered his call.

In the mid '70s, thanks to the VCR, the explosion of the adult film industry was so dramatic that soon it was generating nearly as much revenue as the big Hollywood studios. As fast as they could be made, pornos found healthy circulation in all of the stores that would carry them. And adult film stars were garnering fame and fortune like never before. For a time it was as though anyone merely associated with the adult film industry was becoming a millionaire. And this new breed of beautiful, young nouveaux riches partied in a way that gave even the rock 'n' rollers a run for their money.

Predictably, however, old Hollywood's receptiveness to porn was nothing short of frigid. As had been the case with the wild rockers, the hard-living, sex-obsessed porn types were simply not welcome in the finest restaurants and bars.

Fortunately, a solution already existed for this problem: the Rainbow Bar and Grill.

A Perfect Union

By 1975, the Rainbow had earned its reputation as the favored haunt of the rock 'n' roll elite. With the incredible success of the Roxy next door, the Rainbow was a seasoned veteran of unbridled hedonism and had become a personal playground for its loyal crowd of rock star regulars. Rod Stewart had even recruited a "soccer team" out of the Rainbow called the Rainbow Hollywood Vampires. Comprised of fellow musicians/heavy drinkers Alice Cooper, John Lennon, Keith Moon, Ringo Starr, Mickey Dolenz, and Harry Nilsson, the team claimed the Rainbow's fabled crow's nest as their official lair and made a point of wreaking debauched havoc there at least twice a week.

So, when the porn industry came knocking, the Rainbow merely considered it a welcome addition to its carefully cultivated culture of decadence and mayhem. Certainly it could handle whatever these well-endowed sexaholics would bring.

Soon the biggest names in porn, such as John Holmes and Ron Jeremy, were calling the Rainbow home, and hot adult actresses, such as Seka and Marilyn Chambers, instantly shot to the top of the groupie ranks. It was as though rock and porn had been destined to marry, and with the Rainbow they'd finally found their church. For the Rainbow, this was truly the dawn of a golden age.

Bringing with it an avalanche of cocaine and nude women, the porn industry quickly made the Rainbow more than just a place to party; it became a place to audition as well.

"I still see a lot of dancers here getting into adult movies," says Ron Jeremy. "The Rainbow is by no means a casting facility for adult films, but a lot of dancers congregate here. This is also where Heidi Fleiss became the famous Hollywood madam."

Indeed, just next door at On the Rox, the private club located directly above the Roxy Theatre, Heidi would frequently throw lavish, anything-goes bashes featuring high-end call girls she recruited from the Rainbow. Her best friend Victoria Sellers (who was conceived during the brief marriage of Peter Sellers and Britt Ekland) served as the manager of On the Rox for a short period and helped to facilitate these affairs, which attracted some of the biggest (male) names in music, film, and television. An invitation to one of Heidi and Victoria's private parties soon became as much a status symbol for the happening Hollywood player as a spot on Hef's preferred list of mansion guests.

Walking through the Rainbow, Captain Ron, as he's often called, points out sites where he's held his own private auditions:

"I've had lots of sex up there," he says, pointing to a secluded spot on the Rainbow's upper floor. "That's the balcony, and inside there's a little alcove that people already know about. But I like to be creative. I like to find places no one has ever been to. Like the bathroom—ha!

"I have on many occasions taken a girl into the downstairs bathroom under the guise of just helping her clean off the seat. I'll dust off the seat with a little rag, and say, 'Okay, honey. The bowl is all yours.' Then right before I leave, it's like, 'Just one little kiss.' Next thing you know, we're having some kind of hard-core sex right there in the bathroom, trying not to make any banging noises. If someone knocks on the door, I'm like, 'Hold on, I'm taking a dump!'"

Caressa Savage, a porn starlet who has won awards for her intense girl-girl scenes and proficiency with immense dildos, recalls the effect the Rainbow scene first had on her:

"The Rainbow is so hot," proclaims Caressa. "That's where I started being sexually unrepressed. And I know that's where a lot of the other girls started, too. It's a good place to meet people who can introduce you to other people. It's just a good place to fuck and have a good time."

She continues, "Last time I left the Rainbow, I came in with a pair of blue jeans on, and I walked out with a skirt. Somebody just completely ripped my jeans open, right there in the dining room. I was having such a good time that it was a skirt by the time I left."

Ferret Talk

After years of frequenting the Rainbow, Ron Jeremy says he and his best friend, the late Sam Kinison, figured out the key to picking up ladies there. As Ron puts it:

"If you have to talk to a girl all night long, she might be high on speed or alcohol or something. But a guy has to put up with it if he wants to get laid at the end of the evening. So you see guys at the Rainbow Bar and Grill just sitting at tables leaning on their hands.

"One time this girl was spending hours talking to a guy about her pet ferret. Sam Kinison laughed and said, 'Look, look, he has to listen to everything she says and act interested or he's not going to get any later.' The guy across from the girl was going, 'What kind of cage does it have? What do you feed it?' This guy was going crazy; I mean, he was begging for cancer. After all night long just talking about ferrets he was just ready to die. But, finally, after he showed enough interest in that fucking ferret, later that evening they had sex. So it was all worthwhile. So that became our constant joke at the Rainbow Bar and Grill. Going to the Rainbow and talking about ferrets."

STONED ON SUNSET

May 21, 1977

Holy shit. It's actually happening. The Roxy is being busted. Unbelievable. Another rock 'n' roll idol showing feet of clay. How depressing.

No one saw this coming. But should it really be such a surprise? It was bound to happen eventually. Local authorities could only turn a blind eye for so long to all the flagrant misdeeds taking place nightly along this block of Sunset. In recent weeks, things have really gotten out of hand. Not simply drug dealing, but actual usage on the sidewalk during hours of peak foot traffic, in plain view of respectable civilian and lawman alike. Every Saturday and Sunday morning, empty baggies, coke straws, and half-used rolling papers flutter along the sidewalk like the remnants of a tickertape parade. Neighboring merchants and residents have finally had enough and are starting to complain publicly. Op-ed pieces in the *Times* and the *West Hollywood Courier* have grown more strident in criticizing the lackadaisical police response to the situation. The department is losing face. Decisive action must be taken, and tonight the shit is finally going to hit the fan.

It's time for Operation Shoot the Moon.

Alas, the bust is not going all that well. In more precise language, it's a complete fiasco. The commanding officer, Sergeant
Stedenko of the LAPD's crack undercover narco squad, watches in
artery-clogging agony as his carefully crafted operation, months in
the planning, falls apart due to incompetence.

Needing to vent before he blows a capillary, Stedenko zeroes in
on his favorite target, junior narc officer Harry, who has been a constant burr under the sergeant's saddle from day one.

"Look at yourself! You're stoned, you are very, very stoned!
You've got food all over your uniform, you've got no self-control
whatsoever. What do you have to say for yourself, Harry?"

Harry is consumed with the messy process of wolfing down two
double-stacked slices of the Rainbow Bar and Grill's highly lauded
pizza. His mouth is so crammed with dough and cheese, he's
unable to offer a prompt reply, and, besides, he has a vague idea
the question is rhetorical. Most of Stedenko's questions are. Pretty
much everything that comes out of his mouth when addressing his
subordinates is designed to be answered by the Sarge himself; that
way, he can perpetuate his ongoing monologue of reproach and
abuse.

Stedenko shoves the 215-pound Harry up against a large green
van parked illegally in front of the Roxy. The van has been tagged
as evidence in the bust, but it is rapidly collapsing into a fiery
wreck. Large plumes of bluish gray smoke gracefully billow out of
its tailpipe, gaining momentum from a cool eastward breeze. Some
of the fumes are sucked into the Roxy's ventilation system, while
the rest linger low in front of the club, trapped under the illuminated
marquee. You'd think Stedenko would be worried about this monumental loss of key evidence, not to mention the possibility of
gassing a large number of innocent pedestrians, but his main concern at the moment is getting a satisfactory reply from his junior

officer.

He tries to grab Harry by the lapels and shake, but the lapels aren't there. Harry is not wearing his normal undercover uniform (tweed jacket, ultrawide patterned tie, and polyester slacks) this evening. Instead, the portly policeman is dressed in a light beige muumuu that covers his ample frame like a tarpaulin thrown over a customized VW bus to protect against rain and bird droppings. Sergeant Stedenko himself is sporting similar garb. This is known in the narcotics field as "deep cover." The element of disguise is only one small facet of the intricately designed doper-catching mousetrap known as Operation Shoot the Moon. It all looked so good on paper.

"Why don't you guys admit it, you've got the munchies!" Stedenko shrieks, wheeling away from Harry to direct his wrath at the two other men on his squad, Officers Clyde and Murphy. They too are camouflaged as Hare Krishnas, though their full heads of hair, black leather shoes, and shoulder holsters immediately give them away to any potential doper over the age of four. Not even bothering to stand anymore, Clyde and Murphy both sit on the sidewalk in front of the club's entrance. Feasting. Two empty Rainbow pizza boxes lie at their feet, and they are working their way through a third.

"I've never seen anything so disgusting in my entire life. You're a disgrace to the force. You've let me down, boys!"

Stedenko turns back to Harry, the tone of his voice subtly shifting from rant to plea. He appears to be on the verge of weeping.

"I'm stoned!" he bellows, spewing spittle into Harry's round, sweaty face. "Do you understand that, Harry? I am stoned!"

Harry offers him a consolatory slice of pizza. "So go with it."

Stedenko knocks the slice from his hand, sending a small shower of toppings onto Officer Murphy, who doesn't seem to notice, or to mind if he does.

"You tell me to go with it?!" Stedenko roars. "You almost botch the entire operation! You lose my best dog! Two guys piss on my leg! I'm on the verge of a total pig-out, and you tell me to go with it??!!"

For a long, interesting moment it looks like Stedenko might reach under his muumuu to pull out his gun and pop a cap into his tubby junior officer. Instead, he rips open the pizza box in Murphy's lap and grabs four slices with both hands, clawing the pie with his fingers as if it were the leering face of a particularly vile drug kingpin.

"I'll go with it!" Stedenko screams, stuffing all four slices into his mouth at once. It's a gross, unnerving spectacle. The sergeant moans and coos with obscene gratification as he literally gorges himself on the hot, delicious pie. Hunks of cheese, meat, and vegetables fall from his mouth, but that doesn't slow him down a bit. He's totally lost in the joy of unbridled gluttony. His subordinate officers are too stunned by Stedenko's voracious display to do anything but continue eating.

This is definitely not how the operation was intended to go. What a pitiful sight. Four of the city's finest, ripped to the tits on the Sunset Strip, surrendering to a bad case of the munchies as a two-ton van constructed entirely of marijuana goes *Up in Smoke*.

Just as this scene really starts to strain credulity, Lou Adler yells, "Cut!" The entire thirty-person crew, which has been biting their tongues in agony for the past five minutes, explodes in boisterous laughter and applause. Stacy Keach immediately steps out of his role as the psychotic Stedenko and bows deeply, his face still covered with food.

Adler himself has been so crippled with silent tremors he's gotten a cramp in his side. It's been incredibly hard to keep a straight face on the set of this movie, even for a director with a million things to worry about. Adler has taken to stuffing a napkin in his mouth to avoid interrupting the action with laughter. That's what happens when you attempt to shoot a feature-length comedy based upon a handwritten three-page "script." The spontaneity of impromptu performances can produce magic on the screen, but it can also create untold challenges during the production. When you have no idea what's coming next, it's easy to be caught off-guard. It was with a heavy heart that Adler fired a likeable and highly proficient gaffer during the first week of shooting. He had no choice; the guy kept ruining takes with uncontrollable outbursts of gut-rupturing guffaws.

"That was great, Stacy," Lou says, clapping. "All you guys were great."

Keach accepts a towel from a young production assistant and wipes the greasy food from his face. "All in service to the muse, my good sir."

Though Adler is nominally the director of *Up in Smoke,* he shares the task of creatively guiding the movie with its two writers and stars, Richard "Cheech" Marin and Tommy Chong. The three men work extremely well together. It's the comedy duo's first time acting in a movie and Adler's first time directing one, but their natural rapport sustains them through the tensions that are naturally bound to crop up on a tightly budgeted production like this one. Lou's respect for them as performers, every bit as deep as his feelings for the musicians he's worked with over the years, is really the glue that keeps the whole thing together.

As director, Adler is most concerned with facilitating the transition of Cheech and Chong's phenomenally popular brand of spaced-out humor from live standup to the medium of film. That is the mandate behind all his creative decisions on this project. Adler's tendency is to allow the scenes to unfold at their own hazy pace, giving his performers the time they need to let the absurd situations develop in front of the camera within long, sustained master shots. Adler doesn't shoot many close-ups and there are virtually no cutaways. Working with director of photography Gene Polito, he fills the wide-angle frame with a panoply of carefully placed comedic details and lets the audience discover them as they may. There's to be no spoon-feeding of gags through obvious, predictable editing techniques.

The idea is to create a shooting technique that matches the loose improvisational tone of the material as it is performed before a live audience. Content determines style. The films of Robert Altman are a major influence. Having worked with the Cheech and Chong team for almost six years, producing four hugely successful comedy albums, Adler has a keen appreciation for the syrupy timing their schtick requires to be not only funny but realistic. You just can't rush a joke about smoking a joint full of dog shit.

So, by habit, Adler is hesitant to cut off Keach's pig-out scene too soon. He's curious to see how far the actor will take it, though he's also a little worried that someone in the crew might have to perform the Heimlich maneuver before all is said and done. Keach has a habit of attacking his roles in a heavily physical manner, and it was a little disconcerting to watch the way he choked those pizza slices down his throat with seemingly no concern for his well-being.

Behind the camera, seated in director's chairs emblazoned with their names, Cheech Marin and Tommy Chong have been watching the scene unfold. They love it. It's always nice to take a break from carrying the movie with their on-camera antics and just watch the process happen.

Decked out in faded denim from head to toe, with his trademark red bandana, bushy beard, and John Lennon glasses, Chong is very enthusiastic about Keach's performance.

"That was fuckin' great, man. It's like Stacy's really ripped, the way he tore up that pie." Chong laughs, a classic pothead rumble echoing up from the back of his throat. "Had *me* fooled."

Cheech nods in agreement. "Nice to have at least one real actor in the movie."

"I'm not so sure he's acting, man."

Cheech reaches up to adjust the red wool cap that will forever be associated with him after this movie is released. He likes the brim to ride snugly over the top of his earlobes like a headband. Smoothing his thick mustache, he looks around the set and idly wonders if there are any women he hasn't hit on yet tonight.

Chong tries to get the attention of the director, who is watching with keen interest as a few brave grips, handkerchiefs held over their faces, douse the green van's flaming tailpipe with buckets of sand. They will need to conserve as much of the flammable material as possible for the rest of the shoot.

"Hey, Lou," Chong says. "You sure that's dry lettuce they're burning over there, man?"

Adler turns, smiling. "You think we've got the budget for anything stronger?"

"I dunno, man. Stacy's got me wonderin'. Nobody straight should be able to force-feed himself like that."

"He's a pro. He'll do whatever it takes." Adler walks over and gives Chong a playful chuck on the arm. "Pay attention, Tommy. You could learn something from him."

He's kidding, but there's an element of truth to what he says. Stacy Keach is in fact a classically trained thespian, having studied Shakespeare at Yale's prestigious drama school in the early '60s. What his former teachers would make of his performance tonight can only be guessed. Regardless, Stacy is the only member of the cast with any real acting experience—or at least the type of acting that involves remembering lines and responding to calls of "Action!" and "Cut!"

Not that Cheech and Chong are greenhorns to show business. They have been performing their standup routine onstage together since 1969, and they were doing comedy separately for years before their paths first crossed at a titty bar in Vancouver.

Adler takes a minute to consult with the director of photography, Gene Polito. Polito suggests setting up a quick reverse angle on the last scene for protection. Though Lou doesn't plan on cutting away from the perfect master he just got in the can, he likes this idea, since it gives him time to go into the Roxy and rehearse the several hundred extras packed inside. He gathers his two stars and sends them into wardrobe to prepare for the big musical finale.

Both guys have put a lot of thought into what they should wear for the performance. Cheech has decided on a lacy pink tutu that he used to incorporate into the stage act with great success. He likes the way it shows off his muscular calves. Chong is a bit more reserved. A devoted student of comedy, he realizes there can't be two equally outrageous members in any successful duo. Neither member of the team should step on the other's toes; they should complement rather than contradict each other. So Chong chooses to go for the more subtle laugh and dresses up as a human Quaalude.

A cute young production assistant named Debbie enters the dressing room with a tray of sodas and snacks. She is greeted with warm flirtation by both performers, especially Cheech, who makes her sit on his lap for a minute or two the way he does every time she comes in here. Debbie, who owns all their albums and has gotten them to autograph every one, gets a huge kick out of these guys and how similar they can be to their alter-egos.

Chong, in particular, has a habit of staying in character even when the cameras aren't rolling. Though he's got substantially greater mental wherewithal than Man Stoner, his on-screen persona, he still ends every statement with the word "man." Also, Tommy is high for most of the shoot, just like Man. (But that's hardly anything unheard of. Lou Adler's good buddy Nicholson is reported to have smoked several dozen joints in a single night's shooting of *Easy Rider,* and that was seven years ago.)

Cheech also has some things in common with his character, Pedro de Pacas, including a custom license plate that reads "MUF DVR." But overall he's more of a traditional performer who turns it on as soon as the cameras roll and reverts to a quieter fellow between takes. He takes comedy seriously, and he's not the only one.

In the latter half of the 1970s, there is a strong feeling among cultural movers and shakers that comedy will surpass rock 'n' roll as the dominant form of live performance, not only as entertainment but as artistic expression. The two sometimes merge with each other to such a degree that making a clear classification is impossible. Case in point: Steve Martin's "King Tut," a goofy two-minute tune about America's hysterical reaction to the Tutankhamen exhibit touring the country's museums. The song, written as a throwaway bit to be used during lags in his live act, has gone gold.

The current tidal wave of high-profile live comedy has put performers like Martin, Richard Pryor, the cast of *Saturday Night Live,* and Cheech and Chong in a pop-culture position rarely enjoyed by comics of previous eras. They are not only selling out large venues and cranking out chart-topping albums, they are being written about as serious artists on the social landscape. People who get paid to gauge the temperature of the nation and write about it in glossy magazines are actually composing think pieces about the comedy stylings of Cheech Marin and Tommy Chong. Viva la '70s.

Even in light of this trend, it's been no picnic bringing *Up in Smoke* to the screen. Just getting a studio to consider a full-fledged dope comedy took several years. Many a coke-snorting executive told Adler that they couldn't possibly release such a vile product on the youth on America. Then they took a peek at Cheech and Chong's record sales, which by the third album were starting to rival those of multimillionaire bands like Zeppelin and the Stones. Suddenly, the dealmakers of Hollywood decreed in their wisdom that the American moviegoing public was ready for a thirty-five-millimeter dose of unapologetic drug humor after all.

And yet even with studio backing, this has been a highly unconventional production closer to that of an independent project. Shooting has been spread out unevenly over almost a year, depending on the variable availability of funds and personnel. Shoot for a month, break for six weeks, then shoot some more until the next break—that's been the pattern. Though the total budget will come in somewhere under two million, the film will go on to gross many, many times that and will be recognized as the best comedy of its kind ever made. Since it's a stoner comedy, that may be a dubious distinction, but it's one that will make Cheech and Chong very rich men. And Lou Adler an even richer one. The cinematic reverberations of this modest little project will spread far and wide, from Sean Penn's defining turn as surfing pothead Jeff Spicoli in 1982's *Fast Times at Ridgemont High* to the streak of drug humor running through much of Quentin Tarantino's work in the '90s.

Not that anyone at tonight's shoot has such lofty ambitions in mind. It's been a long, generally low-paying endeavor, and most people involved are tired. Tonight's scene is part of the grand finale, in which Stedenko's ultrasquare narco squad receives their poetic comeuppance while our two protagonists break out of their impoverished existence by winning a battle of the bands at the world-famous Roxy Theater. The clever name of Cheech and Chong's quasipunk quintet is Alice Bowie. It includes a three-man horn section featuring none other than Miguel Maurillo of the Rainbow's kitchen.

Of course, any good story requires some sort of unforeseen challenge to come up at the last minute, adding a dose of dramatic tension to the climax. This comes in the form of a fistful of downers Chong swallows backstage, leaving him essentially dead on his feet just as Alice Bowie is getting ready to perform. The scene calls for Cheech to run out first and warm up the crowd with some acrobatic footwork and ass-waggling in his tutu. Then the rest of the band files out, with Chong being awkwardly propped up by the same chick who fed him the downers (played by one-of-a-kind comedienne Zane Buzby). Just as the band is set to begin their number, Chong slips into a full drug coma and falls into the drum kit, creating havoc on the stage and garnering angry boos from the crowd.

The scene plays beautifully as written in the script: "Tommy collapses into drum kit. Audience boos." But the logistics of the gag make Chong a little uneasy now that they are ready to shoot. How exactly is he supposed to face-plant into a set of metal drums without hurting himself? A stunt double is out of the question. No one on the set, or in all of L.A. for that matter, looks enough like Chong to make a believable stand-in: his rare genetic combination of Asiatic facial features and rangy six-feet-one-inch Scot-Irish frame qualifies him as a true freak of nature.

Cheech offers the use of his kneepads, but Chong points out that they might prove inadequate to protect his face. Polito suggests that the stunt can happen off camera with a sound cue, and they can simply cut to a shot of Chong lying under a pile of drums.

No one's too happy with that idea. Cutting away from the gag seems to undermine the whole gonzo spirit that is the hallmark of this movie. Someone who can't be thinking very straight suggests using a dummy.

Finally Chong puts an end to the debate. "Fuck it, man. Let's just be sure to nail it on the first take."

Cheech beams with admiration for his partner's showmanship, but Adler won't have it. They still have six shooting days left, and Tommy is needed in every scene. They can't afford to lose him to the emergency ward; that would really throw the production into turmoil. Adler proposes a compromise: wouldn't it be just as funny for Chong to fall backward off his stool and completely disappear from view behind the stage? It'll be a cinch to rig some padding back there, and he can perform a full pratfall in one take without risking injury. Polito and Cheech agree it's a good alternative. Chong is less convinced. He doesn't want to get hurt, but he doesn't want to water down the material, either. However, over the next ten minutes, the other three men gang up and talk him into the compromise.

Adler and Polito decide to set up two cameras to double their chances of getting something usable—one in front of the stage and one directly behind the drum kit at a slightly elevated angle. This takes the proverbial eternity.

In the duration, the burly assistant director gives the crowd of extras in the audience directions on how they should react. There's a mob of women crushed against the front of the stage, vying for pole position. None of them are as concerned with getting a good view of the band as they are with finding a prime spot in front of the camera. The majority of these fiercely competitive ladies are the crew's wives, girlfriends, and/or casual bunkmates. After endless promises that they'd have the chance to appear in the film, they finally have their chance, and they are determined to make the most of it.

At last all the preparations are made and the actors take their places. Stacy Keach, all cleaned up, stands in the wings next to Adler watching the scene. Cameras roll. Adler yells for action. Cheech runs out and does his opening bit, giving it his all. Following the assistant director's instructions, the crowd is apathetic at first, waiting to see what this unknown band is all about. Miguel and the two other horn players assume their marks. Finally Chong weaves out onto the stage, supported by Miss Buzby. He really looks like he's having a bad drug experience, from his lidded eyes to his soft spaghetti knees. The guy knows wasted.

Meanwhile, the cameras keep rolling. Zane guides him around to the back of the drum kit and helps him lower his butt onto the stool. Then, with a kiss on the cheek, she leaves him to his own devices.

Cheech grabs the mike and tells the audience to get ready to hear some heavy shit. Polito stands squinting into the A-camera in front of the stage. His key light hits the foreground, keeping Cheech well lit in the left third of the frame. Chong and the drum kit are clearly visible in the background off to the right.

So far so good. On impulse, Adler glances down at his watch, wondering if they'll be able to wrap before dawn. During that tiny moment in which his eyes leave the action, he hears a thundering crash followed by a diminishing series of smaller metallic clangs. It's exactly like the sound cue Polito was suggesting earlier. Looking up, Adler sees Chong lying face-down on the stage amid dozens of scattered pieces of the demolished drum kit.

How about that. The crazy bastard did it anyway.

And everyone in the room clearly loves it. Cheech is laughing so hard his whole body is doubled up. Chong lies prone for a moment, milking it. After the appropriate dramatic pause, he allows his partner to help him to his feet. The crowd starts to boo and throw stuff on the stage, screaming for these amateurs sullying the good names of both Alice Cooper and David Bowie to pack it up and go home. It's a perfect take. The director yells, "Cut!"

Adler is mildly annoyed by the change in plans, but he's got to focus on one thing at a time. He briskly walks over to Polito. "Tell me we got that, Gene."

All Polito can do is nod mutely and give the thumbs-up. He's completely beside himself with laughter, tears running down his face. Adler tells him to check the gate and move on to the next setup. There will be no protection takes for the drum kit gag.

After things settle down a bit, Adler corners Chong backstage and demands to know, with gentle reproach, why Tommy ignored his directions and risked ruining the rest of the shoot.

Chong shrugs casually. "Just felt right, man."

Lou Adler can't argue with that logic. He walks away to prepare for the next setup. They still have a lot of work to do tonight.

Ode to a King

When Lou Adler sold his famous Dunhill label to ABC back in 1967, many questioned the wisdom of giving up so much control inside such an incredibly competitive industry. Sure, the sale had made him an enormously wealthy man, but at what sacrifice?

However, Lou Adler saw it much differently.

Free from the demands of a huge catalog of successful artists, he was now able to refocus his energies on discovering and developing new talent. And with his expanding fortune (money was also rolling in from the success of Monterey Pop), he had incredible flexibility to take chances on artists others may have deemed too risky for the cutthroat pop market.

So, when the sale of Dunhill was complete, Lou Adler promptly created a new label: Ode Records.

One of the very first acts Adler signed to Ode was a young woman few would have given any chance of becoming a pop star. A freckly-faced Earth mother from New York City, she sang and played piano but was afflicted with a paralyzing case of stage fright. However, upon hearing demos of her performing simple renditions of her own songs on a piano, Lou was so charmed that he insisted on recording her.

Her name was Carole King.

Born Carole Klein in Brooklyn, New York, on February 9, 1942, Carole King was hardly a newcomer to the music industry when she first met Lou Adler. In fact, for several years she had been half of one of the most successful songwriting duos in history. With her partner, Gerry Goffin, she'd penned more than a hundred hits during the 1960s, including such megahits as "One Fine Day," "The Loco-Motion," and "Natural Woman." Their songs were recorded by everyone from the Beatles to the Monkees to Aretha Franklin. But, when King started a three-piece band of her own called the City, her stage fright prevented them from touring to support their album, and they subsequently flopped.

But Adler believed in her talent and convinced her that she should go it solo without any backing band. He felt that her magic lay in the intimacy heard on her demos—that of a songwriter alone at the piano.

"I knew that her demos were more popular than her records," remarked Adler. "People in the business collected Carole King demos. You couldn't get them back once you'd sent them to a producer."

Heeding this advice, Carole King went back to the studio—this time completely alone. The first result was an experimental album called *Writer.* In an effort to compensate for the stark nature of the recording, King tried writing songs that were more complex than her usual style. The album sold a bleak six thousand copies. But she and Adler simply regarded it as a misstep.

For the second album, she went back to basics, recording the songs alone at her piano with only the slightest musical accompaniment, just as if she were creating a demo to give to another band. The result was *Tapestry.*

Released in May 1971, *Tapestry* was an instant sensation with both critics and the public. By June, it had reached number one on the American charts. For fifteen consecutive weeks, in fact, the album remained at number one, spawning four Top Ten hits, including the number-one gold single "It's Too Late"/"I Feel the Earth Move."

For a woman, the album was an unprecedented success. That year Carole King became the very first woman to capture the Grammy grand slam: Album of the Year, Record of the Year ("It's Too Late"), Song of the Year ("You've Got A Friend"), and Best Pop Vocal Performance, Female. And songs from *Tapestry* covered by other artists also won Grammys: James Taylor's version of "You've Got A Friend" scored Best Pop Vocal Performance, Male (and was a gold-certified, number-one single), and Quincy Jones' recording of Carole King's "Smackwater Jack" won Best Pop Instrumental Performance.

The same year it was released, *Tapestry* went platinum and, at the end of 1971, was still selling an unbelievable 150,000 copies per week—all astronomical figures for those days. Carole King was officially a superstar, and Lou Adler's Ode Records was quickly becoming a heavyweight.

To this day, *Tapestry* remains one of the most important albums of the rock era for having proved the commercial viability of the singer/songwriter—especially the female singer/songwriter. Since its release in 1971, *Tapestry* has sold more than twenty million copies worldwide, and its songs are some of the most covered in history.

Stoner Comedy

Riding high from the success of Carole King and *Tapestry*, Lou Adler and his Ode Records were ready to take on more musical long shots.

Acting on a tip from Dinah Shore's daughter, Melissa Montgomery, Adler went down to the Troubadour in late 1971 to check out a little-known comedy duo that had recently moved to L.A. from Canada. Calling themselves Cheech and Chong, the pair took the stage in a cloud of pot smoke and destroyed the audience with skits about getting stoned, getting laid, playing rock 'n' roll, and living in East L.A.

"We were doing one of those hootenanny things on Monday nights at the Troubadour," recalls Cheech Marin. "It was about the eighth or ninth one we'd ever done. Originally, it was set up for a guy from Warner Brothers, but Melissa Montgomery came up to us and said that Lou Adler was in the crowd. She said he wanted us to call him the next day, so we did. Tommy didn't know who he was, but I did."

Convinced that this pair of blissed-out musical stoners just might have a future, Lou invited Cheech and Chong down to Ode's offices, where he promptly signed them to a multi-album deal. Surely, he figured, if they could make him laugh, they could make America laugh, too.

Topless Improv

The road to that now fateful night at the Troubadour started in very different places for Richard "Cheech" Marin and Tommy Chong. Cheech, whose nickname comes from *cheecharone,* a Chicano delicacy made of deep-fried pork skins, was the son of a cop and raised in the barrios of East L.A. with his seven brothers and sisters. A self-described "low-rider" in high school, he spent most of his days playing hooky in order to practice with his two bands, Captain Shagnasty and His Loch Ness Pickles and Rompin' Richie and the Rockin' Robins.

Unable to land a record deal, Cheech somehow managed to graduate from high school in 1968 with a straight-A average and get into California State University, Northridge, where he washed dishes to pay his tuition. After earning a degree in English, Cheech decided to move to Vancouver and study pottery.

Tommy Chong, on the other hand, was raised in the tiny Canadian town of Dog Patch, just outside of Calgary. The son of a truck driver, Tommy was born to a pure Chinese father and a Scotch-Irish mother, a mixture that accounts for his unusual appearance. As Cheech puts it, "He was the first kind of whatever it is he is that I'd ever seen."

Like Cheech, Tommy was interested in music; in fact, he was even part of Calgary's first R&B band, the Shades. However, the

Shades were involved in a fracas after one of their shows at Calgary's Canadian Legion Hall, and the mayor of Calgary officially banned them from ever playing in the city again. Undeterred, the Shades relocated to Vancouver, where they promptly split up. But Chong, an excellent guitar player, was quickly picked up by a popular Vancouver band called Bobby Taylor and the Vancouvers. After getting signed to Motown Records, the Vancouvers pumped out a solid hit called "Does Your Mama Know About Me" and hit the road for a cross-country tour of the U.S.

It was on this tour that Chong first discovered the art of improvisational comedy. One night after playing a gig in Chicago, Tommy and the band were invited to see Chicago's famed Second City improv troupe. Chong was so inspired by this freeform comedy that he actually decided that night to quit the band and start an improv troupe of his own. Back in Vancouver, Chong bought into his brother's strip club, and decided to turn it into a home for his new act, known as City Works.

"It was a topless joint, and I didn't have the heart to fire the strippers," recalls Chong, "so when I turned the show into a comedy troupe, I put the girls in the skits. We had the only topless improvisational theatre in Canada."

It was during a tryout for local comics to come in and test their skills that Cheech Marin walked through the door.

The chemistry between Cheech and Chong was electric from the first meeting, and together they turned City Works into one of Vancouver's most popular attractions. For two years, the duo worked out original material onstage, most of it based on their mutual interest in rock 'n' roll.

"We were musicians all our lives," says Cheech, "and so our

comedy really represented a musician's sense of humor. We tried to keep music in our act because it was part of our generation and a mutual love of ours."

In 1970, the pair decided to disband City Works and take their highly successful local act out on the road as Cheech and Chong. But life on the road as a musical comedy duo proved not to be as easy as they had hoped.

"There were no comedians doing it when we first started," recalls Cheech. "Clubs would tell us, 'Oh, rock 'n' roll bands only. There is no such thing as rock 'n' roll comedy. Go away.' So we had to sort of pioneer that whole thing."

After driving to one-night stands all over Canada and the northern United States, Cheech and Chong at last decided to take their act to Los Angeles, where they hoped the warm weather and free accommodations with Cheech's family would suit them better.

As it turns out, it would be a perfect fit.

Counterculture Heroes

When Ode Records released Cheech and Chong's eponymous debut album in late 1971, not even Lou Adler could have anticipated the stunning reception it received. Although derided by critics, the album was almost instantly a massive hit with the aging hippies, rockers, and dazed-and-confused teens that made up the underground drug culture in America at the time.

With sketches like "Waiting for Dave," "Cruisin' with Pedro" (about drug-deal paranoia), and "Trippin' in Court," Cheech and Chong were branded counterculture heroes, and, within months of its release, their debut went gold. Suddenly, this unlikely stoner pair was the hottest new act in the U.S.

Cheech recalls what it was like to suddenly be a part of the in crowd:

"The great thing about Lou Adler was he used to give *the* Christmas party at his house every year . . . and the first year we signed with him we got invited to this party. We were just two schmoes off the street, you know? And we go to this party and every single person there was somebody famous. It was like the world of God. You'd turn around and there would be John Lennon and Ursula Andress and John Derek and Peter Sellers, and it went on and on. It was like, 'Wow, man!' I'd forget I was supposed to be there, so I was, like, collecting people's drinks to take them into the kitchen, you know?"

In the spring of 1972, when Cheech and Chong released their followup album, *Big Bambu,* they were hardly "two schmoes off the street" anymore. Neatly wrapped in a giant rolling paper, *Big Bambu* shot to number two on the U.S. charts and was voted the year's number-one comedy album. With a much-hyped third album due out in early 1973, Cheech and Chong were well on their way to becoming superstars.

Their third album, *Los Cochinos* ("The Pigs"), won a Grammy, and their fourth, 1974's *Cheech and Chong's Wedding Album,* featured the monster musical hit "Earache My Eye," a song that would become part of the duo's enduring legacy.

As Cheech recalls:

"Another musician we started with in Canada named Gabriel played that riff for me in my kitchen one time on an acoustic guitar. I just went, 'That's it!'—*dunadun-dunadun-dun-dun-dun*—

it was perfect. It was like hearing 'Louie, Louie' for the first time. I can't tell you how many bands have played that riff. Van Halen used to use it for their encore. Sound Garden recorded it. It's one of those Rock 'n' Roll Hall of Fame riffs. I'm mounting a campaign to get Cheech and Chong in the Rock 'n' Roll Hall of Fame as the quintessential rock 'n' roll comedians."

Toast of the Strip

Living in L.A. as the poster children of the 1970s stoner culture, Cheech and Chong became as much a fixture at the Rainbow as the club's trademark red leather booths.

Taking up residence in the Rainbow's exclusive Over the Rainbow and the Roxy's ultraprivate upstairs haunt On the Rox, the duo saw the mayhem that took place during these golden years firsthand.

"Anybody in Hollywood who was hot was hanging out at the Rainbow and the Roxy," recalls Cheech. "Ryan O'Neil, Cher, Warren Beatty and Jack Nicholson, Michael Jackson, Michael Douglas, I mean, anybody that Lou knew—and he knew everybody. What was interesting was that Lou and those guys owned the places, so we kind of by association took them to be our hangouts, too. We basically went through the staff—it was like our own private fishing pond. My first wife was a waitress at the Rainbow who put me off for quite a long time. The waitresses at the Rainbow were always the most beautiful girls in town."

He continues, "And the Roxy had On the Rox, which was kind of like our own little private club. That was like fishing in a hatchery. Oh, baby."

Cheech also recalls his first impressions of Mario Maglieri:

"I was good buddies with this girl who worked the front door, so I used to go down there and hang out with her. Mario was always there, too, so I would bullshit with him and hear the history of Hollywood. He was just the greatest guy. He's just no bullshit. 'You want something to eat? Something to drink? Let me take care of it.' He's the man."

The Dope Scene

After releasing four phenomenally successful albums, Cheech and Chong spent the next four years touring the country in sold-out arenas. Out on the road, they realized how pervasive drugs had become in America.

"The '70s were really where the '60s got played out," Cheech recalls. "When we first started traveling around the country, you'd go into every city and tell them to take you to the hippie section. Every city had a hippie section, like a ghetto. When we'd go back then, it was still kind of peace and love, and it was a big deal to have long hair and stuff. And then pretty soon there were other elements, cocaine elements.

"We saw it turn from the pot-smoking generation to the cocaine generation real quickly. It just cut a swath through all our friends, man. When speed started coming in, it became a whole different scene, and we saw a lot of our guys, especially the most successful ones in entertainment, really go down hard. It rendered them all blithering idiots."

Up in Smoke

In 1978, after four years on the road and more than ten million albums sold, Cheech and Chong returned to Los Angeles with the feeling that there was only one place left to perform their act: the big screen. Lou Adler agreed and soon raised two million dollars to let his prized comedy duo do whatever they wanted with a movie camera.

The result was *Up in Smoke*.

"We were basically trying to figure out how to put in elements from our records and our stage act and just make up the story as we went along, you know?" says Cheech. "We were really kind of loose, but it flowed."

"For the ending of the movie," recalls Cheech, "we just figured we'd do a battle of the bands and do this tune, you know, and it would bring down the house, and in fact it did. You know, it was funny because nobody had ever seen us play. It blew the guys in the band away when we came out and did it."

Miguel Maurillo, the Rainbow's head chef for the past thirty years, put the whole backing band together about twenty minutes before the shoot.

"Lou comes to me," recalls Miguel, "and says he's making this movie, and I'm going to be in this band. And [laughs] I say okay, you know, so I get in there, they give me my uniform and my trumpet, and I start playing! It was the funniest thing I've ever seen."

Incredibly, among the other punk bands in *Up in Smoke*'s competition were future L.A. punk icons Bobby Pyn (AKA Darby Crash) of the Germs and Exene Cervenka of X.

"The Cheech and Chong movie was where I met Bobby Pyn," says Exene. "It was an open call, fifty bucks for a couple of hours, so it was a big score for me."

The film created the formula for a string of follow-up movies that would become a veritable cottage industry for Cheech and Chong. Over the next five years, the duo put out 1980's *Cheech and Chong's Next Movie,* 1981's *Nice Dreams,* and 1983's *Still Smokin'.* All told, the movies would gross nearly a half-billion dollars.

Eventually, with the advent of the "just say no" attitude of the mid 1980s, the appeal of the pair's brand of humor did wane. Regardless, Cheech and Chong endure as cultural icons, and their own memories of hitting it big on the Sunset Strip will always remain a source of inspiration.

As Cheech puts it:

"The Roxy and the Rainbow and the Whisky were the center of the center of Hollywood during those days. You couldn't get more inside, and we were right in the pocket with the owners.

THE
STRIP REBORN

When Elmer Valentine, Mario Maglieri, and Lou Adler celebrated the Whisky A Go-Go's fifteenth anniversary in January 1979, it must have seemed as though a lifetime had passed since Johnny Rivers first plugged in opening night.

Johnny Rivers, the Byrds, the Doors, Janis Joplin, Jimi Hendrix, Led Zeppelin, David Bowie . . . too many great musicians to name all had played the club, all had partied in its booths, all had left the ghosts of greatness behind to forever haunt its stage.

And, though the Whisky had met with a period of decline during much of the 1970s, it still managed to capture the imagination of every young band that performed there, and its reputation as the world's most legendary rock 'n' roll club remained solidly intact.

So, with fifteen years of wild times, great music, and extremely hard work to look back on, you might assume that Elmer, Mario, and Lou would think about resting on their laurels and cashing out. Luckily for the world, this never entered their minds. As the '80s and '90s would prove, the odyssey of the Whisky was far from over.

NIHILISM AT 45 RPM

December 22, 1979

Santa Claus is on smack. Well, maybe not. But the skinny vagrant who almost weaves into heavy traffic off the corner of Sunset and Clark *is* dressed up as everyone's favorite gift-dispensing elf boss. And why not, it's the most wonderful time of the year, even for heroin-crazed street crawlers with nothing better to do than stagger along the Strip and wait to get arrested or killed.

Clarence, the Whisky's mountainous, recently hired doorman, grabs the costumed freak by the shoulder before he can lurch into the street.

"Whoa dere, Kris Kringle," Clarence says in his deep West Indian baritone. "Like to git youself plowed."

If the junkie in the Santa suit realizes his life was just saved, he makes no sign of it. Clarence looks down into the poor wretch's sightless saucer eyes and sighs ruefully. Where did this lunatic get his hands on the costume? he wonders. Then he decides he'd rather not know. A man whose heart is probably too kind for his new line of work, Clarence still hasn't gotten used to seeing so much human wreckage on such a regular basis. He's only been in L.A. for a few months, and he actually thought the Sunset Strip was supposed to be glamorous until he started working here.

Clarence makes the guy sit down on the curb while he tries to flag down a passing cop car. Except there are no cops cruising the Strip tonight. It's a Sunday, after all. The keepers of the peace are hoping maybe it will be a slow night. They couldn't be more wrong.

Santa starts warbling an off-key rendition of "Jingle Bells" and Clarence considers cramming him into the dumpster behind the club until he comes down a bit. He has no business hanging out in front of the Whisky, especially right now. Things are about to get hectic. A stupefied junkie dressed in a red pom-pommed cap will be far too tempting a target for the denizens of the night soon to be flooding the street.

The doorman can already feel the vibrations coming from inside the club. The walls aren't thick enough to contain all the amped-up rage on the other side. Clarence glances up at the newly restored marquee above the Whisky's front door. It seems almost impossibly bright, powered by row after row of ultra high-watt bulbs. Stark black letters crawl across the white-hot glare in such great contrast they appear to be carved into the sign:

TONIGHT ONLY: THE RETURN OF
DARBY CRASH AND THE GERMS

Preferring calypso to punk rock, Clarence can't decipher much meaning from those words. But to the several hundred people already packed inside the club, they represent both a revelation and a promise kept.

Christmas is coming a few days early to the Whisky in this Year of Our Lord, Nineteen Hundred and Seventy Nine. Tonight is the night a lot of twisted prayers are about to come true. One look around the crowded dance floor confirms it. Safety pins are hung from earlobes with care, in hopes that St. Darby soon will be here. The excitement anticipating his arrival travels through the room like an electric current.

Everyone's gonna get their stocking filled tonight, one way or another. Darby Crash always delivers, though he hasn't been seen in these parts for quite some time. In his absence, his myth has grown. To the hordes of the faithful presently assembled, he really is as crucial a figure as Kris Kringle was during less troubled eras of their lives. He is both provider and punisher, a shadowy figure to be loved but also feared.

You're never really sure what Darby might pull out of his tattered bag of tricks. But there's always hope for a big payoff. Who knows, if you've been really, *really* bad, he might reward you with a sucker punch to the ribs or a big gob of spit right in your face. Word on the street is that in the twenty-some months since the Germs last played the Whisky, the band and its scabrous leader have only grown more rabid in their quest for sonic anarchy.

So the fans are pretty keyed up. Up by the foot of the stage, a kid with a six-inch blue Mohawk smashes an empty Bud bottle against his temple. For kicks. As the blood trickles down the side of his face, his friends laugh fuzzily. Over by the bar, a shaved girl with a nail running through her lower lip starts screaming Darby's name over and over until she realizes the room is too loud for anyone to take notice. Mildly frustrated, she stubs out her cherry-tipped cigarette on her freckled left forearm, barely wincing at the pop and hiss of burning skin. Quite a few people are sporting similar "Germs burns." It's common knowledge among the initiated that Darby Crash is obsessed with circles and urges his followers to scar themselves with as many round spots of scorched flesh as they can fit onto one arm. Ashtrays are for pussies. Like any field general worth his salt, Darby doesn't ask the troops to do anything he's not willing to do himself. His own neck, torso, and back are pockmarked with scars rendered by broken glass, rusty blades, and fire.

It is the twilight of the '70s, a time some thought would never come, and the punks rule Sunset. Beyond any doubt. This is their turf, as fiercely protected as any demilitarized zone in the Western Hemisphere. An army of disenfranchised, disaffected, and, in many cases, diseased soldiers have made their conquest with an almost demonic show of force and sheer numbers that make the hippie invasion of the mid '60s look like a schoolyard game of kick-the-can.

With them, the punks bring a very different vibe and a host of problems the old-timers of the Strip simply aren't used to dealing with. Amazingly, the Whisky embraces these unsightly champions of social disorder in the same manner as it embraced the hippies before them. As during that earlier epoch, which seems like a centuries-old, hazy daydream, the Whisky shows an unparalleled ability to change with the times. "Keep moving or die" seems to be the rule. If today's kids want to pay for live acts of self-mutilation and horrendous atonal screaming every weekend, so be it. It's not like the Whisky can really complain; the punks are responsible for bringing the club back to profitable life after almost a half-decade of consistent decline and near obscurity.

But the Whisky will only go so far to thank the punks; their voracious support is a mixed blessing at best. Yes, their constant patronage over the past two years has put a lot of greenbacks in the register. But, for every dollar earned, at least a quarter must be spent repairing the physical damage they inflict upon the club on a nightly basis. It's an impressive catalog of carnage: from the innocuous (food and paper projectiles) to the dangerous (shattered glass and piles of abandoned syringes) to the flat-out vile (splattered blood, vomit, urine, and semen, all deliberately liberated from the bodies that contained them). Early on in the punk revolution, Mario, Elmer, and Lou unanimously agreed to double the salary of the Whisky's clean-up crew. It was an act of conscience rather than cost-sensitive management.

So, although the punks are allowed to celebrate the Christmas of '79 at the Whisky, they aren't being treated to much in the way of decorative frills. For tonight's show, the club has refused to offer any holiday adornments. Mario is quite sure the place will be reduced to a wreck by the end of the performance, so he doesn't see much point in hanging tinsel and colored lights or, God forbid, planting a highly flammable fir tree anywhere within the building.

But that's okay. The silver-haired Grinch can't steal the excitement of this evening. The punks have brought their own Yuletide cheer. On this balmy December eve, it's actually snowing. Inside. A fine powder of cheap speed is packed up a wide assortment of tack-pierced nostrils and jammed into extruded veins with rusty hypodermics. And, for every wasted, horny, angry, drugged-up punk inside the club tonight, there will soon be at least three more standing outside. Poor Clarence the calypso-loving doorman will be alone in keeping these deprived hordes at bay.

It's a special breed that is brave or insane enough to mix with this crowd. The miscreants and losers, the misfits and wastrels, they all hold sway here. Standing outside the Whisky without the means to enter is an exquisite form of torture to the devoted punk. But they all carry the same warped faith; even if they are unable to get inside to see the show, the great Darby Crash will somehow be able to communicate his message of nihilistic depravity to them.

How stunned those die-hard Germs fans would be to learn that their antihero is in the grip of a mild panic as the show draws near. The singer sits shirtless on a stool in a dark corner backstage with his buzz-cut head clenched in his hands. None of the other Germs try to approach him. They all know Darby's body language well enough by now.

It takes a fair amount to rattle a guy who drinks lighter fluid and gouges his own body with sharp objects as a matter of routine. But Darby Crash is truly nervous. His jitters have two sources, both equally troubling.

First of all, the Germs' drummer Don Bolles is nowhere to be found. He should have been here an hour ago for the sound check. No one panicked when he didn't show up on time, because for a band like the Germs, sound checks are little more than a chance to show off fresh scabs and get blitzed in unison before the show. But now the curtain is set to rise on a major comeback performance and a key member of the group is still MIA. Not even Bolles's girlfriend Dinah Cancer knows where the drummer could be, though she's betting he's in police custody (and her hunch is right on the money). One thing everyone agrees on is that the crowd will go absolutely *apeshit* if the Germs don't perform. That doesn't worry Darby in and of itself. Indeed, the night will be a bitter disappointment if it fails to culminate with a respectable display of mindless destruction. He's just panicked that the Germs won't even be able to play a single tune before everything falls apart.

The makeup of the crowd itself is his other cause for concern. It's not just the expected collection of hard-core punks out there. A few minutes ago, Darby took a cautious peek from behind the curtain and was dismayed to see an intimidatingly large representation of Huntington Beach surfers in the audience. Darby knows what their presence portends. These bronzed, muscle-bound crackers, all undoubtedly jacked up on Boone's Farm apple wine and brown Mexican weed sprinkled with PCP, have not traveled two hours from their seaside shacks to enjoy some down-home punk. In fact, the surfers loathe everything remotely connected to the Hollywood punk scene. The feeling is mutual.

Though not more than a few years old, this feud is practically Balkan in depth. It's a class war between equally marginalized kids, a race war fought entirely among whites, a conflict that sustains itself on sheer hate and misdirected energy. Tonight, the surf rats have decided to bring the fight directly to their foes' doorstep. Not content to stay where they belong, shredding waves and hanging freshly doffed bikini bottoms from their bedposts, these overgrown, long-haired thumpers are here to rumble.

For the past few months, this increasingly violent trend has spread along the live music circuit, from the Whisky and the Troub on the west side all the way east into punk strongholds like the Masque, the Garage in Silver Lake, and even Chinatown's venerable Madame Wong's. Cadres of surfers, who under normal circumstances wouldn't be caught dead within a five-mile radius of Hollywood, are blowing through and leaving a smoky trail in their wake. Left to their own devices, the punks are obviously capable of generating more than their share of mayhem. But when mixed in close quarters with dozens of red-eyed beach mutants who bus themselves in all the way from Orange County for the express purpose of starting shit, the chance for an actual riot becomes substantially greater than fifty-fifty.

The surf rats have their formula for pandemonium down pat. Entering a club en masse, they jostle and elbow their way right up to the foot of the stage. This prime positioning serves two purposes. It gives them ideal real estate from which to heckle and harass the musicians, and, more importantly, it aggravates the punk faithful who depend on those few front rows to get close enough to trade fluids with those onstage. If you are a Germs fan and leave the show without being spit on by someone in the band (even stone-faced bassist Lorna Doom), you might as well have stayed home.

Thanks to the drummer's absence and the surfers' presence, tonight has "train wreck" written all over it. A cloud of gloom hangs over the band and its meager entourage as they nervously pace the floor backstage. Guitarist Pat Smear is the only one showing a trace of optimism. It's just inconceivable to him that the usually reliable Don Bolles will pull a no-show.

As Darby broods in the corner, the Whisky's stage manager, Jimmy "Beefeater" Corso, charges backstage. Not looking anyone in the eye, he booms out an ultimatum: find a goddamn drummer and get on the stage within ten minutes or face decimation. He means every word. Though it would be a six-against-one brawl, the ex-prizefighter Corso has no doubt about his ability to mop up the floor with these malnourished waste products.

Corso exits the dressing room as rapidly as he appeared. The man feels nothing short of utter revulsion for the Germs, and his feelings are not without some basis. He practically begged the management not to book tonight's show but was voted down by Elmer Valentine, who has shown a stronger streak of tolerance for the punks than the Whisky's other owners.

When it comes down to it, it's amazing the Germs are even allowed to set foot in the club. The Whisky already imposed one lifetime ban on them in the aftermath of the Great Punk Rock Weekend of 1977. Put together by revered promoter Kim Fowley, that event is still considered one of the milestones in the history of L.A. punk. Fowley brought together a handful of local bands, each of which proved to be responsible in some measure for the explosive popularity of the new musical movement: the Weirdos, the Dickies, and the Screamers were among the more notable names. All of them played with ferocity, paving the way for short, intense, and influential careers. But the Germs were by far the most impressive performers. Equally impressive were their fans, who put on an explosion of mosh pit rage that had the Whisky reeling. The cost of the damage they inflicted on the club ran into the thousands.

By the end of the three-song set, they had trashed the place so badly that Jimmy Corso collared everyone in the crowd, demanding to know who had come to see the Germs. The fact that no one lied testified to the magnetic loyalty the band imbued within the withered hearts of their followers. Everyone who answered in the affirmative was made to stay late and clean up the mess. A few balked at the order, naturally, but most were glad to get a couple more hours inside the great, revitalized hall of music and mayhem. It's not like there was anything waiting for them at home. Though informed by Jimmy Corso that he would never perform at the Whisky again ("until the day you fucking die!"), Darby Crash still looked upon the night as an unqualified success. It was the first time the Germs were able to capture a decent live recording, released a few years later on an LP called *Germicide*.

Strike one.

Not long after the Punk Rock Weekend debacle, the Germs were invited to take part in the battle-of-the-bands climax scene of *Up in Smoke*. Considering their ban at the Whisky, inviting them to participate in the shoot at the Roxy was a fairly ludicrous casting decision. Nonetheless, the Germs were delighted to get another shot at despoiling one of the Sunset Strip's most well-regarded nightclubs. After playing only two songs, Darby was up to his old tricks again, smashing amps and using his mike stand as a spear. The Germs were quickly booted from the Roxy, and the footage of

NIHILISM AT 45 RPM

their implosion was never used in the film.

Strike two.

In light of this spotty record, the Germs' current promoter Brendan Mullen must have employed some kind of Vulcan mind control to convince the Whisky to give the band another chance for tonight's show. Whatever his methods, Mullen succeeded. Both he and the band consider it a crucial opportunity to prove they can play a professional gig at a respected venue. Anarchic, yes. But in a professional, contained way. Only after getting the green light did Mullen stop to consider the ramifications of his bold play. By then, of course, it was too late.

And now the crowd wants their Germs. Half of them are waiting for the show to start so they can hear their idols play. The other half is just slavering for an excuse to throw a fist and get it on. Another excruciating seven minutes pass with no sign of the missing drummer. Darby considers holding an open audition; there must be at least a few people in the audience who can keep a four-four beat for two minutes at a time.

Just as Jimmy Corso is ready to charge backstage again and exact the punishment he promised, Don Bolles walks in the Whisky's front door. He is immediately swamped by fans who greet him with welcoming sucker punches and raised middle fingers. Some unseen prankster, probably from the surf crowd, deliberately trips him. Muscling his way through the throng, it takes him five intensely unpleasant minutes to reach the dressing room.

Once backstage, Bolles doesn't have much time to explain his late arrival. His initial story about being detained in the Hollywood police station's drunk tank will later be called into question, but right now everyone's just happy to see him. They grab their instruments, administer final dosages of whatever they rely on to get through the gig, and prepare to make their grand entrance.

Darby rises from his stool in the corner and walks over to Bolles casually, like he never felt the slightest qualm.

"So you want to play after all," he says, a cigarette dangling from his lips. "Sure you wouldn't rather just slit your wrist and be done with it?"

Bolles shrugs. "After the show, maybe."

"Good. I'll join you."

Darby takes the cigarette from his mouth and holds the burning tip an inch or so from Bolles' neck. Close enough for the heat to make its presence clearly felt. Their eyes stay locked as the cigarette hovers in place. Bolles is really sick of Darby's persistent, vaguely homoerotic taunts. In light of his tardiness, he doesn't feel he can rebuff the singer right now, but he'll be damned if he's going to flinch or look away.

"Do it," the drummer finally says.

Darby just smiles. He slowly retracts the cigarette and extinguishes it on his own left nipple. His lower lip trembles just slightly at the pain, and Bolles can't help averting his eyes.

"Do it yourself," Darby says, letting the dead cigarette fall to the floor. He walks away.

And with that, the Germs take the stage, ready to ring in the spirit of the season. As anyone might guess, it's a fiasco from the opening minute.

The band doesn't even complete their first song, the apocalyptic ballad "Forming," before they are pelted with dozens of bottles and glasses. So many projectiles are hurled onstage it's impossible to tell if they are being thrown in tribute by the punks or in attack by the surfers. What's the difference, anyway? It's all the excuse Jimmy Corso needs for pulling the plug. Halfway through the song, he kills the stage lights. The band keeps grinding away until Darby tells them to cool it. The leader of the Germs draws a line at performing in the dark. How are the fans supposed to feast their eyes on all his nihilistic glory? For a suicidal sociopath, Darby Crash has a lot of the same image-conscious characteristics as your standard rock 'n' roll diva.

The audience is not happy with the interruption. They fill the club with outraged boos and even more flying debris. As if receiving a preordained signal, a wiry surf rat standing by the left corner of the stage drains the beer bottle in his hand and goes into a low crouch. Steadying himself against an onslaught of boots and knees, he pulls a gasoline-soaked rag out of his jacket and stuffs it into the bottle. Instant Molotov cocktail. Lighting the wick with a trembling grip, the surfer springs to his feet and throws the bottle overhand like a pitcher zeroing in on the strike zone. The bottle barely misses Lorna Doom's head and shatters on the rear wall behind the stage. A balloon of flames instantly bursts forth, and the stage is on fire.

Ernie the bouncer sees the whole thing happen. Shoving people aside like cardboard cutouts, Ernie grabs the scrawny arsonist by his stringy blond mane and slams him hard onto the cement floor. Seeing this act of justified violence, Pat Smear unhooks his six-string from the shoulder strap and brings it down heavily on top of Ernie's head. The bouncer is only stunned for a brief moment before wheeling around to face his attacker. The look on his face expresses more surprise than rage. Why would Smear attack Ernie, who's only trying to punish a surf rat who almost set Smear and the entire band on fire? The fact is, Pat Smear has a slightly pathological reaction to all forms of authority, be they his parents, policemen, meter maids, or, especially, bouncers. Whether Ernie laid a lick on a loyal Germs fan or a surfer bent on the band's annihilation matters little to Pat. When he saw Ernie attack the flamethrower, he went into Pavlovian mode and struck back on behalf of the fallen surfer.

As Ernie pulls himself up onto the stage with murder in his eyes, Pat wisely beats a retreat to the rear exit. One of the other bouncers struggles through the crowd with a fire extinguisher, a group of surfers forming a human chain to block his progress. About a dozen more are engaged in a group brawl with some punks a few feet away. A teenage girl starts to get trampled under-foot and is dragged off to a safe corner by some merciful soul.

As the Whisky burns once more, Darby Crash stands silently in the middle of the stage, rigid behind his mike stand. This wasn't how the night was supposed to unfold. The events are fine, but the sequence is all out of whack. There should not have been a fire onstage until at least the third song. If anyone was going to assault a bouncer, it should have been Darby himself. Now there's absolutely no question the Germs will never play this club again, and the star of the night didn't even get a chance to shine. It's bru-tally unfair, yet such are the dangers of being a punk on the edge. This is a movement in which music is secondary to madness, and it can sometimes be impossible for a performer to share his talent with the audience.

After a few more minutes, the stage is a truly dangerous place to be, and the Germs scatter. Lorna Doom jumps into the crowd and swings her bass like a truncheon, taking out surfer and punk alike as she tries to clear a path to the exit. Don Bolles follows in her wake, throwing elbows indiscriminately. No one sees Darby leave. The rumor spreads almost instantly that he has perished by flame or assault, but, in truth, he manages to escape out the front door unnoticed in a wave of bodies.

Pat Smear is somehow able to clear out the back door into the Whisky's parking lot. After a quick camouflage job, he starts sprint-ing south and doesn't stop for fourteen blocks. It's by far the most exercise he's gotten since mandatory phys ed in high school. His feet don't halt until he arrives at an ex-girlfriend's crummy apartment complex on La Cienega. After being shaken out of a warm bed by manic pounding on her door, she opens it to see a sweat-soaked apparition in a filthy Santa Claus costume that she doesn't even recognize as her former lover. (Pat swiped the suit from the catatonic junkie in the dumpster behind the Whisky, figuring it would be less likely to attract the attention of cruising cops than his leather-studded punk garb.) He manages to talk his way inside the girl's apartment and ends up screwing her on the sofa while her current boyfriend slumbers obliviously in the bedroom.

There will be a total of sixteen arrests and seven hospitalizations before the night's over. The damage to the Whisky's stage will necessitate the cancellation of at least three shows planned for later in the week. In a fitting conclusion to the whole awful experience, some loyal Germs lover will express his hatred of surfers with a message scrawled along the men's room wall with his own excrement.

Strike three, and the Germs are out. Permanently banned from playing not only the Whisky, but also any other half-respectable venue on the Sunset Strip ever again. Which turns out to be a short sentence, since Darby Crash will die from an intentional heroin overdose in roughly a year. His body will be found in a rent-by-the-hour room in the bowels of Hollywood, laid out in a faux crucifixion pose with a note pinned above his head reading "Here Lies Darby Crash." All but the most slavishly devoted of Darby's followers have to concede his lyrics sometimes verge on the maudlin.

The Germs will dissolve within a week of the unsurprising news. A few days before Christmas 1980, the surviving band members and a few dozen fans will gather in a barren, windblown cemetery to spit on the casket as it is being lowered into the cold earth. Everyone agrees Darby would have wanted it that way.

The Whisky's New Identity

When the Whisky A Go-Go first opened in 1964, its meteoric success established it almost immediately as the progenitor of virtually every future rock club in America. It was the first discothèque, the first club to offer a stage dedicated to live rock 'n' roll, and the first venue to embrace the tolerance and flexibility necessary to sustain success in the turbulent 1960s.

For nearly a decade, the Whisky A Go-Go ruled L.A.'s musical landscape and earned its reputation as a star maker.

But, when the Whisky burned in 1971, its fortunes dramatically shifted and other clubs quickly emerged to fill the void the Whisky left behind. State-of-the-art concert clubs such as the Troubadour, the Roxy, and later the Starwood soon became the venues of choice where up-and-coming bands could build their following. And smaller bars such as the Rainbow and for a brief time Rodney's English Disco were the chic new celebrity hangouts on the Sunset Strip.

So, for much of the early to mid 1970s, the Whisky was simply viewed as a dinosaur drowning in the sea of competition its success had helped create.

As Elmer Valentine remarked at the time:

"We can't get big crowds regularly," he said. "We are competing with every little rock 'n' roll club and every concert. Only when we have a big name is business very good. But you can't get a big star every week."

Struggling simply to maintain profitability, the owners of the Whisky made several desperate attempts to forge a new identity for their prized club. For a while they turned the club into a theater and cabaret, offering such eclectic productions as *Tarzana Tanzi*, a musical comedy set in a wrestling ring. When this failed, the owners decided to remove the stage altogether and convert the Whisky into a DJ-only dance hall. But this also failed. Soon, a new stage for live rock 'n' roll was back. But when a rowdy band accidentally burned down the new stage in November '76, Elmer and Mario decided to shut the Whisky down for a few months to reevaluate things.

It was at this time that Elmer ran into the Runaways' producer/songwriter, Kim Fowley.

"One day in the summer of '77," remembers Fowley, "Elmer Valentine said to me, 'We need a gimmick to get tickets sold. What do you have?' And I said, 'Well, punk rock,' and he said, 'What's that?' 'English stuff,' I said. 'Oh, yeah, we'll put punk rock in here—whatever it is.' I said, 'Okay.'

"So I called up Rodney Bingenheimer [L.A.'s famed KROQ DJ] and said, 'Rodney, you gotta put me on the air so we can invite all the garage bands to show up at the Whisky. We'll call it punk rock no matter what it is, okay?' So I went on Rodney's show and said, 'Attention unsigned new bands in garages! Guys and girls who are playing weird underground music. Whoever shows up at the Whisky this Friday will automatically be guaranteed a spot. In other words, if you show up, you get to be onstage, even if you're horrible, I don't care.'"

What showed up, in Kim Fowley's words, was a crowd of "urine-stained, safety-pin-wearing, shit-ass motherfucker out-of-control fuckboys and fuckgirls, pissing, puking, shitting, and farting. It was anger, angst, madness. White punks on dope. It was like Kosovo meets Auschwitz."

Nevertheless, the concert sold out and Elmer and Mario saw it as a big success. From that moment, the Whisky had found its new identity. For the next several years it would be the home for punk rock in Los Angeles.

From Pop to Punk

Back in the olden days of 1967, when Iggy Pop first shouted obscenities into a microphone, rubbed peanut butter and raw steak all over his body, and sliced his chest open with broken glass, he had no idea that each one of these violent, primitive moves would be studied and duplicated by a future generation of rockers barely out of preschool at the time. Nor did he know or even care that he was the only rocker in the world putting on a nightly show of self-mutilation. To Iggy (formerly James Osterberg), it was simply how he vented the angst of growing up poor and abused in a trailer park near Ann Arbor, Michigan.

His was the true spirit of a punk, and along with his band, the Stooges, Iggy Pop brought punk rock into the world.

Unfortunately for Iggy, it was the Summer of Love and punk rock was not exactly what the world was looking for.

Incredibly, the Stooges' originality did manage to land them a recording deal with Elektra in 1968, but their only two albums, *The Stooges* and *Funhouse* (now considered classics) completely bombed. In 1971, discouraged and mired in drug addiction, the band split up.

But Iggy and the Stooges had built a small but die-hard following, and many fans were deeply moved by their albums.

One such fan was David Bowie.

Glam Rock

In 1971, David Bowie (formerly David Jones) was already a rising star in England after two successful albums and a hit single, "Space Oddity." But he was growing increasingly disenchanted with a music industry almost exclusively dominated by the easy-listening singer/songwriter types (such as Carole King, the Eagles, and Crosby, Stills, and Nash) and the lead-guitar-driven heavy-metal bands (such as Aerosmith, Led Zeppelin, and Black Sabbath).

So Bowie mounted his own personal rebellion against the status quo and transformed himself into Ziggy Stardust, an androgynous, bisexual rock star from another planet. Sporting a dress, heavy makeup, and spiked, bright orange hair, Bowie declared himself gay to the press and in late 1972 released his new record, *The Rise and Fall of Ziggy Stardust and the Spiders from Mars*. Glam rock was born.

Remarkably, the album and its lavish, theatrical concerts became a sensation throughout England, and soon Ziggy Stardust would become a word-of-mouth hit in the United States as well. In fact, Bowie's rerelease of "Space Oddity" would go on to reach the American Top Twenty.

Suddenly, from New York to Los Angeles, cross-dressing bands playing Bowie's brand of glam rock (or glitter rock as it was often called in the U.S.) began popping up everywhere, and groups such as the New York Dolls, Silverhead, the GTOs, and the Berlin Brats all got in on the action.

On the Sunset Strip, famed underground L.A. disc jockey

Rodney Bingenheimer opened a club dedicated to glam rock called Rodney's English Disco. Boasting Bowie as one of its board members, it was considered by far one of the hippest clubs in L.A from 1972 to 1974.

Despite the groundswell glam created, the phenomenon proved to be short-lived. By the end of 1973, Bowie had abandoned the Ziggy persona, as it was all too clear that the cross-dressing fad was no longer hip. Meanwhile, the best bands to emerge from the movement, the New York Dolls and the Berlin Brats, succumbed to heroin addiction.

But the brief success of glam exposed quite clearly that a substantial base of people were desperately searching for something beyond what was being offered in the mainstream.

Once again, David Bowie had an idea of just what to give them.

Raw Power

After retiring Ziggy Stardust, Bowie decided to go back into the studio. This time he would perform not as a musician, but as a producer.

Convincing the newly clean and sober Iggy Pop and the Stooges to get back together, Bowie agreed to have his MainMan Management Company handle the group and subsequently landed them a new recording deal with Columbia Records. Within months Bowie was at the mixing boards helping the Stooges record what would become one of the most influential punk rock albums of all time: *Raw Power.*

As Chris Ashford, founder of the punk label What? Records, puts it, "*Raw Power* became the godhead album for these new postglitter kids."

Punk diva Belinda Carlisle of the Go-Gos was one of them:

"I was born and raised in Southern California," says Carlisle. "Growing up, I listened to schlocky radio—the Doobie Brothers and Chicago, pop music. One day I walked into a record store and I saw the cover of *Raw Power.* And I said, 'Who's that?' And I bought the album and it opened up a whole new world that I didn't know existed. Discovering Iggy led to discovering the Velvet Underground and Roxy Music. I started going into L.A. to see bands. Postglitter bands."

Another postglitter kid was former Germs, Nirvana, and Foo Fighters guitarist Pat Smear:

"We would look through the cut-out bins and buy records for the covers, and that's how we discovered *Raw Power* by Iggy and the Stooges. The cover had these horror-style dripping letters and showed Iggy with his shirt off with makeup and platinum hair. The record was cool, but it didn't even matter. The cover made it. It wouldn't have mattered what it sounded like."

After *Raw Power* was released, Iggy and the Stooges moved to Los Angeles, where they made a huge impact on the fledgling postglitter L.A. scene by playing a string of five straight sold-out nights at the Whisky. A reviewer from the popular music industry rag *Back Door Man* called the performances "the best live rock 'n' roll I have ever witnessed."

But despite the obvious impact of *Raw Power,* the album failed to sell well upon its release. Dejected, Iggy Pop again took to heroin and other hard drugs, and the band again broke up.

The Dawn of L.A. Punk

Though less well-known than its New York and British cousins, the punk scene that sprung up in Los Angeles from late 1976 to 1982 produced some of the most gifted and timeless bands of the entire genre.

Because the nicer concert venues refused to book punk bands and there were absolutely zero DJs playing punk music on local radio, the punk scene in L.A. was slow to get started. It wasn't until Rodney Bingenheimer began playing the New York and British punk bands such as the Ramones and the Sex Pistols on his new weekly KROQ radio show that the trashy garage scene really began to claim its identity.

The scene was further strengthened when writer Brendan Mullen opened up the Masque, L.A.'s first all-punk venue/rehearsal space/crash pad. Basically an illegal club located in the ten-thousand-square-foot basement of the abandoned Hollywood Center building, the Masque was a place where any aspiring punk rocker could party, thrash, and rehearse to all hours of the night without the threat of parents or police.

Then, out of the primordial mix of hard drugs, indiscriminate vandalism, and generally weak musicianship that was the hallmark of early L.A. punk, some genuine genius began to emerge.

The first punk group to surface from the Masque was the Germs. Helmed by brilliant lead singer Darby Crash (who supposedly had an IQ of 180), the Germs played their first gig without ever having had a single rehearsal or even really knowing how to play any instruments. Just hitting the stage, screaming, and thrashing about chaotically, the Germs "played" for about fifteen minutes and then were thrown out.

But Darby Crash had made an impression on the audience with his reckless unpredictability. Though that gig had been a disaster, when the Germs announced they were going to play again, crowds came just to see what Darby Crash might do.

At the Germs' next show, Darby once again delivered. Cutting his chest with razors and smearing peanut butter all over his body, the crowd was delightfully surprised when the Germs actually performed some inspired original songs with potent lyrics. Darby Crash and the Germs' reputation quickly grew, and, before long, they were mythologized throughout the scene.

At the same time, other groups were forming as well. Bands such as the Weirdos, the Screamers, the Dils, the Gun Club, and X all began attracting acclaim.

As former Black Flag lead singer Henry Rollins puts it:

"There were some really great bands to come out of L.A. in those early days. Like that seminal Masque-era shot of X, the Weirdos, the Germs, and the Screamers, for sure—their genius was just incredible. The Gun Club was a great Hollywood band. You play those records now, they totally stand up.

"I mean, the Germs' Darby Crash was kind of that generation's Arthur Rimbaud. Just a stunning lyricist. You read that stuff now, it makes you jealous as a songwriter. He was really, really talented and died young . . . so I think there will always be a small cult around him."

The scene in L.A. was definitely starting to take shape. However, incredibly, no major record labels paid any notice to the L.A. punk bands. In their opinion, if it wasn't from England or New York, then it wasn't for real.

Famous KLOS DJ Jim Ladd (AKA the Lonesome L.A. Cowboy) echoes the attitude at the time:

"When the punk movement came along, I understood it as something legitimate in England, in working-class Birmingham or wherever. A legitimate stage in rock 'n' roll. But except for L.A. bands like X, Black Flag, and a few others that I really thought were great, because they were good, and they believed it and they lived it, the L.A. punk scene was basically a joke. Most of the punks out here—I mean, if you're a kid from the Valley . . . come on. What the fuck are you so angry about? So I never took that seriously. I saw it as mostly posers. It was basically fashion without a real foundation."

But whether the establishment was paying attention or not, the L.A. punk bands were watching their popularity grow. Performances at the Whisky were perpetual sellouts, and a new club, the Starwood, was making punk its bread and butter. Meanwhile, *Slash* magazine, a weekly punk review put out by writers Steve Samiof and Claude Bessey, began steadily increasing its circulation to the point that they needed to open a larger office to handle the demand.

Still, no record labels called.

It finally reached a point where people in the scene simply decided to pool their money and begin their own independent punk labels. Soon Slash Records, Bomp! Records, What? Records, SST Records, and Dangerhouse were born.

All of them went to work producing and distributing the best young punk bands' albums and sending the groups out on tour. Money was tight, budgets were low, but at least the bands were going to get heard. And their ally at KROQ, Rodney Bingenheimer, would have something to play.

Once on the road, these early L.A. punk bands began to make an impression on their East Coast counterparts. As Henry Rollins, who was raised in Washington, D.C., and was living there at the time, recalls:

"My friends and I all knew who X and the Germs were, the Weirdos and the Dils and the Dead Kennedys. We were all record collectors, so we had everything on Dangerhouse Records and What? Records, and we knew who Rodney Bingenheimer was. And the bands all toured, so we saw them play and we met them. And little by little I got to actually meet all these people finally, and it was really cool, you know? To meet Brendan Mullen, Jeffrey Lee Pierce [lead singer of the Gun Club], and Exene Cervenka, because all of these people from three thousand miles away were sort of legendary."

The L.A. scene was given an extra jolt when New York punk supergroup the Ramones were booked into a renowned string of shows at the Whisky.

"Los Angeles was great," recalls Joey Ramone. "We blew their minds. We were an instant hit. They totally related to us. A sick bunch. The L.A. kids were really wild and insane, much more like the English audiences than the hip New York crowd."

Broadcast live on Rodney Bingenheimer's radio show, the Ramones' gigs became a watershed for the entire L.A. punk movement. Soon bands such as Black Flag from Huntington Beach (thirty-five miles south of L.A.) and Vicious Circle (later TSOL) from Malibu began to emerge and make their way to the Hollywood clubs.

Punk Turns Ugly

Unfortunately, as the mix of fans and bands from different regions grew, so did the instances of fights breaking out at virtually every punk concert. In the past, the Hollywood punkers had generally kept the violence onstage, with the performers destroying their own equipment and mutilating their own flesh. But soon every punk concert was turning into a bloody brawl with people being seriously injured in "slam pits" and vicious fights.

As Mark Truelove, a legendary tattoo artist and former punk, remembers:

"I started going to the Whisky in '79 when they started booking punk bands like Black Flag, the Circle Jerks, the Blasters, Agent Orange, all the old L.A. punk. Black Flag, who brought out a certain surfer/jock element, started playing there Friday nights as the house band. So you'd get confrontations between the jocks and punks. We hated them and they hated us."

According to Henry Rollins, it was primarily the new fans coming from other regions who were causing the trouble:

"What I think happened was that punk rock became popular as a cultural thing, and you had the jocks checking it out because of KROQ or whatever. It happens in any city scene, you know, the suburban types come in—the bridge-and-tunnel crowd. In Washington, D.C., where I came from, you had the Maryland-Virginia element coming in for shows, and immediately fights started. And it was always the suburban jockuloid types versus the locals. But when the Orange County punk rockers—you know, very capable surf types—started coming to those shows in Hollywood, I think that's when you started having the mix-ups. I don't think Hollywood punk rockers were ever going to give you any stick—not in those days."

Rollins continues, "The Hollywood punk rockers, as far as I could tell, were not really worth beating up in that they were just these weenie-armed intellectuals wearing tuxedo jackets and not looking for trouble. It was not about 'tough guy.' It was more these kind of well-read people who were too smart for the football team."

The Black Flag Whisky Riot

In any case, the hostilities steadily grew, and with bands such as TSOL and Black Flag incorporating the fights into their acts, things really started getting out of hand.

"TSOL was a pretty scary unit," says Henry Rollins. "I mean, it was intense music, but their audience was *really* intense. And they followed them everywhere. So, whenever TSOL showed up, everyone knew there was going to be this element that was going to give it back to the security guys. These guys were not afraid of bouncers. They were into mixing it up. TSOL would come to play in L.A., and the place would be packed out—the Whisky, the Palladium, Florentine Gardens, whatever—and, with all those guys in tow, shit would happen pretty immediately."

As the violence escalated, police began showing up before every punk show. Soon, confrontations between the cops and punks became almost routine.

"The cops hated Black Flag," says Truelove. "Raymond Pettibone [Black Flag's renowned artist] was doing flyers of people sticking guns in the cops' mouths and saying 'Suck me off now, cop!' And that infuriated the sheriff's department. They started hassling people at the Whisky, and they started hassling us on the streets."

According to Henry Rollins, the punks became a favorite target for the cops:

"The Hollywood punk rock scene definitely had a problem with police," he says. "Police Chief Daryl Gates really had it in for punk rockers in L.A. There were some heavy clashes. Whenever you'd go to the Whisky, the cops would come out with a video camera and try to video-ID people just so they could kind of put you on file or drive by and try to take your photograph or tell you to keep moving. You'd be in front of the Whisky and they would go, 'Okay, move.' And so you would just walk down to Tower Records, cross the street, make a right near the Viper Room, walk back up across the street, and then go back for, like, another twenty minutes before they came around with the bullhorn and told you to take that walk again."

West Hollywood Deputy Sheriff Bruce Thomas gives his impression from those days:

"You used to see a lot of punkers on the street," says Thomas. "Every now and then the punkers and the rock 'n' roll guys would clash, and you'd have fights. But for the most part, they had their own little agenda, whatever they were doing. It seemed to work out some nights, and other nights it didn't work out. Some nights you'd take people to jail, other nights you wouldn't. And you'd see the same people every Saturday night. The same punks, the same rock 'n' roll people. And you would know who your problematic ones were. So you'd say, 'Okay, goodbye, guys. See you next Saturday night.'"

But everything came to a head one night in 1979 during a

particularly violent Black Flag show at the Whisky.

"The cops came in to kind of break up the show," recalls Rollins, "and it got out of control. People were arrested, and I think police vehicles were vandalized, so they closed off part of Sunset Boulevard. Apparently it was the first time it had been locked down like that since the riots on Sunset many years before. Black Flag ended up not playing there again until 1982 as a surprise guest. But other than that we were banned from the Whisky."

Glen Friedman, a photographer who was at the Black Flag riot, recalls the tense night:

"All of a sudden the Sunset Strip was closed off. Cops were beating the fuck out of kids. They put their faces into the ground, handcuffed them to newspaper vending machines on the sidewalk. That shit was nuts."

For the owners of the Whisky, this was the final straw when it came to punk bands, and they decided the nightly fights and degenerate crowds were just not worth whatever money they were getting at the door. After more than two years as a punk mecca, the Whisky closed its doors.

Mario Maglieri comments on the decision:

"With punk rock, people were so vicious, so destructive. Not only inside, but outside. They'd break windows, car windows, all kinds of nonsense. So I closed the Whisky for two years. Just closed it, 'cause of that element. I can't have that. And even today, I take a look at a band, who are they, what do they bring in here? I gotta find out, or I won't have it. You don't wanna go destroying people's property, knockin' on people's doors, shittin' on their lawns, know what I mean? You gotta watch that."

Punk rock, at least on the Sunset Strip, had been dealt a heavy blow. It wouldn't be until 1981, after the age of punk rock and then new wave and hard-core punk had essentially passed and a new era of spandex, teased hair, and makeup emerged, that the Whisky would once again put out the welcome mat.

BIG HAIR WILL GET YOU LAID

March 4, 1982

"Jesus, kid. You don't look so hot," Mario Maglieri says with a quiver of genuine concern in his voice. "When's the last time you had a good meal?"

John Belushi doesn't answer the question. He's not ignoring Mario, he's simply too preoccupied with the task of trying to fish one last bent cigarette out of a badly crumpled pack in the breast pocket of his sweaty, open-necked shirt. Belushi squints and bites hard on his tongue, which pokes out luridly from the confines of his wide mouth. In the dim glow of the limousine's backseat light, the tongue looks completely obscene—grayish and mottled and covered with a visible film. Mario has to look away and wait for Belushi to return his tongue to where it belongs.

Staring out the smoked window at the raucous display of humanity pressing in on all sides, Mario desperately wishes he could step out of the limo and breathe some fresh air. Mingle with the crowd and share the excitement that's come with the early arrival of spring this year. But he knows the incredibly sensitive Belushi would read that simple act as nothing short of utter aban-donment. So he just shifts uncomfortably in the padded leather seat and sits it out.

Belushi grunts softly. The process of manipulating his pudgy fingers into the pack and grabbing the reluctant Marlboro Red commands every bit of the movie star's limited attention. He's actually sweating from the effort. Or possibly from the eight lines of coke he snorted right before the limo pulled into the Rainbow Bar and Grill's driveway, where it now sits.

Finally extracting the reluctant smoke, Belushi's eyes light up with hammy pride. He raises one brow in a classic Bluto Blutarski leer as he sticks the cigarette in his greedy maw. Now all he has to do is find a lighter. Mario steels himself for another long wait. He's actually feeling relieved just to have seen a glimmer of life in Belushi's eyes. Every other part of the comedian's ample being seems utterly dormant. Mario feels a little sad just looking at him. He also feels more than a little ridiculous sitting in this enormous vehicle as it clogs the driveway to his club on a busy Saturday night. He's spent almost twenty minutes trying to convince Belushi to come inside the Rainbow, but corralling the man into any kind of forward motion is no small feat.

"Come on, forget the fucking lighter. I'll give you a whole box of Rainbow matches."

Still he gets no reply. Eventually it dawns on Belushi that the limo has a built-in lighter, and he pounces on it, using a meaty fist to smash the knob into the igniting port. Drumming his fingers impatiently on the armrest as he waits for it to pop back out, Belushi looks like he might not be able to endure the nicotine deprivation; however, he manages to hold out long enough to light the cigarette. Visibly relaxing as he inhales two huge lungfuls of sweet Virginia tobacco, he gradually acknowledges Mario.

"What were you saying?" Belushi asks.

"I said you look like you could use a nice hot meal. Come on inside."

Belushi's eyes blur slightly as he tries to retrieve a lost memory. "Wait a minute," he stammers. "We were taking about something important. What was it?"

Mario doesn't even attempt to conceal a frustrated sigh. "Some lousy punk band."

"Right, right," Belushi says, leaning forward animatedly. "Fear. They're called Fear. This is a great fuckin' band, Mario. *Great* fuckin' band."

Maglieri's patience seems to instantly evaporate. "I keep telling you," he almost barks, "you're talking to the wrong guy. I'm the last person in this whole goddamn town who'd ever spend a dime on punk rock. I hate that shit. Find another sucker."

"These guys are different. Seriously. This band Fear's really got the goods. They're like *real musicians.*"

The sincerity of his pitch softens Mario a bit. It's like dealing with an overeager kid who desperately wants to please but just won't acknowledge the word no.

"Listen to me, Johnny," Mario says with a friendly pat on Belushi's grapefruit-sized knee. "You're not the first guy who's tried to get me to back some band that's sure to be the next big thing. I'm not interested in that, okay? And I've turned down some acts that really *did* blow up. Why would I put money into something that's caused me nothing but a big fuckin' headache from day one? Besides, punk rock is dead, in case you hadn't heard. It's over, and good riddance. Just take a peek out there."

He points through the limo's window, which offers a picture-frame view of the Rainbow Bar and Grill's driveway and parking lot. Unwilling to give up the fight, Belushi nonetheless feels compelled to at least pretend to look.

It's actually quite a sight. The Rainbow's parking lot has in recent months become the biggest open-air party in town. The action that goes down out here on a nightly basis is so heavy there's hardly any reason to move inside unless you're dead set on sitting in a booth. It's been like this every weekend night since the advent of spandex metal made the Strip cool again after punk's demise.

L.A. punk is over. Mario's exactly right on that score. A phenomenon as short-lived as it was intense, it left a powerfully unpleasant aftertaste that hung around for quite some time. When the Whisky shut its doors, all the major players on the scene sort of cocooned, waiting for a change in the weather. For the first time in decades, the Sunset Strip was talked about in the past tense among Hollywood hipsters, who sought out new territories of undiscovered cool. Local columnists started composing grandiose obituaries to this once great boulevard of dirty dreams.

Thank God a new subspecies of locally generated music cropped up when it did, before L.A. became virtually obsolete on the national scene. And with it arrived a new influx of fans who were actually more interested in hearing music than disturbing the peace. What a refreshing change of pace that was. The Whisky's reopening in '81 signaled a rebirth of not only the Sunset Strip, but also of rock 'n' roll itself.

The fate of the Rainbow has always been inextricably linked to its sister club down the block. When the Whisky tanked, the Rainbow also went into a downward spiral of sorts. While it could always rely on its notoriety to draw a solid dinner crowd, the last few years of the '70s and the first one of the '80s constituted a period of relative slumber for the venerable 'Bow.

But it only takes a passing look at the parking lot tonight to see that the Rainbow Bar and Grill has been born again. It has entered a second golden age, confirming its title as the world's greatest rock 'n' roll bar/restaurant. The fact that it doesn't have much competition for the claim does not undermine the achievement. The Rainbow earns its rock 'n' roll credentials nightly. There are few posers to be found around here. These folks are the real deal, and this is where they come to let it rip. It's a bad place. It's a good place for bad people.

And right now there are so many of them that the parking lot is overflowing with huge hair, fake tits, studded leather, cowboy boots, and spandex. There's no way all these people can fit into the Rainbow at the same time. Not even the newly added patio can accommodate the demand. So the parking lot serves as an extension of the building, and it is jam-packed with the rock 'n' roll faithful until well after closing. Many are minors. The Rainbow's parking lot is where you hang out on a Saturday night in Hollywood if you're a seventeen-year-old kid without a decent fake ID. A male kid, that is. Females of virtually any age are admitted, since the Rainbow has not tightened its door policy regarding underage girls since the glory days of Lori Mattix and her *Star* magazine sisterhood.

"Tell me something," Mario says as he looks out into the crush. "Do you see a single punk rocker out there?"

Belushi takes a final drag on the Marlboro, sucking right down to the filter. Stubbing it out, he sighs in resignation. "Shit, maybe you're right. You've been in this racket a lot longer than I have."

"Don't let me piss on the parade, kid. I'm sure there's plenty of rich dopes out there who'd love to put some green into this band of yours."

"It's not my band. I'd just like to see them get a break, that's all. Forget it."

Mario shrugs. "Okay with me. Ready to get out of this glorified meat wagon, or what?"

BIG HAIR WILL GET YOU LAID

"Sure. All of a sudden I feel the need for some lentil soup."

"That's the first sensible thing you've said all night."

Belushi raps on the partition behind the driver's head and tells him to open the door. Mario would much rather get out by his own doing, but if Belushi demands the movie-star treatment, so be it. At least the kid's agreed to put some hot food in his stomach. Mario is less convinced of Belushi's willingness to abandon his fundraising pitch for his latest pet project.

And Mario's suspicions are entirely accurate. Belushi has always been a natural manipulator, with a wide arsenal of moods to call upon. Whether he has to assume the guise of raging bull, sad clown, or overgrown little boy, he usually ends up getting what he wants. So he has shrewdly opted to leave Mario alone about Fear for the moment and resume his campaign at a later hour.

The two men emerge from the limo and work their way toward the Rainbow's entrance. They are almost identical in stature, if you were to replace Belushi's flab with Mario's aging muscle. Sadly, though the club owner has a good twenty-five years on the actor, he still looks a lot younger. There's certainly no question whose cardiovascular system is in better shape.

Steady Eddie the doorman allows them to pass through into the cozy oak-paneled foyer, where the walls are covered with snapshots taken inside this, place over the past decade. It's a virtual who's-who of the rock 'n' roll Strip. Mingled together in a colorful jumble are the famous and the obscure, the beautiful and the grotesque, the immortal and the just plain lost. All the faces in the photos share at least one quality: they are plainly having a hell of a good time. Belushi smudges a finger against a snapshot of himself as he passes by.

Tony Vescio stands at his post by the register, a leather-bound menu in his hand. Though he now serves as one of the Rainbow's co-managers, Tony still relishes the task of personally guiding many of the restaurant's higher-profile guests to their tables. He bows deeply as Belushi approaches. "Would you like a table, sir?"

"Is number fourteen open, Tony?" John asks. For some reason, he has designated this quiet corner booth as his lucky spot and is reluctant to sit anywhere else.

"Of course it is. It's always available to our favorite funny fella."

"That's what I love about this place," Belushi says, greatly pleased. "Lead the way, my good man. And let's get things rolling right away with a bottle of Dom."

"Whatever you say."

As Belushi starts to follow Tony into the living room, Mario taps him on the shoulder. "Order the whole fuckin' menu if you want. I'm serious. It's on me, okay?"

A slight trace of panic jumps into Belushi's eyes. "You're not coming with me?"

"I'm on duty, kid. I'll be over to check on you later on."

Belushi grabs Mario's arm, digging his fingers in tight. His strength is surprising, given his almost funereal pallor. "Don't make me sit there alone," he pleads. "I fucking hate that, man."

Mario studies the comedian's pasty moon face closely for a few long seconds. The urgency in Belushi's eyes is real. An aura of loneliness hangs on him like a steel chain, pulling down on his shoulders and sinking his whole sad, fat body toward the carpeted floor.

Mario finally shoots him a wink. "Lemme just check on the kitchen. I'll be right over, I promise."

Hugely relieved, Belushi paints a crooked smile on his face and starts giddily foxtrotting with an invisible companion across the crowded dining room toward his table. Tony seats him and says the champagne will be right over. Cracking open a fresh pack of smokes, Belushi lights up and surveys the room. He's riding a good, strong cocaine buzz and the shimmery veneer of invincibility that comes with it. He feels completely in charge.

True to his word, Mario shows up and takes a seat in the booth. He knows it's going to be a long night, but at least he'll be able to give his aching feet a rest.

They stay there for hours. Bullshitting. Actually, Belushi does most of the bullshitting and Mario does most of the listening. A huge spread of food encompassing most of the menu covers every inch of the table. Maybe four bites have been taken, total. Belushi's far too busy drinking, talking, and smoking to pay much attention to dinner. He's also excused himself to go to the bathroom at least a half-dozen times, telling Mario he's got a bad case of the trots. The lie is so transparent it lowers the whole scenario to the level of bad farce. Though Mario feels that his intelligence is being grossly insulted, what he mainly feels is a sense of helpless compassion.

Belushi does manage to consume at least one item from the menu. The lentil soup he mentioned earlier is mild enough to be digested by his wildly churning stomach. Lifting the bowl to his face to slurp down every last drop, Belushi emits a tooth-rattling belch that would make his *Animal House* frat brothers proud. He sets the bowl down and energetically wipes his face with an otherwise unused napkin.

As Belushi stands to make his sixth or seventh trip to the toilet, Mario puts a firm hand on his arm and pulls him back into the booth. He holds him there as a tense moment of silence prevails.

"What the fuck are you doin', John?"

Belushi sputters out a fake laugh totally devoid of mirth. "Hey, if you want to get in my pants, why don't you just ask? I should warn you, though, I never go all the way on the first date."

Mario isn't smiling. "Look at me, asshole. What the fuck are you doin' to yourself?"

Hemming and hawing, Belushi unhooks himself from Mario's grip. "Just trying to have a good time, you know? Live it up a little. Otherwise, what's the point?"

"You mean there's a *point* to putting that garbage up your nose? Take a look at yourself. I've seen too many of you stupid fucks waste away. All the talent in the world, all the money, all the cooze, and it still ain't enough. Nothing's *ever* enough. Not until you're broke, insane, or dead. I don't want to say that about John Belushi."

Impassioned reason isn't the ideal weapon to use in confronting this particular addict. It would be much more effective to just slap him across the face and flush his stash down the toilet.

And yet Belushi is visibly moved by Mario's concern. Slumping in his seat, he delivers a few vague apologies. Then he lurches back to his feet. Only now the spring is gone entirely from his step. He says he's feeling tired, and it's obvious he's telling the truth. The coke has plateaued, and no matter how much more he does tonight, he won't be able to get high again. Only more irritable and paranoid. It's time to call it a night. Mario shakes his head as he looks at the massive amount of food that sits as a doleful testament to Belushi's life of excess. The memories of an impoverished childhood still fresh in his mind, he hates to see waste. Oh well, he can give it to the busboys.

As Mario guides Belushi across the dining room floor toward the exit, the sad clown sort of sags against him. He tries to assure Mario it's just a bad night and that he'll come back in a day or two an entirely new man. Even while heavily intoxicated, it's clear he's worried about what the owner of the Rainbow will think of him. Mario tells him to just get some sleep and take it easy for a while. Maybe a long while.

The parking lot is still booming with crazed activity. Belushi looks into the crowd longingly, scoping out all the kids who are still at that early stage of their experience with drugs, when getting loaded is actually fun. John left that stage behind long ago. Standing by the limo, he wraps Mario in a suffocating bear hug. As Mario tries to extricate himself, Belushi keeps repeating that the Rainbow makes the best lentil soup in the world. Mario tells him he's welcome to come have some any time he likes. The more the better.

Then, performing one last warped Bluto-esque pirouette that is actually funny despite being pathetic, Belushi whirls into the back of the limo and slams the door shut.

At roughly three o'clock the following afternoon, John Belushi's corpse is wheeled out on a gurney from bungalow number three of the Chateau Marmont Hotel, just a mile or two up Sunset from the Rainbow. The coroner's report will reveal massive amounts of cocaine and heroin in his bloodstream. The only contents in his stomach are the remnants of a bowl of Scarlett Maglieri's famed lentil soup. When Mario hears that, it just about makes him weep.

A New World

When the Whisky reopened its doors in 1981 after nearly a two-year hiatus, it was to a world far removed from the angry punk rock scene that had dominated the Sunset Strip in the late '70s.

The punk movement had been a victim primarily of its own nihilistic creed. Persistent violence and clashes with cops had made punk concerts nearly impossible, and the punk world's deadly devotion to heroin had claimed several of its icons, most notably Sid Vicious in 1979 and Darby Crash in 1980.

The petulant punk movement had also been pushed out of the mainstream club scene by the late '70s disco craze and the astronomical success of heavy-metal acts such as Van Halen and the resurgent Ozzy Osbourne with guitar god Randy Rhoads.

Though some hardcore punk bands such as Black Flag and John Belushi's beloved Fear did manage to forge successful careers in the early '80s, with the turn of the decade and the election of Ronald Reagan as president, it was clear that a new era was dawning. Izod shirts and Jordache jeans were becoming all the rage, and the business of music was quickly and dramatically being reshaped by the new popularity of an old idea: the music video.

The explosion of the music video created a new kind of rock star. Suddenly, how musicians looked was just as important as the music they played. For many bands that were short on talent but long on style, dreams of rock stardom were now within reach.

I Want My MTV

The idea of building music videos out of popular songs was by no means a fresh concept in 1981. The Monkees had demonstrated the technique with amazing success on their weekly TV show back in 1966. And many other acts, including the Beatles, Rod Stewart, and David Bowie had also created short films around their songs for use as promotional tools. But in 1975, when Queen released an elaborate made-for-TV clip to go along with their operatic masterpiece, "Bohemian Rhapsody," the music video was immediately cast into a new light.

All of a sudden music videos were seen less as promotional tools and more as a new means of entertainment. Soon groups such as ABBA, Devo, and Blondie were creating extended-length videos of their songs featuring ornate props and advanced special effects. Television shows in Europe and Australia began airing special segments devoted to these "pop clips," as the videos were called.

But music videos were slow to catch on in the United States. It wasn't until ex-Monkees guitarist Mike Nesmith decided to get back into the game that a breakthrough into the massive American market occurred. Realizing that the U.S. simply had no on-air forum for showcasing music videos, he decided in 1978 to produce his own thirty-minute music video show, aptly called *Pop Clips*. Having made an unsuccessful bid to sell *Pop Clips* to the major networks, Nesmith was encouraged by Warner Records executive Jac Holtzman to pitch his idea to parent company Warner Cable. Warner Cable had recently established the Movie Channel to compete with HBO and was building a new kids-only channel called Nickelodeon. Meeting with execs at Nickelodeon, Nesmith was offered a chance to produce a variety of *Pop Clips* episodes for airing in a Columbus, Ohio, test market. When *Pop Clips* debuted on Nickelodeon in 1980, it was an immediate sensation.

Enormously impressed by these results, Warner Cable decided to create an entirely new channel devoted solely to *Pop Clips*. Incredibly, it was at this point that Mike Nesmith decided to opt out of his role in the music video world and explore other unrelated projects. However, Warner Cable continued with the plan and hired a dedicated staff to produce the all-music video channel.

Finally, on August 1, 1981, a revamped *Pop Clips*, sporting the new name MTV, went live into the national market. The very first music video aired was appropriately titled "Video Killed the Radio Star" by the Buggles. As the music started to play, a voice proclaimed, "Ladies and gentlemen . . . rock and roll."

And with that simple announcement, the music world would never be the same.

Breaking the Band

Originally MTV's format was modeled exactly after a radio station's, with videos being introduced by a VJ much like a DJ would introduce a song. The videos were streamed twenty-four hours a day and were meant to showcase a variety of different musical genres. Unfortunately, limited quantity and poor quality hampered MTV in its early stages. The fact was that in 1981 very few bands had actually filmed music videos. Many of the best videos were often replayed multiple times every few hours.

"When we went on the air," reflects MTV Networks chairman and CEO Tom Freston, "we had 168 clips. And thirty of them were Rod Stewart."

But the rock 'n' roll subject matter and novelty of its programming format gave MTV instant appeal to America's teenagers. Soon the channel was reaching tens of millions of American homes. And the bands that did have high-quality videos benefited immensely from consistent play, even if their songs weren't played on mainstream radio.

One band that reaped fame and fortune during the early days of MTV was the Stray Cats, a new-wave rockabilly trio from the East Coast that had been enjoying a modest degree of success in Great Britain.

"We'd made videos in England before MTV," says Stray Cats' drummer Slim Jim Phantom, "because you had to make them if you were there on tour. They would play them on kids' afternoon shows and the popular British TV show *Top of the Pops*. You couldn't appear on *Top of the Pops* unless you had a video to show on it. So, when MTV started, we had, like, two or three videos already finished. They didn't have that much content back then, so they had to play whatever they had."

He adds, "What was cool about MTV then, which really isn't the case anymore, was that it could break a band. We weren't on the radio at all in the early '80s; we were selling records in the U.S. purely because of MTV. Eventually American radio said, 'Wow, these guys are good.' Then they had to start playing us."

With their high-energy act and cool look, the Stray Cats quickly nailed the formula that spelled success on MTV. Their two videos "Rock This Town" and "Stray Cat Strut" both became number-one videos, and, as the channel blossomed, the band got famous in the U.S. Soon both songs reached the Top Ten on the American radio charts.

Moving to Los Angeles at the height of their MTV success, the Stray Cats melded perfectly into the Sunset Strip scene, which was gaining new momentum after a post-punk lull.

"I had never been to L.A. before," says Slim Jim. "We did a show with the Rolling Stones here on the '81 tour, and the Stray Cats were booked for a solo weekend at the Roxy. Jack Nicholson was in the audience dancing in the front row getting pushed around by all the rockabilly kids. I didn't even know there was a rockabilly scene on the West Coast. So I met Jack Nicholson the first time I was ever here. You just think, it's true, man, everything they say, it's all true. In L.A., there's palm trees and movie stars and blondes. At that point, I just said to myself, this is where I'm gonna live. So that was my first introduction to the Sunset Strip."

He also recalls his first trip to the Rainbow:

"The first day we arrived, a guy from L.A. who was working for us told us to go to the Rainbow. So that night we walked down the Strip, and Brian Setzer [the Stray Cats' lead singer] and I met Mario. He came up to us and says, 'Are you the two kids who are gonna work for me tomorrow night?' I didn't know who he was, and I didn't really know what he was talking about—'work for him' apparently meant we were playing his club. It was kind of an old-school way of presenting it. So we said, 'Well, yeah, we guess.' He says, 'Well, you're too fucking skinny. Come in the back with me,' and he proceeded to bring all of this food for Brian and me. We weighed like a hundred pounds back then— we had just gotten to town and were hanging out, so we weren't really into eating that much—this was back in the time of the hundred-dollar-a-day South American diet. So we kind of pushed the food around the plate, and Mario was all, 'You're not fucking eatin', you got two shows for me tomorrow. How are you gonna make it through without eating?' So we tried to eat for Mario."

The Rise of the Hair Bands: First Wave

If you look at how MTV and the Sunset Strip have evolved since 1981, it's hard to tell which had the bigger impact, MTV on the Strip or the Strip on MTV. It's hard to tell for one simple reason: Mötley Crüe.

When MTV officially launched in 1981, Mötley Crüe had already established itself as the hottest and most influential band on the Strip. Their look, their stage show, their sound—all of it was part of their carefully crafted vision of being the first quasi-punk-rock/heavy-metal hybrid band. A style they called glam metal.

BIG HAIR WILL GET YOU LAID

"In '81, the kings of the Sunset Strip were definitely Mötley Crüe. They were all about publicizing themselves and creating an image," says Guns N' Roses guitarist Slash. "What was I doing in 1981? Oh, shit. I was hanging out. I was selling Quaaludes and trying to get gigs."

Somehow managing to attract both punkers and heavy-metal rockers to their notoriously wild shows, Mötley Crüe hit the stage each night with an explosion of teased hair, loud makeup, ultratight jeans, and cowboy boots.

As Pleasant Gehman, the punk-rock author and former roommate of Go-Gos singer Belinda Carlisle, recalls:

"Belinda and I went to the Whisky on acid to see Mötley Crüe because we couldn't believe a band who looked like that would actually exist. We were the only people at the show who had short hair. But, by the end of their set, we were really into them."

Comprised of bassist Nikki Sixx (born Frank Ferrana), drummer "Tommy Lee" Bass, guitarist Bob "Mick Mars" Deal, and singer "Vince Neil" Wharton, Mötley Crüe were unsigned Sunset Strip superstars. Known for their outlandish, sexually charged stage theatrics and out-of-control after-parties, the band routinely sold out the Whisky, the Roxy, the Troubadour, and even larger venues such as the Palladium and the Palace. When they released their debut album *Too Fast for Love* in 1981 on their own label, Lethur Records, it sold a surprising twenty thousand copies in a matter of months.

With all this success, it didn't take long for larger record companies to take notice, and in 1982 Mötley Crüe signed a major deal with Elektra. By early 1983, the band was ready with their second album, *Shout at the Devil*, featuring the song "Looks That Kill."

The Crüe's video for "Looks That Kill" went to number one almost instantly. There was just something about the band's energy and exotic image that left MTV's audience awestruck. The video's huge success spilled over into album sales and the record went platinum within a year.

Immediately, all of the major labels started mining the Sunset Strip for other glam-metal bands to promote. Soon an entire wave of Mötley Crüe look-alike bands started to appear. Led by the outrageously brash bands Ratt and Quiet Riot and the demonically misogynistic W.A.S.P., glam-metal videos began dominating MTV's airwaves. By 1984, they had helped the once tiny cable channel turn into one of the most powerful entities in rock 'n' roll.

Unfortunately for W.A.S.P., however, MTV didn't always return the favor.

"MTV was no good to us at all," says W.A.S.P. guitarist Chris Holmes. "After our first couple of videos, they ended up banning us because they said we were demeaning to women, just because one of our videos had a naked woman on a torture rack. To me, man, it's just entertainment."

In Los Angeles, perhaps more than ever before, Sunset Boulevard became absolute ground zero for the music industry. And the party on the Strip surrounding the glam-metal bands became bigger than anything it had ever seen.

"Have you ever seen one of those shows on the Discovery Channel with the guy who's covered in bees?" asks Nikki Sixx. "That's what it was like when we were on the Strip. Wherever we went, it was like a swarm of bees around us. People had to be close to us and touch us, and girls were like, 'I'm gonna fuck you tonight,' and guys were like, 'You're gonna do my drugs tonight,' and it sort of became the norm. I didn't think anything about it. Narcissism is a wonderful disease, I guess."

The Rainbow Bar and Grill was indisputably the most popular bar in town and, on a nightly basis, played host to twisted depravity not seen since the days of Led Zeppelin.

"Someone said I fucked the cigarette machine once there," recalls Chris Holmes. "It probably didn't give me any smokes."

"Another time," according to one longtime Rainbow waitress, "this girl over by the fireplace just lifted her dress and started playing with herself in front of all the customers. And the manager went up to her and said, 'Honey, you're gonna have to stop that 'cause people are trying to eat.'"

But the mayhem was not only inside the Rainbow, it was outside in the Rainbow parking lot as well. Often showing up with their own cases of beer, hundreds of partiers of all ages would rage until deep into the night, not even thinking about ever going into the bar.

"The party outside was so incredible, you never had to go inside," remembers Maria Perdue, a bartender at the Rainbow who used to party nightly at the club as a teen. "So one day when I was twenty-two years old, I walked in here and went, 'Oh, this is a fuckin' restaurant.'"

Frank Sedloev, a longtime Rainbow patron and distant cousin of Rolling Stones guitarist Keith Richards, sums it up best:

"It was like every night was the weekend and every weekend was New Year's Eve."

The scene on the Sunset Strip was exploding. Glam metal had

completely taken over, and everyone wanted to be part of it. "We started playing in, like, 1982 and '83," says Tracii Guns, founder of the successful mid-'80s glam-metal group, the L.A. Guns. "When the Crüe and Ratt and Quiet Riot were getting big, when those three bands started popping, everything in town got groovy. I must have been around fifteen or sixteen, and I would see Blackie Lawless [lead singer of W.A.S.P.] walking down the street. I would see Nikki [Sixx] driving a giant car. And the girls—I mean, I'm sixteen, and there are all these hot girls with big boobs everywhere. I had to be a part of that, somehow."

In only a couple of years, he would get his chance.

As the first wave of glam-metal bands went on world tours to support their albums, the door was opened for a second wave of big-hair bands to take the spotlight. Led by bands such as Poison, Warrant, Faster Pussycat, the L.A. Guns, and the mighty Guns N' Roses, this second wave would push the image-is-everything mentality and the hard partying lifestyle to its limits.

METAL, THE SEQUEL

September 1, 1987

"Did anyone get their names?"

The mouth that asks the question belongs to Slash, but it's hidden under an impenetrable mask of curly black hair that creeps down from under the brim of an oversized top hat like Spanish moss hanging from a rooftop in the deep South. Slash has been cultivating this look for about a year, and he's really starting to like it. The hair not only minimizes eye contact, which the introverted guitarist avoids like the plague, but it also acts as an organic shield protecting against ultraviolet rays. And that comes in handy, since Slash can't seem to hold onto a pair of sunglasses for more than a day or two without losing them, breaking them, or giving them away. An essentially nocturnal creature, he's not a big fan of direct sunlight.

Slash is wondering if anyone knows the names of the two teenage girls who just stepped off the bus licking their lips. He doesn't get any straight answers from the other thirteen guys on the bus. Instead, his bandmates in Guns N' Roses, along with their seven-man road crew, reply by heaping piles of verbal abuse on the guitarist. All except Axl Rose, who is too preoccupied refilling his beer cup and probably would remain silent even if he weren't. The others more than compensate for Axl's silence, ripping Slash mercilessly for being soft enough to ask the chicks' names. What an amateur move.

The bus they're sitting in is painted a classic bright yellow. It is the property of Laidlaw Education Services, which the Los Angeles Unified School District contracts for the purpose of ferrying small children from their homes to hallowed halls of learning and then back again in one piece. It's really no different than any school bus you'd find in big cities and small towns all across the country. Except those vehicles usually aren't rented out by ascendant rock bands who don't have the means for more glamorous modes of transport.

As the autumn of '87 starts to simmer off from the heat of the summer, the Gunners have not yet arrived at the stretch-limo level of stardom. All in good time. The current situation is actually fine with them, because it's a lot easier to fit two kegs of beer into a school bus than a limousine.

One silver barrel is already dead, lying forlornly on its side in the back of the bus. A few inches next to it, the other keg is still kicking. Barely. Axl Rose pumps the tap with a steady vicious hammering of his tattooed left arm, like an oil derrick plumbing the Earth for hidden reserves, while he clenches a red plastic cup in his right hand. The tap hisses and gurgles on the verge of extinction. Axl keeps leaning on it until the keg can produce nothing more than carbonated air. Satisfied he's gotten the last drop, Axl wordlessly returns to his seat while the rest of the Gunners continue to go to work on Slash, which they do at great volume.

Indeed, as it idles in the right lane of Sunset a half-block west of the Rainbow, chugging out lungfuls of carcinogens, the bus practically sways with the auditory force of blaring music intermingled with wild jeering and laughter. Guns N' Roses is capable of making a hell of a lot of noise, with or without the aid of their musical instruments and a good P.A. Right now they are relying only on a small boombox and their own haggard vocal chords, but they're still generating enough decibels to piss off the neighbors. They really need to either disembark from the parked bus or get it in gear before the cops show up. But no one seems in much of a hurry to do anything right now. Except taunt Slash.

Sitting in the second-to-last seat on the right side of the aisle, within his customary arm's reach of the beer, Slash accepts the barbs with stoicism. Being a member of Guns N' Roses involves taking a bag of shit from your bandmates on a pretty regular basis. A certain strain of mutual hostility, thinly veiled by laugher, is an essential dynamic of the band, and a thick skin is almost as important as musical ability if you want to survive in this outfit for very long.

After a few minutes, the conversation switches from insulting the lead guitarist to the next pertinent subject: dinner. The band seems content to leave Slash alone for a while, until fellow six-stringer Izzy Stradlin takes up the banner again.

"I got an idea," Izzy says, reaching across the bus's gum-specked aisle to slap Slash on the shoulder. "Why don't you hop out and try to track those chicks down? They can't move very fast on full stomachs."

This vile remark produces gales of laughter and a resumption of the trash-talking.

"He's right," says drummer Steve Adler (no relation to Lou, as far as either man knows). Adler struggles to speak as he tugs on a smoldering joint until it disappears into a fragment of ash. "We'll meet you at the 'Bow, dude. If you don't show up by morning, we'll know you're in love."

"You guys are fucking hilarious," Slash says in his low-pitched mumble. "Do you rehearse this shit or what?"

"Okay, okay," Izzy says to Adler. "I think he's had enough." Izzy punches Slash on the arm and returns to his seat. Still, he can't resist adding, "But, really, *asking their names?* What the hell?"

Meanwhile, Steve Adler has returned to his own spot on the bus and is hammering his drumsticks against the padded back of the seat in front of him. Under no circumstances does Steve relinquish his drumsticks—or his role as a drummer for that matter. He's constantly tapping out a beat on whatever surface presents itself. Right now that happens to be the back of Axl Rose's seat. Steve's really getting going until Axl reaches over his shoulder without turning and yanks the sticks from his hands.

"C'mon, Axl! Fuck!"

"I told you to give it a rest."

Steve is usually too stoned to get angry about anything, but he really doesn't like anyone messing with his sticks. "Give 'em back, dickhead!"

Axl takes an unhurried sip of beer. His voice is calm. "They're mine now, Steve."

"I'll fuckin' *take* 'em if I have to."

"You want them? Go fetch, bitch."

Axl tosses the drumsticks out the window directly into oncoming traffic. Steve Adler watches them spiral through the air, his jaw slack with shock. One of the sticks clatters against the windshield of a passing BMW, causing the car to swerve into the adjacent lane. With an angry honk, the driver slams on the brakes and pulls over. A balding geezer in an argyle sweater and tasseled loafers steps out to get a look at the punk who had the nerve to launch a wooden projectile at his car. Seeing not a lone teenage delinquent but an entire busload of tattooed rockers, the old man decides to let it slide. He gets back in and peels away, but not before flipping G N' R a gnarled middle finger.

Watching through the open window, Axl laughs. "That guy was all right."

"Are we gonna get out of this fucking bus or *what?*" bassist Duff McKagan wants to know. "Beer's gone, so what the fuck?"

Though the band is need of a meal and the culinary delights of the Rainbow's kitchen beckon from less than a block away, everyone seems a little reluctant to leave the bus. They've become almost irrationally attached to it.

G N' R finished a blistering gig at the Whisky about an hour ago, as planned. They knew perfectly well that the postperformance dinner would be held at the Rainbow, all of two blocks away. A rented vehicle is hardly necessary to make the trek. But the Gunners are rock stars on the rise. Their debut LP *Appetite for Destruction* was released only two months ago, but the band has been touring behind it nationally, opening for the Cult, and building an increasingly large and delirious fan base with each show. Though they won't emerge as bona fide monsters for another year, they are too far along in their upward climb to be seen walking down the sidewalk like a bunch of unsigned hackers. Especially on the Strip, where they are sure to be noticed. So they rented the only vehicle they could find that met both their capacity and budgetary requirements. On a certain level it makes sense. The bus will get its fair share of use before the night is over, as the boys will almost certainly opt for a late-night mission to the Seventh Veil, the infamous strip bar located about three miles east on Sunset.

From the moment they lifted the kegs through the back doors at five this afternoon, everyone took a liking to the yellow school bus. It just seemed to emit a good vibe. But in light of what happened after the show, they have grown more attached to it than they would have ever thought possible. For the rest of their highly combustible careers, both together and apart, the original members of Guns N' Roses will remember tonight and the big yellow vehicle known simply as "The B.J. Bus." It earned this moniker about twenty minutes ago, when two stiletto-heeled maidens casually approached from the sidewalk and asked if they could get autographs. Upon gaining entrance to the bus, these ardent G N' R boosters promptly proceeded to give head to everyone inside.

Slash is still stunned by the matter-of-factness of the whole encounter. The girls didn't see the need to introduce or explain themselves. They simply went to work. Each taking an aisle, they started with the musicians sitting at the back of the bus and worked their way forward. Even the sweaty, barrel-chested driver, Vic, a full-time Laidlaw employee rented along with the vehicle, was treated to some joy. The girls must have figured he was the official bus driver for Guns N' Roses and therefore worthy. After all fourteen flies had been rezipped, the girls stood up and left, sweetly waving goodbye. They never even bothered to get autographs.

A year from now, Slash will be a lot more jaded about the perks of rock 'n' roll stardom. Such antics won't even raise a hidden eyebrow on the guy. But right now, it feels like he's won the lottery and been named president of *Hustler* at the same time. Slash is the only one in the band honest enough to admit it. Everyone else is equally shocked by the episode; they're just so hardwired into acting cool, they are no longer able to express genuine emotions like surprise and gratitude.

"Those chicks didn't even *want* anything," Slash mutters, recklessly inviting more abuse from the other guys. "No backstage passes, nothing."

"Nope," Axl says quietly. He slyly reaches into his leather jacket to grab a fresh pint of Jack Daniels he's been hoarding for when the beer runs out. He takes a pull and passes it to his guitarist. "That was an act of pure fan appreciation."

"Fourteen acts," Slash says, accepting the pint.

"Let's get some goddamn grub!" Duff McKagan bellows from the front of the bus. He's leaning with all his weight against the folding door, desperate to leave. McKagan is starving, having forgone lunch as a result of forgetting to set his alarm last night. Lurching out of bed at the crack of 3:00 P.M., he had to frantically shake himself awake and hustle over to the group's shared studio/crash pad on Gardner Street ("the Hellhouse") in time to assemble the gear and be picked up by the bus. It's been a long night already, and Duff is pretty impatient to slide into a cozy booth at the 'Bow and get some pizzas working. But he doesn't even consider stepping out of the bus by himself. That would be completely unacceptable.

The Gunners are an extraordinarily tight-knit bunch. Like many bands who've had to scrape and struggle to make a dent, they embrace an "us against the world" mentality that announces itself in everything they do. They take the stage together. They take drugs together. Girlfriends and habitations are shared. Rehearsals and sound checks don't start until everyone is present (which isn't a problem since these guys are still so hungry that they always manage to show up on time). If tonight's two oral starlets had entered the bus and insisted on servicing only the lead singer, they would have been immediately sent to the curb with a barrage of misogynistic insults.

One for all and all for Guns. Learn it. Know it. Live it. Now and forevermore.

Still, in this band of equals, some are more equal than others. Axl and Slash are unquestionably the musical nucleus of G N' R, and they tend to hang pretty close to one another. Their relationship is sometimes described as "closer than brothers," and, like many siblings, they are mutually driven by competition as well as affection. Astute students of rock 'n' roll, they have consciously crafted a partnership based on the great duos of the past: Lennon/McCartney, Jagger/Richards, Page/Plant, etc. What neither Slash nor Axl has stopped to consider is that all those iconic collaborations, fruitful as they may have been, ended with bitter acrimony and the total collapse of the bands themselves. (Okay, Mick and Keith are still ostensibly together, but given the quality of their work post–*Tattoo You,* more than a few true-blue Stones fans wish the band had dissolved long ago.)

Besides, the two leaders of Guns N' Roses, still in the starry-eyed phase of their careers, can already see their future: they will hang tight and continue to crank out immortal rock tunes until they both die, sometime in late middle age, in the same sprawling French villa, surrounded by adoring adolescent waifs and piles of money. That's the game plan, and no one close to either Slash or Axl has the nerve to poke a hole in it. The other musicians resent their rapport and superior attitude, but what are you gonna do? Being in a band on the rise has its price, and everyone in G N' R is more than willing to pay it.

Slash passes the bottle of J.D. back to Axl, who shakes his head when he sees there's only about an inch of fluid left. He drains the dregs and chucks the empty pint out the window without caring to look where it lands. By some small miracle, the street is momentarily empty and the bottle shatters harmlessly on the pavement.

Axl sticks both pinkies between his yellowed front teeth and lets out a whistle loud enough to deafen a Collie. "Okay, Gunners," he says, conscious of not raising his voice now that he has everyone's attention. "Let's move out."

With this edict, all twelve seated members of the entourage rise to their feet in unison. Axl always has the last word, and he rarely has to repeat it. The driver pulls the lever to open the door and Duff McKagan, who is still absentmindedly leaning against it, falls out ass over teakettle. It's quite a drop to the cold, unforgiving sidewalk. His reflexes badly dulled by numerous substances, Duff is unable to break the fall with his hands and greets the cement squarely with the side of his face.

"Holy shit!" cries his guitar tech, Ricky, who shoves people aside and runs to assist the fallen bassist. Everyone else is laughing too hard at Duff's smooth move to be of much help. Their hoarse guffaws ring out into the night over McKagan's prone form.

Ricky turns him over on his back and winces at the sight of a four-inch gash running from Duff's forehead into his left eyebrow. Blood pools around his eye. After a few tense seconds, Duff snaps awake and screams in shock at the momentary sensation of blindness. Ricky uses his favorite Zeppelin T-shirt to wipe away the blood and assures Duff his eyes are fine. He cautiously suggests medical attention, but Duff won't have it. Instead, he tells Ricky to take off the stained T-shirt and tie it tight around his head as a tourniquet. What choice does the loyal guitar tech have?

Duff smiles as he is helped to his feet. He bows theatrically to his hysterical bandmates as they applaud his potentially crippling pratfall. It was a good one, but probably not the most blatant performance of legless buffoonery they're likely to see this evening. After all, it's not even eleven. Still, it's a solid start that qualifies Duff as an early lead for tonight's FUBAR award. And, on top of that honor, Duff is pretty confident he can turn this nasty little spill to his advantage. The chicks at the 'Bow are sure to cream at the sight of fresh blood.

After a couple of minutes, the rest of the Gunners have gotten their hilarity under control and are filing out of the bus in an appropriately disorderly fashion. Axl tells Vic to keep it parked here and not to take any shit from cops telling him to move.

Stepping onto the curb, Slash inhales the night air into his lungs as deeply as his three-pack-a-day habit allows. Just feeling the Sunset Strip underneath his leather boots sets him straight. He grew up here, literally. He's been cruising these sidewalks since he was old enough to figure out where his parents hid the spare key to the front door of their house. Considering his father worked for David Geffen, whose label signed Guns N' Roses in March of '86, Slash was born into rock 'n' roll.

The other guys clamor out of the bus and cut a wide swath across the sidewalk as they move toward the Rainbow. Axl is stopped for an autograph before he's advanced ten feet. A few passing cars honk their horns in tribute. A girl in the back of a pick-up lifts her top for the band's benefit before being yelled at by her boyfriend and sheepishly lowering it.

A green Chevy Impala low-rider carrying two Latino die-hard Poison fans pulls up to the curb where Slash is pausing to light a Marlboro. The *hombre* in the passenger seat yells out, "Gunners suck dick!" His buddy hits the gas and the low-rider veers into traffic, cutting across two lanes and almost causing a pile-up. Even as the car barrels west out of sight into Beverly Hills, Axl has to be forcibly restrained from chasing after it. In truth, he's not really that angry, because any kind of recognition counts. It's the ultimate compliment to the rising star status of G N' R that they can't walk half a block down Sunset without causing a minor scene.

But the real havoc doesn't start until they enter the parking lot of the Rainbow Bar and Grill.

Two teenage German tourists with absurdly exaggerated mullets and loaded down with torturously heavy photographic equipment are milling about underneath the 'Bow's famous neon sign. One of them stands by the entrance holding a hand-painted sign over his head that reads "Das Haus der Lemmy!" with a crudely drawn arrow pointing toward the front door. His buddy crouches with a camera, trying to find an angle that will capture as much of the hallowed building as possible. Tony Vescio stands calmly in the doorway, waiting for them to finish. After firing off a half-dozen shots, the photographer orders his buddy to remain in position ("*Schwarzweiss, schwarzweiss!*") as he reaches for another camera to preserve their fleeting brush with greatness in black and white. They are so involved with getting a good shot, they don't even notice when G N' R walks by.

As the Gunners work their way through the crowd to the restaurant's entrance, they are openly gawked at and embraced. Slash puts a fresh Marlboro in his mouth and a half-dozen lighters instantaneously appear. He leans forward to get a light from a Zippo in the hands of an hourglass brunette in fishnet stockings. Grabbing her free hand, he pulls her along as he tries to get closer to the building.

Up by the front door, Axl is amused and mildly irritated to bump into a kid mimicking his look down to the last detail: long red hair, storm trooper boots, black tank top revealing pale, heavily tattooed arms, and of course the red bandana tied over the head with a pair of sunglasses riding on top. The wannabe is too shocked to be standing face to face with his idol to react in any specific way. After a long, fairly tense moment, Axl just nods and says, "Pretty cool." He walks on through the front door, leaving the copycat to go running over to his disbelieving friends so he can tell them he just hung out with Axl Rose.

Once all the members of G N' R get inside, they tend to do their own thing. The Musketeers unity only goes so far. Everyone is starting to get on each other's nerves, and there are ample diversions within the rowdy confines of the Rainbow. Steve Adler is still pissed about losing his drumsticks, so he plants himself at the bar and doesn't say much. Within a year's time, Steve will have developed a serious heroin habit. While it is difficult to map out the absolute low point in his career, most would agree it comes in 1988 when Guns N' Roses are playing with Mötley Crüe during the "Girls Girls Girls" tour and several members of the Crüe trick Steve into snorting a substantial amount of toilet disinfectant. In early 1990, he will be unceremoniously and permanently booted from the band. But right now all he's thinking about is exacting revenge upon Axl for throwing away his sticks.

Meanwhile, Duff McKagan is thoroughly enjoying himself tonight. He starts chatting up a blonde waitress whose brow is wrinkled with concern for his bleeding head. It's all Duff can do to keep from laughing out loud; he's getting exactly the kind of leg-spreading sympathy he'd hoped for. Staring into her worried blue eyes, Duff considers injuring himself more often.

Upstairs, Izzy Stradlin gets into a heated debate with a threesome of drunken Scots about who was the best drummer to emerge from the British Invasion. Izzy stubbornly insists it was John Bonham, ignoring the strident complaints of the Scots that Zeppelin wasn't technically part of the British Invasion and therefore doesn't qualify. Their unanimous vote goes to Keith Moon. The argument rages on well into the night.

For his part, Axl has planted himself in a recessed booth in the dining room, where he is joined by Slash and the Zippo-bearing brunette. Axl isn't in any hurry to find a companion. He's content to enjoy a mellow late dinner and reflect on what's happened tonight. Of all the Gunners, Axl is by far the most conscious of the band's status and progress. He may be a rock 'n' roll bad boy, but he's also a ruthless careerist who recognizes the extraordinarily rare opportunity he and his cohorts face. It's not just incredibly difficult to start a band and generate a major buzz; it's more like a statistical impossibility. Yes, in the ongoing frenzy of the metal explosion, a lot of young bands are getting signed. But how many of them will ever have a hit single? And how many of that small percentage will be around in two years? These are the questions that haunt Axl's mind even as he should be enjoying a memorably raunchy night.

For a while, he even forgets about the two girls on the bus. Until it's time to pick up the meal tab and he reaches for his wallet. It won't be too long before Axl and the rest of the guys in Guns N' Roses will stop carrying wallets altogether. The richer they get, the less they will actually need to spend money on things like meals, guitars, hotel rooms, and the like. It's a weird inversion of means versus expenditures that seems to accompany the rise of every rock band, until the bills get so staggering that the requisite sycophants and hangers-on are no longer willing or able to cover the debt.

Be that as it may, on this particular September evening in 1987, Axl graciously decides to pay for dinner. But when he reaches into the hip pocket of his frayed Levis, he feels nothing but his own skinny ass. And then he remembers the way the girl on the bus (she seemed to be the older of the two, but it was hard to tell in the low light) wrapped her arms all the way around his torso and squeezed while she went down on him, providing more than enough distraction for a sly act of petty theft.

Axl leans back in the comfortable booth and smiles in spite of himself. It seems he's got one or two things to learn about being a rock star after all. Just wait till the other guys get a load of this. He'll never hear the end of it.

Big Hair and Spandex: The Second Wave

In the mid 1980s, when Mötley Crüe and the rest of the first wave of glam-metal bands took to the road, it seemed, for a little while at least, that the party on the Strip had left with them.

It was as if the entire record industry was collectively holding its breath to see if the hair metal craze was just a fad or if its insane popularity was the real deal. Luckily, at least for all of those bands who'd just paid for hair extensions, the sold-out arenas around the world provided an easy answer.

Though there was a temporary lull in the action on the Strip, it didn't take long for an entirely new crop of big-hair bands to pick up and run with the white-hot torch Mötley Crüe and the others had left behind.

Leading the charge of this second wave of glam-metal rockers was a band from the East Coast called Poison.

"I had nothing but respect for the bands that had come before us," says Poison lead singer Bret Michaels. "You know, Mötley Crüe , Ratt, W.A.S.P. I thought they were great, but those bands had made it and were out playing on the road, so there was this big void in L.A. When Poison came out in '84, we just became the premiere party band. I mean, we were the event to go to. If you loved us, you showed up. If you hated us, you showed up even earlier. And, believe me, we had both. Eventually, people realized that it didn't matter if they liked us or not, it was always a huge party, because even on the smallest stages we made a big event out of it."

Originally composed of singer Bret Michaels, bassist Bobby Dall, drummer Rikki Rockett, and guitarist Matt Smith, Poison had arrived in L.A. with absolutely no money in their pockets. By necessity, they earned their reputation as literally the hungriest band on the Sunset Strip. Raiding thrift stores for spandex pants, vests, and scarves to concoct their own cheap version of the traditionally leather-based glam look, the band managed to forge their own unique identity.

"We were what I called street glam," says Michaels. "We were living in a poor area of L.A. in a warehouse behind the back of a dry cleaners, so it wasn't like we could go pick out designer clothes. We just threw together stuff from the Salvation Army. The look came strictly out of wanting to be colorful, to sort of beat the gray depression that was around us every day. I mean, we lived in an awful environment, so our fantasy, the only fantasy we had in all of it, was the show. So that was what we made as bright and vivid and colorful as we could. It kind of gave us something to look forward to."

Amazingly, Poison made their street-glam look work so well that it caught on with the other emerging bands and ultimately became the new look for the whole glam-metal scene.

The Flyer Barrage

Poison also brought with them an incredible drive for self-promotion.

"We spent all of our effort and time making these flyers, which were this infamous color called Poison Green. The reason it was called Poison Green was that it was the ugliest color Sir Speedy Printer had at the time. They couldn't get rid of it, so it was the cheapest paper. That's how we afforded it. So we just put flyers everywhere. Everywhere we'd go, we'd cover everything with this green and black. It was great, because everyone knew when you saw that color, it was a Poison show."

This forced Warrant, Faster Pussycat, and all the other unsigned bands trying to get noticed to try to match Poison's output.

As Slim Jim Phantom recalls:

"Bands were putting flyers everywhere. Poison at the Troubadour, Warrant at Gazzarri's—wherever you went you were getting handed a fucking flyer. And those bands were out at every show, every club, constantly self-promoting, because there was a lot of competition, but at the same time there was room. So everyone was working hard at it. And everyone looked incredible. Whether you dig that kind of style or not was another story. But they were done up twenty-four hours a day, seven days a week."

For Poison, the intensity finally started to pay off with sold-out shows and interest from various record labels pouring in. However, a crisis occurred when guitarist Matt Smith was forced to leave the band and move back to the East Coast after getting his girlfriend pregnant. Poison had to move fast to find a new lead guitarist.

"We had a huge tryout," says Bret Michaels, "and all these people came. It was narrowed down to C. C. DeVille, Slash, and one other guy. Some of the tension that's always been between me and C. C. comes from the fact that I chose Slash when we voted. The truth is C. C. is a really great guitar player, but at the time he didn't want to play any of our songs, and it pissed me off. Slash came in and played all of our stuff note for note and had one of his own songs, which eventually became 'Welcome To the Jungle.' I was like, 'This guy is great.'"

Slash recalls the audition:

"Poison was sort of the band that was going to carry Mötley Crüe's torch," say Slash. "Now, I did audition for Poison; that is true. There was a point where I was willing to do anything, and as much as I hated what Poison was about, you have to do whatever it takes to make it. So it came down to me and C. C. DeVille auditioning to replace their old guitar player, and C. C. was perfect. I could play the shit out of their material, but I definitely didn't look the part. I don't think C. C. was really the greatest guitar player, which you didn't need to be in that band, but he had the look."

So against Bret's wishes, Poison selected C. C. Deville, a decision that ultimately proved the perfect move for everyone concerned. Slash would shortly thereafter join future '80s supergroup Guns N' Roses, and C. C. would help Poison write and produce their breakout debut *Look What the Cat Dragged In*.

Making It

Released in 1986 on the tiny independent label Enigma Records, Poison's debut was an unbelievable smash from the start. Netting three hit videos and Top Ten singles with "I Want Action," "Talk Dirty to Me," and "I Won't Forget You," it sold an astonishing two million albums in the first year.

"Our second video, 'Talk Dirty To Me,' just went through the roof," recalls Michaels, "and it kind of set a standard for rock on MTV. In other words, I think it made people realize how many fans were out there jonesing to hear rock music."

Poison had proven that audiences were still desperate for more glam-metal, and soon music-industry powerhouse Capitol Records bought out Poison's contract from Enigma.
As Faster Pussycat guitarist Brent Muscat remembers:

"Poison was the first band to come out of the second wave, and they had shown they could sell out shows and sell records. As soon as Capitol picked them up from Enigma and said they were going to get behind them, all of the other major labels just said, 'Okay, who in L.A. right now is a part of this new scene?'"

As a matter of fact, every band that was popular on the scene at the time, including Warrant, Metallica, Jet Boy, the L.A. Guns, Faster Pussycat, and Guns N' Roses, received a major record deal.

"When I first saw the aftermath of the second generation of bands," says Nikki Sixx, "I was a bit bitter. I was like, 'These fucking bands like Warrant and Poison, awwww! You gotta be kidding, man! They're not serious.' And there they were, giving interviews where they talked about partying and being crazy, and I was like, 'They don't know. They're faking it.' But the bottom line is that we did spawn some of those bands."

And Poison and the other bands definitely were not faking it. The party on the Sunset Strip was raging full steam ahead.

"What happened," recalls Bret Michaels, "is that the scene on the Strip started to really come back. By '86 you couldn't even move. I mean, if you tried to go from the Whisky up to the Rainbow or to Gazzarri's and the Roxy, it was just like a huge party on the street. At the Rainbow, half the time the party was in the parking lot. It was out of control. And one of the things that Poison did after every show is invite people back to the Rainbow Bar and Grill to party with us. You know, back then there was really no law. You would just be out in the parking lot drinking and handing cases of beer out if you could afford it."

And the good times just kept on rolling.

"The second scene that we came out of," says Brent Muscat, "was all about sex, drugs, and rock 'n' roll. Oh, we had songs, too, but those were also about sex, drugs, and rock 'n' roll. Everything was about looking good, partying, being cool, being part of the scene."

He continues:

"Rock 'n' roll is the ultimate aphrodisiac for girls. If a guy is really popular and has a number-one video, he could be bald and the fattest guy in the world, and he could walk into the Rainbow and every girl would be like, 'Wow, he's so cute.' By the time you make it, you get so jaded sexually because you can bang any girl you want anytime you want. You see so much pussy, you're like a gynecologist. After a while, it's hard to get excited by just normal sex; you almost have to experiment to keep it exciting."

And the Rainbow Bar and Grill provided the perfect forum for experimentation.

"The girls at the Rainbow Bar and Grill are some of the prettiest in the world, bar none, because they come from around the world to that place," says Bret Michaels. "And, I can tell you this, I have gotten to meet and enjoy some of the prettiest women in the world there."

Michaels recalls his attempts to emulate the antics of his idols:

"I unfortunately never got to do the 'Zeppelin in the bar,'" he says, "but I did get to do the 'Poison in the bathroom.' As our albums started to sell, somehow I got the magical kitchen bathroom key. Who knew that it would be in the Rainbow kitchen, where they're cooking, like, chicken soup and pizza, that I'd meet some of the prettiest women in the world and have some of the quickest and most intense sexual encounters? That became Poison's infamous place—the Rainbow kitchen bathroom. You'd pray that no one had been in there before you who was really using it, if you know what I mean."

Mandy Lion, lead singer of the band World War III, fondly remembers the Rainbow during this period:

"Underwear was not very popular," says Lion. "Once I was sitting at the round table in the back, and some really sleazy bitch sits down next to me. That's how I met my wife. In the beginning it was a casual thing, but eventually I realized that, in addition to being a really sick bitch, she was also highly intelligent. So I fell in love, big mistake, and got married. But one day she found God, and the panties came back on, and that was that. I should've kept her at the Rainbow."

From Glam to Grunge

Eventually, just as the first wave of glam-metal bands had done, Poison and the rest of the second wavers left the Sunset Strip for world tours. But, throughout the last half of the 1980s, they were undeniably dominant on both MTV and the radio.

However, as brightly as Poison, Guns N' Roses, Mötley Crüe, Metallica, and all the other bands had burned, the entire glam-metal genre was virtually snuffed out in 1991 when the Seattle-based group Nirvana released their pioneering grunge-rock masterpiece, *Nevermind.*

Almost overnight, any music even remotely connected to the glam-metal scene was considered patently uncool. Many music aficionados' hostility toward glam metal turned into near-denial that the movement had ever even existed.

"The '80s hair bands were a musical hiccup," declares Los Angeles DJ Jim Ladd. "Those bands cared more about who was gonna do their makeup than how much they practiced guitar. I always hated that. Music was just this annoying thing they had to learn to put on the costume to get the girls."

For the vast majority of the glam-metal groups, survival was impossible. But some of the bands—Mötley Crüe, Poison, Guns N' Roses, and, later, Metallica—did manage to prove with their music that they were more than just an image. They had true staying power. And, in Poison's case, they even helped grunge gain a foothold.

"Poison never had a fight with grunge," says Bret Michaels. "Music has to constantly change and have new life breathed into it from new bands. When grunge came out, Poison took Alice in Chains out on the road with us during our 'Flesh and Blood' tour. We could've taken anyone at that point. We took Alice in Chains because we thought they had a cool album. Grunge had a rhyme and a reason—and some great music."

Born in Seattle, grunge made its influence felt worldwide—and the Sunset Strip was no exception.

"All these L.A. bands that were positive, hard-rock-show bands all of a sudden tried to act grunge," says Michaels. "But there's a dilemma with that. L.A. is sunny three hundred-plus days in a year, and people come out here to party. I think they were being grunge in the wrong city. And it killed a little bit of that L.A. vibe that just now is finally coming back again."

Meanwhile, though glam metal may be gone, it's certainly not forgotten:

"I always dug the whole vibrancy of it," remarks Slim Jim

Phantom. "It was fun. I didn't have to be into the music or into what they looked like or played like. I just liked the whole time. People were dressed up—it wasn't how I dressed, but I liked it— and there were girls everywhere. And it was pretty much the last time I remember sex, drugs, and rock 'n' roll. Because after that came that whole scene from Seattle, which was, like, the anti-rock-star thing, even though they OD'ed, right? That anti-rock-star thing is worse than being a rock star, I think, because it is denying what it is that you do."

Glam Metal's Permanent Home

In many ways, the Sunset Strip in the 1980s marked the grand crescendo of a scene that was nearly two decades in the making. It was a decade of incredible decadence that continues to have a profound impact on music and pop culture in general. And much of the identity of the clubs along Sunset Boulevard still harkens back to those mid-'80s glory days, when life seemed to be about nothing but a good time.

"I had my birthday party at the Rainbow last year," says Bret Michaels, "and it was huge. We just closed the place down—it was insane. So it truly is my second home. I love going there. They always treat me great, and there's sort of that warm feeling. If you're a rock musician, you're always kind of an outcast, and for some reason the Rainbow always makes you feel like you're coming home."

To honor the Rainbow Bar and Grill, Bret recently wrote a song about it that appears on Poison's most recent album, *Hollyweird*. Appropriately enough, it's called "Home."

HOME (BRET'S STORY)

Saturday night, Rainbow Bar and Grill,
Where there's cocaine lines and a little white pill.
A beer and a gin, now I can't see straight,
Slip it in, no glove, oops, too late.
I remember her face but forgot her name,
She forgot mine, too, ain't that a shame.
Smell like reefer and my hair's in a mess,
I left my love running down her dress.

Dave from Drowning Pool is here,
Steals my women and he drinks my beer.
Buys me a pizza and a shot of Jim Beam
And asks who the fuck is Angelyne?
I go to piss in the parking lot,
Well, I get in a fight, but I don't get caught.
Hell, no problem, cuz the night's still young,
I wanna little more, gonna get ya some.

Rock stars, movie stars, a Hollywood scene,
I eat dinner with Nick Cage and Charlie Sheen.
Nick asks me what the hell "Unskinny Bop" means,
It's slang for C. C. banging a porno queen.
Mario, Michael, Tony, and Steady,
RV, won't ya get table six ready?
My platinum records hang all around,
Rainbow's home when I'm in this town.

NO EXITS FROM THE FAST LANE

January 16, 1999

"Like a trrrrooooo nature's chiiiyyyuuulldd,
I was baaaawwwwnnnn,
Bawn to be wiiiyyyuuulllddd,
Gonna fly so high,
Nehvuh wanna diiiiiiiieeeeeee!"

Wait a minute. Where are we? Is this really happening? Are we actually standing here in the Whisky A Go-Go at the bitter end of the twentieth century, watching a silver but still sexy Nancy Sinatra gyrate onstage in a black leather miniskirt and boots made for walkin'? Is this live or a tape delay? Is it reality or just a cerebral misfire, synthetically produced by three decades of acid intake?

These are reasonable questions, given the events unfolding tonight. A few of those in attendance wonder whether they are experiencing a flashback or simply the long-awaited onset of senility. As they drink their outrageously overpriced cocktails and yearn desperately for a cigarette (forbidden fruit inside the Whisky these days, as in all other L.A. drinking establishments since the passing of antismoking legislation in 1998), they can't help feeling like they're trapped in a time warp.

"Baaaaawwwwwwnnn toooo beeee wiiiiiyyyyyyuuuulllld-ddd!!!!" The Whisky is having its thirty-fifth birthday party. The psychedelic '60s are back, at least for one night. What a long, strange trip it's been—and not a cheap one, either. For some, the debt could be settled with mere currency. Others had to forfeit their marriages, their sanity, their lives. But of those who were lucky or strong enough to survive, the gang's all here. Sort of.

Johnny Rivers is in the house tonight. Yes, that Johnny Rivers. He kicked the evening off with a roof-raising set almost identical to his now mythic performance on the Whisky's opening night. Rivers is still the consummate show-biz professional. He can rip through shagadelic throwback tunes like "Secret Agent Man" without the slightest trace of irony. The guy doesn't even look like he's aged all that much. In fact, you could argue he's in better shape than the building itself.

Robby Krieger is also here, looking perhaps not as well preserved, but still every bit the six-string hero. He's waiting for Nancy Sinatra to surrender the stage so he can close out the night with some rockin' Doors chestnuts, backed by his son Waylon on rhythm guitar and John Densmore on the skins. Also in attendance is the surviving member of Jan and Dean, though it's not entirely clear which half of the songwriting powerhouse is still above ground. Whoever he is, he's glad to be here.

As Nancy switches from her elevator-worthy rendition of "Born to Be Wild" to a cover of "Like a Rolling Stone" à la Guy Lombardo, the night threatens to spiral irretrievably into a surreal bad trip. But she keeps it together, and you have to hand it to her: Nancy's still got that indefinable *it*. She's downright slinky as she works the mike stand like a masseuse in pursuit of a happy ending, belting out Dylan's iconoclastic lyrics and projecting the full force of her personality. It's a hell of a show, and it pushes the whole shindig beyond pastiche, beyond even nostalgia, and into the realm of loopy greatness. She gets a huge ovation.

Tonight's entertainment is not confined to the main stage. The old aerial go-go cage, which was retired when the Whisky was rebuilt after the fire in '71, is back in business. Inside, a girl in a lacy negligee spins and shimmies, conjuring up some of the white-hot magic Patty Brockhurst used to floor the crowd so long ago. Those sultry gyrations may not generate many scandalized gasps anymore, but it does imbue the night with a powerful whiff of history. Where Ms. Brockhurst is today no one can say, but tonight her randy spirit lives on in the nightclub she helped make famous.

The revivalist groove extends beyond the Whisky's interior. The outside of the building has been repainted a faithful facsimile of the purple-and-gold checkerboard pattern that was the absolute pinnacle of groovy haute couture back in the late '60s. The cost of the building's facelift was picked up by Twentieth Century Fox for the production of a feature film about the L.A. rock scene set in the glory days. The movie, accurately if unimaginatively titled *Sunset Strip,* will end up being a straight-to-video casualty, knocked out of theatrical contention by Cameron Crowe's similarly themed *Almost Famous.* In less than a year, the Whisky will dip into its own till to have the exterior restored to the red-and-black façade that has been its trademark since the '80s. Most people agree the Day-Glo checkerboard look is hideous.

For tonight, however, the purple and gold is ablaze with the glow of rotating spotlights. The sidewalk is choked with a double-file line of bodies stretching over more than three blocks, just as it was the night the Doors played here in '66. But there are no fist-fights or shoving tonight. This crowd is way too weary for that kind of youthful waste of energy. They just want to get through the front door without being asked if they'd like the senior citizen discount.

Back inside, the downstairs bar is almost as loud as the stage. Battle-scarred veterans of the rock 'n' roll wars make hazy eye contact across the crowded floor, trying to establish a connection with the faces staring back. Every few minutes a glimpse of recognition occurs and two people yell out rude greetings and embrace. Some are dumbstruck with disbelief at finding an old partner in crime still drawing breath and walking the streets.

"You crazy motherfucker! Are you out on good behavior or what?!"

"Holy shit, I heard you OD'ed back in '88! Lemme buy you a shot of Jack, you horny sonuvabitch!"

"Dude, did I ever say how sorry I was about balling your ol' lady all those times?"

And so on. It's like a class reunion for survivors of the voyage of the damned. Many people are stunned to be bumping into long-forgotten ghosts from previous lifetimes. Some are even more surprised to be standing here themselves. But the prevailing emotion seems to be a bold defiance of the clock, a kind of forced regression to the crowd's collective wanton youth. The outward manifestations of this urge are hard to miss, and they make the Whisky's walls shake like they haven't in quite some time. No one's taking it easy tonight. Everyone is determined to party like it's 1969. Based on the bar tab alone, this should be a very profitable evening for the club.

Former underage-groupie legend Lori Mattix is over in a corner, dressed in a flowery kimono, sipping a rum and coke and telling everyone who will listen that she and former lover Jimmy Page are now the best of friends and all is forgiven. Even the stuff with the whips and the cat-o'-nine-tails. Across the room is former Long Island mechanic-cum-gadfly Joey Buttafuoco, who worked a brief stint as the doorman for Over the Rainbow after settling in Los Angeles in the early '90s. Though he's since moved on to numerous appearances of note in the entertainment and law enforcement arenas, Joey still holds a warm spot in his heart for the Maglieri family.

The patriarch of that clan is sequestered in the quieter bar upstairs. Mario patiently glad-hands well-wishers while simultaneously giving interviews for a diverse range of TV, print, and online news outlets. Reporters from *Rolling Stone* and VH-1 jostle for position, trying to get a quote or two from the man of the hour. About three minutes of usable footage from the VH-1 camera will have to be doctored before it can air; upon reviewing the tape days after the party, the director notices a flagrantly exposed nipple peeping out from the plunging neckline of an unidentified brunette standing a few feet behind Mario. It's an obviously intentional tit-flash for the camera, and the director wonders bemusedly how it could have escaped everyone's attention at the time. Shades of go-go Flo, all over again.

So many things about this club are the same as they were thirty-five years ago. And yet so much has changed. A quick gander about the room reveals no one of Cary Grant's stature. Indeed, you'd be hard-pressed to make a Corey Feldman sighting in this crowd. The party is not shaping up to be the star-studded event some were expecting. For reasons that may never be fully understood, the majority of Hollywood's A-list invitees have stayed away. Is it because they feared tonight would resemble a wake rather than a celebration? Or were they simply booked with unbreakable obligations?

Whatever the reasons, this event is for the most part comprised of unknown die-hard Sunset Strip devotees. The kind of people who have embraced the lifestyle as a true calling, not some transient fad. Even though the Whisky, Roxy, and Rainbow have attracted the biggest names in entertainment for a solid four decades, the majority of those celebrities were only drawn to the clubs for the cachet that could be acquired by frequenting them while they were on the kind of fatuous "hot lists" that dominate the entertainment trades. It's a far rarer breed that keeps poking their heads into these houses of the holy night after night, year after year. These people are lifers. The folks in attendance tonight have come not in hopes of getting mentioned in the scandal sheets, but to honor an unprecedented run of music, magic, and mayhem. They are the true believers. And maybe they are the only ones who really deserve to be here.

There is, however, one truly notable absentee: Elmer Valentine. A lot of people were really hoping Elmer would make an appearance. No one would be standing here right now if not for him, after all. Yet he's nowhere to be seen.

Elmer's failure to appear may be notable, but it's hardly surprising. He sold out his interest in the Whisky just weeks ago, as did Lou Adler. When the lease on the building came up, they just figured it was time to put it on the auction block and get while the getting was good. The club is still profitable, but, at this late stage in their careers, Elmer and Lou thought it wiser to sell to the highest bidder and rent a Brinks truck to handle the proceeds. Mario stunned them by proposing to buy them out himself. Though the paperwork won't be completed for another month or so, it's a done deal. After negotiating with his former partners, Mario quickly acquired the plot of land directly behind the club that serves as the parking lot. At ten bucks per vehicle seven nights a week, that investment has already paid for itself. This recent flurry of dealmaking has left the Maglieri family the sole owners of the Whisky A Go-Go (though Valentine and Adler still own the Roxy and hold on to their stakes in the ever-lucrative Rainbow Bar and Grill).

Since Elmer and Lou have understandably opted to avoid this celebration, the night belongs to Mario. For a man who has spent his entire career pulling the strings offstage and consistently shunning the spotlight, it is an awkward occasion. In addition to being the Whisky's thirty-fifth anniversary, this day also marks Mario's seventy-fifth birthday. Well, it's actually a few weeks from now, but the dates are so close that Mikeal Maglieri couldn't resist making this evening a dual celebration in honor of his old man. For Mario, the attention being showered on him is at best a mild irritant. At worst, it's a painfully embarrassing ordeal. But he manages to paste on a convincing smile and respond to a local reporter's questions nonetheless.

Mario is asked if, thirty-five years ago, he could have ever predicted this night coming to pass. Hardly bothering to conceal his disdain for the banality of the question, he says, "Well, I never thought I'd own the fuckin' building and the land and everything else. That's the way it goes, I dunno." He shrugs his broad boxer's shoulders, still formidable at age seventy-five, and gives the reporter a look that says, "What do you want from me? I'm just trying to get through this fuckin' party without putting someone's lights out."

When pushed about the source of the Whisky's unparalleled longevity, Mario doesn't bat an eye before answering with his trademark lack of false modesty. "You gotta be here if you wanna run a joint, know what I mean? When I first came on as the manager in '64, the guy who was running the place had his office all the way upstairs. How the fuck can you watch what's going on from upstairs? You gotta be down here, on the floor, to see what's going on. And I see it all. I don't miss nothin'."

With that oblique jab at the no-show Valentine, Mario turns his back on the reporter, letting him know the interview is over. They decide to get a few quotes from Scarlett, who seems to be enjoying the spotlight a lot more than her husband is. Beaming, she introduces dozens of members of the Maglieri clan, spanning four generations. Several of her grandchildren, she explains, are closely involved with the current operations of the Whisky.

Scarlett grabs the elbow of a goateed behemoth in his early twenties and steers him toward the camera. She introduces him as Mike Maglieri Jr., scion to this Sunset Strip dynasty and the best hope for its preservation. A budding promoter, Mike has his own company, M Productions, which he runs out of the Whisky's second-floor offices. Mike shares his grandfather's reticence when it comes to being in the public eye. As he offers up a few obligatory words of praise for the old man, Mike's eyes glaze over just a bit. It's clear he's more comfortable acting behind the scenes, maintaining the Whisky as a showcase for cutting-edge new music rather than exalting in the glory days of old. Days he's too young to even remember. As it happens, Mike's forward-looking approach is the very same one that has kept this club going for so long.

As Mike Jr. talks into the documentary crew's camera about the up-and-coming bands he is promoting, the party grinds on with a growing sense of futility. Drinks are poured down with more urgency, and everyone tries really hard to have the kind of memorable good time that's worthy of the occasion while attempting to discern some significance in it all. No one really seems sure what they are supposed to be celebrating: the Whisky's survival or their own. Anyway, that's not the kind of existential quandary you want to mull over during a party.

Just when it seems like a communal bummer is about to set in, Robby Krieger takes the stage and strikes up the classic

flamenco-inspired riff of "Love Me Two Times." A wave of excitement rolls across the room. Jim Morrison may be a pile of dust in
a Parisian cemetery, but the tune still kicks. Bodies instinctively
start swaying. People sing along with the immortal lyrics about
double gratification that no passage of time nor chemical pollution
can erase from their brains. Amid the vibrations of Robby's
Stratocaster and the crunch of John Densmore's backbeat, everyone manages to forget themselves for a few minutes.

And maybe that's all that can be expected from tonight's event.
No profound realizations. No grand trumpeting across the sky. And
no particular meaning gleaned from the chaotic events of the last
three and a half decades. It seems a little silly to even seek out
such things while standing inside the great Whisky A Go-Go. That's
never been what this place is about.

There are dozens of angles from which the story of the Whisky,
the Roxy, and the Rainbow could be approached. But at its core,
this is a story about the American dream, fully realized. In fact, the
true-life character arc of Mario Maglieri adheres so closely to the
stereotype that only the least imaginative Hollywood hack could
write it with a straight face.

ACT I: Fade in. Immigrant child braves the hazards of a transatlantic voyage to arrive on the shores of the land of opportunity.
Survives a tough childhood on the mean streets of Chicago's east
side. Finds his own Fagin in the form of Al Capone, who takes the
boy under his protective/corrupting wing and introduces him to the
bootlegging business. Reaches manhood and travels back to the
old country to defeat the Nazi scourge.

ACT II: Returning a war hero, he opens a nightclub and soon
earns a reputation as one of the shrewdest impresarios in the
Windy City. Marries his sweetheart and starts a family. Reaches
middle age a wealthy man, has given his children a better life than

he ever had, and never needs to work again. Pulls up the stakes and transplants the entire clan to the sunny climes of Southern California.

ACT III. A little bored with retirement, he is reluctantly recruited by an old friend back into active service on the front lines of a new generation of nightclubs. Saved from premature stagnation by the irrepressible power of a nascent form of distinctly American music. Quickly rises through the ranks from enlisted man to commanding officer of the Whisky A Go-Go in a few short years. Working with his tight circle of partners, proceeds to dominate the most lucrative nugget of real estate in Los Angeles. Launches some of the biggest careers in music. Buys out his partners until he is the sole owner. Passes down the family business to his son and eventually his grandchildren. Honored on his seventy-fifth birthday, still showing no signs of stopping.

Fade out.

Yes, indeed, the story of the Whisky and its unheralded captain is the American Dream writ large. Sure, there's been a lot more rampant drug use, unbridled sex, sleazy backbiting, and untimely death than in most renditions of the perennial tale. But that's rock 'n' roll.

Looking slightly dazed by the riotous reaction from the audience, Robby Krieger gives his band the signal, and they launch from the final chord of "Love Me Two Times" directly into "Light My Fire." It's a little haggard, especially during the lengthy guitar solo with Robby filling in where Ray Manzarek's keyboards usually take over. But the crowd loves it just the same. Even Mario pushes himself up to the front of a small pocket of people so he can check it out. His head bobbing in time with the beat, Mario pulls Mike Jr. close enough to yell in his ear, "I always liked these sons of bitches! Happy music, kinda like circus music!"

Mike smiles at his grandfather and gives the thumbs-up. Personally, he finds the Doors put him to sleep, but he enjoys seeing the old man rocking out. As the solo comes to an end and the song shifts to the final chorus, it seems every single set of vocal chords in the building is belting out the lyrics at full volume. For a fleeting moment, everyone is joyously enslaved to the music. They revel in the purest form of escape: from everyday cares, from harsh realities, from themselves.

That's why people have come here for thirty-five years, and that's why they will keep coming.

Until the music's over.

The Strip in the Twenty-First Century

As the Sunset Strip moves into the twenty-first century, it still looms as the holy grail of rock 'n' roll. Though there is no longer a distinct hippie scene or punk scene or even metal scene, for that matter, the Strip continues to be the ultimate proving ground where young bands from all over the world can come and take their shot at stardom.

And for these young bands, few venues exist on the planet that can capture their imaginations like the Whisky A Go-Go. Performing on the same stage as their idols, the energy surrounding any band's gig there contains a rare combination of excitement and magic.

Singer Greg Martin, whose unsigned band Reactor sits on the cusp of a major record deal, puts it this way:

"Playing the Whisky is a remarkable experience. The ambience and aura of the venue is awesome. To be onstage, playing in front of a packed house, hearing the roar of the crowd—it's unforgettable. Knowing that David Lee Roth, Eddie Van Halen, Alice in Chains, Jim Morrison, George Lynch, and every kick-ass band who ever got famous played there makes you believe in yourself. It gives you hope that you're gonna make it."

One band that's recently succeeded is Depswa. After playing almost exclusively at the Whisky, the Roxy, and the Troubadour for more than two years as an unsigned act, they have finally been discovered by Geffen Records and are on the verge of releasing their major debut record, *Two Angels and a Dream.*

"We grew up in small towns," says Depswa guitarist Dan Noonan, "so I guess the vision of the Whisky matched the whole Hollywood rock-star vision in your head. So when we finally got a chance to play there and tell our friends we were playing, you know, where the Doors and so many other bands got famous, everyone was pretty awestruck and thought that was a major step in our career. The reality was it was just kind of the beginning."

"It was an acknowledgment," says lead singer Jeremy Penick. "Playing the Whisky on a regular basis showed us that our band was making it within the scene."

"The Strip's definitely where it all goes down," continues drummer Gordon Heckaman. "It's where you join bands out in the parking lot or even just promote your band. You meet just about everyone on the scene at the three main clubs—the Whisky, the Roxy, and the Troubadour down on Santa Monica."

Adds Penick, "I noticed that A&R reps for all the major record labels hang out just as much as the artists, sometimes in front of these clubs, and you get to know some of these people that way."

"That's how we got our momentum," says bassist Ryan Burchfield. "Just going back and forth to these three clubs and hanging out in front of them every single night. A lot of nights at the Whisky throwing out flyers."

Though the Strip is certainly still a mecca for the music world, many who were there during the golden years say it's not quite what it used to be.

"The Strip's more like Times Square these days," says Jim Ladd. "It got cleaned up. Which is good, in a way. But it's just not as gritty as it used to be, and I miss that."

Adds Henry Rollins, "Now the Hollywood scene is more like a showcase—you know, like, 'Please sign me.' It doesn't seem to be a hangout so much as just a clump of buildings where people go to see gigs. It used to be that if you wanted to catch up with somebody, chances were they were going to be at the Whisky at some point that night, so just go and wait, and that girl or your drug connection or that guy who owes you fifty bucks is gonna be there. I don't think there's a scene like that anymore."

But it remains up for debate as to whether or not the scene on the Strip is as good as it once was. After all, everyone has trouble relating to the next generation, to that next wave of cool.

The Future

Though the owners of the Whisky, the Roxy, and the Rainbow may be in their twilight years, there is no fade into the sunset for their three clubs. There is a living trust, a strong bloodline bent on preserving and developing the clubs well into the future. At the Whisky and the Rainbow, Mario still keeps a tight rein on the clubs, although his son Mikeal has taken over as president. And Mario's grandson, Mike Jr. (AKA Mikey), has given every indication that running a rock 'n' roll club is in his blood.

"I started off doing raves, stuff like that," says Mike Jr., "trying to get people in one place and charging them money to get in. My first show went real well. I've been going to concerts since I was two or three. I'm sure I was pushed in a stroller to a fucking concert."

He continues, "With the clubs, it's all about the music. It's about what people want to hear. The Whisky has its name, but that's not what's going to bring in the business. Without the acts, all you have is the name. Which is good—it's pretty much the biggest club in L.A. But to keep bringing the new people in, and to bring the rest of the people back, it's the music."

Mikey feels strongly that, for the Whisky to continue to grow, the bands he books have to be fresh and on the cutting edge.

"My goal is to bring the Whisky into the twenty-first century," he says. "To bring people what they want to hear. I'm not here to keep that old stuff alive. I'm here to make a difference and put new music in people's faces."

As for the Roxy, Lou Adler's son Nicholai now runs the operation.

"I'm in a very fortunate position," says Nic, "and I don't want to take it for granted. I think we have the chance to be the best club in the world, and, if you see the people who work here beside me, they all have that same look in their eye, too."

Nic admits that the music scene on the Strip did weaken for a while, but he believes it's entering a new golden age:

"After Guns N' Roses and those kind of hair-metal bands that took over everything, we had a lull at the Roxy, and I think the Whisky, too. But then once '95 came around, and '96, there was this young generation that grew up on Guns N' Roses that came out here. It started with Incubus and System of a Down and Alien Ant Farm and Papa Roach. They're all from here, you know, this is their home. Actually, the Roxy is their home. It's not just one band that's big; there's no gimmick. There is great music coming out of here now, and I think that's just going to build and build."

Nic also reports that the Whisky, the Roxy, and the Rainbow continue to enjoy a relatively good relationship with the authorities:

"The fire department will show up with four trucks during our biggest show, and I'll start going, 'Oh my god, what's going on?' Then they'll come in and say, 'Hello, we just came to watch the show.' They'll walk inside, hold down their little walkie-talkie buttons, and blast it out to every station within the area. And everybody at the station is sitting there listening to like John Cougar Mellencamp because the guys are in there holding down their microphones."

Elmer, Lou, and Mario

After more than thirty years of partnership in the world's most notorious rock block, it's amazing that all three men are still standing, let alone living full and productive lives.

For the most part, Elmer Valentine, the man who deserves credit for starting it all, has retired from the fast lane, content to spend his days smoking grass and listening to jazz in his Hollywood Hills mansion. He does, however, continue to put in daily work maintaining his reputation as a lady-killer. He is regularly seen on dates with women fifty years his junior.

"I know I'm pushing eighty," says Elmer. "The wonderful thing is, with all these girls, music is the common bond. They look beyond the physical."

The youngest of the three men by a decade, Lou Adler is still one of the most influential players in Hollywood and is continuously generating new ideas and projects. Most recently he teamed up with Paul Newman to create the Hole in the Wall Gang, a nature camp just outside of Los Angeles designed especially for terminally ill children. He has also been busy releasing children's albums, as well as anniversary editions and digitally remastered reissues of his full catalog of music and movies. Usually a tough guy to track down, Lou can almost always be seen sitting right next to his buddy Jack Nicholson at every Lakers home game.

As for Mario Maglieri, he continues to be wildly passionate about his clubs. Every week he still purchases the fresh produce and poultry for the Rainbow, and at least four nights a week, he can be found standing in his favorite spot, just outside the Rainbow's entrance, greeting each and every person as they walk inside.

As Nic Adler puts it:

"Mario is amazing. First of all, his age, being almost eighty, coming to work every day—that is amazing in itself. I think Mario has made this Strip. He's kept these three clubs going for more than thirty years. These places were supposed to be open every day, with something new in here every day, and that's what he did, that's how he kept them going. And he shakes people's hands, and he greets them and he knows their names, and if he doesn't remember their names, he'll remember something else about them and bring that up. He makes a connection with every single person and that's amazing, it really is."

The Enduring Mystique of the Strip

To fully understand the magic of the Sunset Strip, you have to first understand its history. Not necessarily just in date and detail, but also as a legacy of dreams fulfilled.

At its very essence, the Strip is a playground for dreamers, where any given night you might brush elbows with a movie star or get discovered by a record-label executive. It is a place where people come to make history or bear witness to history being made.

This mystique has existed on the Sunset Strip for four decades, and it all began with the Whisky A Go-Go.

Today, most of the clubs that have populated the Strip over the years have long since ceased to exist. Replaced by ultrachic, list-only clubs such as the Skybar and Barfly, the Strip has become mostly a spectacle of the pretentious wealth, decadence, and silicon implants that have become the stereotype of Los Angeles.

But, as Jim Ladd notes, "The Whisky is still there on the same piece of ground, doing the same thing it's always done. That's pretty extraordinary for L.A., because L.A. has no landmarks. A landmark is the minimall down the street that's been open for four years. So the Whisky is a real rarity."

For this reason, the Whisky and its sister clubs, the Roxy and the Rainbow, are as relevant today as they were when they first opened. Virtually unmarked by the passage of time, they represent a living history of the Sunset Strip and therefore a major source of what gives the two-mile stretch of boulevard its unique identity.

Thankfully, Mario reassures us that as long as it's up to him, the Whisky A Go-Go will uphold that identity for many years to come:

"The Whisky is a landmark. I would never sell that building. I told my son, my grandson, I want that place to stay a rock 'n' roll haven. And that's what it is."

AFTERWORD

I first went to the Rainbow Bar and Grill on Sunset Boulevard in 1973. I couldn't believe my eyes. All the most beautiful girls in the world seemed to be hanging out there. I thought I'd died and gone to heaven! I decided this was a scene worth exploring.

I've probably pulled more women in the Rainbow than anywhere else (though the St. Moritz in London is a possible contender), and it continues to be an excellent bar and grill.

Mario and Mikeal Maglieri always made me feel welcome. And managers Mike Weber and Tony Vescio are more polite and civilized than almost any other club managers in the world, which is even more special when you consider how many assholes they've had to cope with over the years.

Down the street, the Whisky (the "A Go-Go" was dropped some time ago) has changed a lot. I remember when downstairs was all tables and chairs. This is the place where, annoyed at the slow service and for some reason wearing a Kotex on his head, John Lennon said to a passing waitress, "Don't you know who I am?" and received the reply, "Yeah, you're that asshole with a Kotex on his head!" Both clubs are legendary in the world of rock 'n' roll.

When I moved to Los Angeles in 1990, I made sure I was within walking distance of the Rainbow. And, luckily, it's downhill going home! Long may it rave.

Affectionately,

Lemmy Kilmister

ACKNOWLEDGMENTS

The authors would like to sincerely thank everyone below for their support in making this book possible:

Jeff Stern, Elizabeth Hurchalla, Eric Fulford, Mike Gorey, everyone in the Quisling, Williams, and Maglieri families, Nic Adler, Helen Ashford, Chuck Bernal at Artists Worldwide, Adriana Bonagrazia, Richard Amadril, Katie Archibald, Drew Bourneuf, Jenna Capozzi, Dr. Michael Caulder, Edward Colver, Kevin Curtin, Liam Curtin, Anthony Deluca and his cool folks, Depswa, Pamela Des Barres, Leah DiBonaventura, Headband Dan Gary, Jeff Gilbert, Laurie Gorman, Devon Freeny, Greg Kevorkian, Penny Guyon, Dan "The Anointed One" Hackett, Todd Hallberg, Chris Holmes, Jonathan Hyams, Ron Jeremy, Joseph Weiss at JoeyJetsonMusic.com, Joe Sutton of Club Vodka, Lemmy Kilmister, Rick Kitkowski, Paul Koretz, Mike Krebs, Robby Krieger, Jim "Lord Have Mercy" Ladd, Chad at KLOS, Glen Laferman, the Lakers, Leah Cevoli at Burst Music, Mandy Lion, Dennis Loren, Mark London, Brothers Vance and Rob Lynch, Jerry Mangalos, Cheech Marin, Greg Martin, Lori Mattix, Roger McGuinn, Bret Michaels, Mike Monarch, Brent Muscat, Ozzy Osbourne, Jamie Parker and Randy Fibiger at HOB, Daniel Peacock, Maria Perdue, Slim Jim Phantom, Deborah Radel, John Rake, Pinder Basi, Rob Vossoughi of Acme Printing, Johnny Rivers, Henry Rollins, Ron at the Red Carpet, Caressa Savage, Sue Schneider, Mark Schwartz, Sir Frank Sedloev, Bob of Shattered Music, Sims and the Bianch, James Otto Stack, Karen Sundell, Deputy Bruce Thomas, Stu Toben, Vic Triepke, Mark Truelove, Stefanie Vishab, Waddy Wachtel, Tracy Watkins, Greg "Mega" Watts, Mike Weber, Nora Wong, Tony Vescio, Steady Eddie, Randy Wright, and the Angry Clam.

NOTES

In preparation for this book, we interviewed dozens of people who have played integral roles in the history of the Sunset Strip. These interviews were conducted either in person or over the phone from the summer of 1999 to the fall of 2002. We augmented our primary research by drawing upon the voluminous body of secondary research material that exists on this subject matter. All direct quotes, gathered either through primary or secondary research, are cited below.

Chapter 1

"They had these . . . ": David Kamp, "Live at the Whisky," *Vanity Fair,* 11/00, p. 255.

"She had on a slit . . . ": David Kamp, "Live at the Whisky," *Vanity Fair,* 11/00, p. 256.

"I remember this . . . ": David Kamp, "Live at the Whisky," *Vanity Fair,* 11/00, p. 256.

"It used to be a glittering boulevard . . . ": David Ferrell, "Golden Sunset; Glittering Boulevard: L.A.'s Unique Blend of Glamour and Panache," *Los Angeles Times,* 9/8/91.

"We weren't poor . . . ": Glenn A. Baker, "Johnny Rivers: The Singer Not the Song," *Goldmine Magazine,* no. 290 (1982).

"Gazzarri said to me . . . ": Johnny Rivers, Interview by Authors, 2/27/03.

"When I first saw . . . ": David Kamp, "Live at the Whisky," *Vanity Fair,* 11/00, p. 255.

"Johnny was like . . . ": David Kamp, "Live at the Whisky," *Vanity Fair,* 11/00, p. 255.

"Elmer Valentine said . . . ": Johnny Rivers, Interview by Authors, 2/27/03.

"I remember the Beatles coming . . . ": Steven Hochman, "Taste of Vintage Whisky at Celebration," *Los Angeles Times,* 1/18/99.

Chapter 2

"It was kind of a square scene . . . ": Roger McGuinn, Interview by Authors, 7/8/02.

"The scene got pretty wild at . . . ": Roger McGuinn, Interview by Authors, 7/8/02.

"Gene Clark, David Crosby, and I . . . ": Roger McGuinn, Interview by Authors, 7/8/02.

"The Whisky wouldn't touch us . . . ": Roger McGuinn, Interview by Authors, 7/8/02.

"The Byrds were the . . . ": David Kamp, "Live at the Whisky," *Vanity Fair,* 11/00, p. 258.

"The hippies just sort of . . . ": Paul Koretz, Interview by Authors, 7/8/02.

"We were astonished . . . ": David Kamp, "Live at the Whisky," *Vanity Fair,* 11/00, p. 262.

"We arrived in L.A. . . . ": David Kamp, "Live at the Whisky," *Vanity Fair,* 11/00, p. 262.

Chapter 3

"I was helping a friend of mine . . . ": Mario Maglieri, Interview by Authors, 8/12/99.

"Elmer worked mostly during the day . . . ": Sue Schneider, Interview by Authors, 9/3/99.

"He was kind of a scary guy . . . ": Robby Krieger, Interview by Authors, 9/14/99.

"People smoke a joint, they relax . . . ": Mario Maglieri, Interview by Authors, 8/12/99.

"We were not folk . . . ": David Kamp, "Live at the Whisky," *Vanity Fair,* 11/00, p. 264.

"The Whisky was for . . . ": David Kamp, "Live at the Whisky," *Vanity Fair,* 11/00, p. 258.

"There were seven people total . . . ": Roy Trakin, "A Special Time in Rock: 1966 on the Sunset Strip," *Los Angeles Times,* 4/7/91.

"Fortunately an extremely sexy . . . ": John Densmore, *Riders on the Storm,* p. 79.

"Ronnie said, 'You . . .'": David Kamp, "Live at the Whisky," *Vanity Fair,* 11/00, p. 264.

"I saw that guy Morrison two or . . . ": Mario Maglieri, Interview by Authors, 8/12/99.

"Well, I saw Jim Morrison pull his . . . ": Mario Maglieri, Interview by Authors, 8/12/99.

"Another time I had a black act . . . ": Mario Maglieri, Interview by Authors, 8/12/99.

"Mario got on the . . . ": Pamela Des Barres, Interview by Authors, 9/18/99.

"Mario had so much stuff to . . . ": Pamela Des Barres, Interview by Authors, 9/18/99.

"It was a fun night . . . ": Robby Krieger, Interview by Authors, 9/14/99.

"In between sets we found him . . . ": Robby Krieger, Interview by Authors, 9/14/99.

"When we started to do 'The End,' . . . ": Robby Krieger, Interview by Authors, 9/14/99.

"And then he got to those famous . . . ": Robby Krieger, Interview by Authors, 9/14/99.

Chapter 4

"We used to chase rock bands . . . ": Sue Schneider, Interview by Authors, 9/99.

"It started as a game . . . ": Sue Schneider, Interview by Authors, 9/99.

"Los Angeles was the Babylon . . . ": Mark Spitz and Brendan Mullen, *We Got the Neutron Bomb: The Untold Story of L.A. Punk,* p. 15.

"The first record that I . . . ": *Mojo,* May 2000 (*www.groupiecentral.com/ articlespameladb.html*).

"The girls and I spent a lot of time making lists . . . ": Pamela Des Barres, "Pamela Des Barres on Pamela Des Barres," *Playboy,* March 1989, pp. 121-124.

"Oooooh! I loved the music!": Pamela Des Barres, "Pamela Des Barres on Pamela Des Barres," *Playboy*, March 1989, pp. 121-124.

"At the Whisky you'd have Keith . . . ": Sue Schneider, Interview by Authors, 9/03/99.

"He was always like that . . . ": Sue Schneider, Interview by Authors, 9/03/99.

"I found them incredibly inspiring . . . ": Mark Spitz and Brendan Mullen, *We Got the Neutron Bomb: The Untold Story of L.A. Punk,* p. 15.

"There haven't really been riots . . . ": Transcript of "Find the Monkees Interview" *(www.geocities.com/Hollywood/Set/9847/findthe.html).*

"If you had to put your finger on . . . ": Roy Trakin, "A Special Time in Rock: 1966 on the Sunset Strip," *Los Angeles Times,* 4/7/91.

"It's fuckin' true . . . ": David Kamp, "Live at the Whisky," *Vanity Fair,* 11/00, p. 268.

"Seeing him play at . . . ": Mojo, May 2000 *(www.groupiecentral.com/articlespameladb.html).*

Chapter 5

"It was me, John Phillips, Cass Elliot . . . ": Gina Arnold, "Pop Perfect: The Monterey Pop Festival of 1967 . . . ," *Silicon Valley Metro Newspaper,* 6/14/01.

"John and I had both heard that . . . ": Gina Arnold, "Pop Perfect: The Monterey Pop Festival of 1967 . . . ," *Silicon Valley Metro Newspaper,* 6/14/01.

"The San Francisco groups had . . . ": Gina Arnold, "Pop Perfect: The Monterey Pop Festival of 1967 . . . ," *Silicon Valley Metro Newspaper,* 6/14/01.

"The media coverage was . . . ": Gina Arnold, "Pop Perfect: The Monterey Pop Festival of 1967 . . . ," *Silicon Valley Metro Newspaper,* 6/14/01.

"Artists were used to performing with . . . ": Gina Arnold, "Pop Perfect: The Monterey Pop Festival of 1967 . . . ," *Silicon Valley Metro Newspaper,* 6/14/01.

"The action wasn't only on the stage . . . ": Rusty DeSoto, "The Way to Monterey: Kicking Off the Summer of Love" *(www.stg.brown.edu/~ed/monterey.html)*.

"A vehicle for Phillips' and Adler's . . . ": Rusty DeSoto, "The Way to Monterey: Kicking Off the Summer of Love" *(www.stg.brown.edu/~ed/monterey.html)*.

"To this day, artists say it . . . ": Gina Arnold, "Pop Perfect: The Monterey Pop Festival of 1967 . . . ," *Silicon Valley Metro Newspaper,* 6/14/01.

"This was the Whisky's heyday . . . ": Mike Monarch, Interview by Authors, 7/14/99.

"She was a great entertainer . . . ": Mario Maglieri, Interview by Authors, 8/12/99.

"[Monterey Pop] was an extraordinary . . . ": Gina Arnold, "Pop Perfect: The Monterey Pop Festival of 1967 . . . ," *Silicon Valley Metro Newspaper,* 6/14/01.

Chapter 6

"I picked up . . . ": David Kamp, "Live at the Whisky," *Vanity Fair,* 11/00, pp. 268–270.

"I did what a lot of . . . ": David Kamp, "Live at the Whisky," *Vanity Fair,* 11/00, p. 270.

"With the black man going into white . . . ": Marilyn Bardsley, "Where Are They Now: Charles Manson" *(www.crimelibrary.com/manson/mansonhel.htm)*.

"Charlie said that the Family would survive . . . ": Marilyn Bardsley, "Where Are They Now: Charles Manson" *(www.crimelibrary.com/manson/mansonhel.htm)*.

"It will be our world then . . . ": Marilyn Bardsley, "Where Are They Now: Charles Manson" *(www.crimelibrary.com/manson/mansonhel.htm)*.

"It was so . . . ": David Kamp, "Live at the Whisky," *Vanity Fair,* 11/00, pp. 268–270.

"The only thing Blackie knows is what Whitey . . . ": Marilyn Bardsley, "Where Are They Now: Charles Manson" *(www.crimelibrary.com/manson/mansonhel.htm)*.

"*That was it. That's . . .*": David Kamp, "Live at the Whisky," *Vanity Fair,* 11/00, p. 270.

"*It changed the . . .*": David Kamp, "Live at the Whisky," *Vanity Fair,* 11/00, pp. 268-270.

Chapter 7

"*The frightening thing at Altamont . . .*": Ethan Russell, "The Rolling Stones at Altamont—1969 U.S. Tour" (*www.ethanrussell.com/altamont.htm*).

"*The assassinations of the '60s had aged us . . .*": Michael Lydon, "The Decade That Spawned Altamont," *Gimme Shelter Exploration* (liner notes), Criterion, 2000, DVD.

"*Janis Joplin was at the . . .*": Mikeal Maglieri, Interview by Authors, 10/11/99.

"*I see myself as a huge fiery comet . . .*": Tim Kendall, "No One Here Gets Out Alive" (*www.angelfire.com/rock/doors/*).

"*Nah, it was an accident . . .*": Sue Schneider and Anne Moore, "Mario Maglieri: A Rock 'n' Roll Legend," *Monsters of Rock*, Fall 1992, pp. 87–92.

Chapter 8

"*We were tired of getting fucked over . . .*": Colman Andrews, "Rainbow Bar and Grill," Whisky Archives (*www.whiskyagogo.com*).

"*It opened with a party for Elton John . . .*": Colman Andrews, "Rainbow Bar and Grill," Whisky Archives (*www.whiskyagogo.com*).

"*In 1972 we gave Mick Jagger his . . .*": Mario Maglieri, Interview by Authors, 8/12/99.

"*You name anyone in the history . . .*": Ozzy Osbourne, Interview by Authors, 10/25/99.

"*My wife used to come here . . .*": Ozzy Osbourne, Interview by Authors, 10/25/99.

"*They don't treat you like shit . . .*": Lemmy Kilmister, Interview by Authors, 11/8/99.

"But it's never really been a . . . ": Lemmy Kilmister, Interview by Authors, 11/8/99.

"The best fucking pizza on the . . . ": Ozzy Osbourne, Interview by Authors, 10/25/99.

"The first time I came to the . . . ": Ron Jeremy, Interview by Authors, 11/27/99.

"But the food here is . . . ": Ron Jeremy, Interview by Authors, 11/27/99.

"It was almost like a family . . . ": Mikeal Maglieri, Interview by Authors, 10/11/99.

Chapter 9

"Led Zeppelin used to party here . . . ": Mario Maglieri, Interview by Authors, 8/12/99.

"One night, one of the guys . . . ": Mikeal Maglieri, Interview by Authors, 10/11/99.

"That particular night . . . ": Sue Schneider and Anne Moore, "Mario Maglieri: A Rock 'n' Roll Legend," *Monsters of Rock,* Fall 1992, pp. 87–92.

"I was modeling for . . . ": Lori Mattix, Interview by Authors, 3/7/99.

"I'd gone to the Rainbow with these . . . ": Lori Mattix, Interview by Authors, 3/7/99.

"The room was dimly lit by candles . . . ": Stephen Davis, *Hammer of the Gods,* p. 171.

"Poor little Lori Mattix . . . ": Stephen Davis, *Hammer of the Gods,* p. 223.

"If Led Zeppelin wants privacy . . . ": Stephen Davis, *Hammer of the Gods,* p. 225.

Chapter 10

"They opened up the Rainbow . . . ": Mikeal Maglieri, Interview by Authors, 10/11/99.

"Well, I made more enemies today . . . ": "Roxy: Pop-Rock Takes a Step Uptown," *Los Angeles Times,* 9/22/75, from Whisky Archives (www.whiskyagogo.com).

"In L.A., everyone is a quote . . . ": "Roxy: Pop-Rock Takes a Step Uptown," *Los Angeles Times,* 9/22/75, from Whisky Archives (www.whiskyagogo.com).

"Harry, Harry, who in the hell is Harry . . . ": "Roxy: Pop-Rock Takes a Step Uptown," *Los Angeles Times,* 9/22/75, from Whisky Archives (www.whiskyagogo.com).

"How about that Billie Jean King . . . ": Judith Sims, "Neil Young Opens the Roxy Theatre," *Rolling Stone,* 10/25/73.

"Welcome to Miami Beach!": Judith Sims, "Neil Young Opens the Roxy Theatre," *Rolling Stone,* 10/25/73.

"It played for 63 . . . ": David Evans and Scott Michaels, *Rocky Horror: From Concept to Cult,* p. 78.

"When we did . . . ": *Rocky Horror Picture Show,* DVD Supplemental Material.

"Glam met rock, cross-dressed it, slept . . . ": *Rocky Horror Picture Show,* DVD Supplemental Material.

"The success of Rocky Horror . . . *":* *Rocky Horror Picture Show,* DVD Supplemental Material.

Chapter 11

"I still see a lot of dancers here . . . ": Ron Jeremy, Interview by Authors, 11/27/99.

"I've had lots of sex up there . . . ": Ron Jeremy, Interview by Authors, 11/27/99.

"I have on many occasions taken a . . . ": Ron Jeremy, Interview by Authors, 11/27/99.

"The Rainbow is so hot . . . ": Caressa Savage, Interview by Authors, 8/13/99.

"Last time I left the Rainbow . . . ": Caressa Savage, Interview by Authors, 8/13/99.

"If you have to talk to a girl all . . . ": Ron Jeremy, Interview by Authors, 11/27/99.

"One time this girl was spending . . . ": Ron Jeremy, Interview by Authors, 11/27/99.

Chapter 12

"I knew that her demos . . . ": Rachel Louise Snyder, "Will You Still Love Me Tomorrow?" Salon.com *(www.salon.com/people/ feature/1999/06/19/king/index1.html).*

"We were doing one of those . . . ": Cheech Marin, Interview by Authors, 9/25/02.

"He was the first kind of whatever . . . ": Nice Dreams Press Kit, Columbia Pictures, 1981 *(www.cheechandchong.com/ biography.html).*

"It was a topless joint, and I didn't have the heart . . . ": Nice Dreams Press Kit, Columbia Pictures, 1981 *(www.cheechandchong.com/biography.html).*

"We were musicians all our lives . . . ": Cheech Marin, Interview by Authors, 9/25/02.

"There were no comedians doing it . . . ": Cheech Marin, Interview by Authors, 9/25/02.

"The great thing about Lou Adler . . . ": Cheech Marin, Interview by Authors, 9/25/02.

"Another musician we started . . . ": Cheech Marin, Interview by Authors, 9/25/02.

"Anybody in Hollywood who was . . . ": Cheech Marin, Interview by Authors, 9/25/02.

"And the Roxy had On the Rox . . . ": Cheech Marin, Interview by Authors, 9/25/02.

"I was good buddies . . . ": Cheech Marin, Interview by Authors, 9/25/02.

"The '70s were really where the . . . ": Cheech Marin, Interview by Authors, 9/25/02.

"We were basically . . . ": Cheech Marin, Interview by Authors, 9/25/02.

"For the ending of the movie . . . ": Cheech Marin, Interview by Authors, 9/25/02.

"Lou came to me . . . ": Miguel Maurillo, Interview by Authors, 9/28/02.

"The Cheech and Chong movie . . . ": Mark Spitz and Brendan Mullen, *We Got the Neutron Bomb: The Untold Story of L.A. Punk,* p. 109.

"The Roxy and the Rainbow . . . ": Cheech Marin, Interview by Authors, 9/25/02.

Chapter 13

"We can't get big crowds regularly . . . ": Dennis Hunt, "Whisky, On Rocks, to Become Disco," *Los Angeles Times,* 3/23/75.

"One day in the summer of '77 . . . ": Mark Spitz and Brendan Mullen, *We Got the Neutron Bomb: The Untold Story of L.A. Punk,* p. 109.

"Urine-stained, safety-pin-wearing . . . ": Mark Spitz and Brendan Mullen, *We Got the Neutron Bomb: The Untold Story of L.A. Punk,* p. 109.

"Raw Power became the . . . ": Mark Spitz and Brendan Mullen, *We Got the Neutron Bomb: The Untold Story of L.A. Punk,* p. 35.

"I was born and raised in Southern . . . ": Mark Spitz and Brendan Mullen, *We Got the Neutron Bomb: The Untold Story of L.A. Punk,* p. 35.

"We would look through the cut-out bins . . . ": Mark Spitz and Brendan Mullen, *We Got the Neutron Bomb: The Untold Story of L.A. Punk,* p. 35.

"The best live rock . . . ": Per Nilsen and Dorothy Sherman, *The Wild One—The True Story of Iggy Pop,* p. 92.

"There were some really great . . . ": Henry Rollins, Interview by Authors, 10/11/02.

"I mean, the Germs' Darby Crash . . . ": Henry Rollins, Interview by Authors, 10/11/02.

"When the punk movement came along . . . ": Jim Ladd, Interview by Authors, 9/17/02.

"My friends and I . . . ": Henry Rollins, Interview by Authors, 10/11/02.

"Los Angeles was great . . . ": Mark Spitz and Brendan Mullen, *We Got the Neutron Bomb: The Untold Story of L.A. Punk,* p. 113.

"I started going to the Whisky in . . . ": Mark Truelove, Interview by Authors, 11/03/99.

"What I think happened was that . . . ": Henry Rollins, Interview by Authors, 10/11/02.

"The Hollywood punk rockers, as . . . ": Henry Rollins, Interview by Authors, 10/11/02.

"TSOL was a pretty scary unit . . . ": Henry Rollins, Interview by Authors, 10/11/02.

"The cops hated Black Flag . . . ": Mark Truelove, Interview by Authors, 11/03/99.

"The Hollywood punk rock . . . ": Henry Rollins, Interview by Authors, 10/11/02.

"You used to see a lot of . . . ": Deputy Bruce Thomas, Interview by Authors, 8/17/99.

"The cops came in . . . ": Henry Rollins, Interview by Authors, 10/11/02.

"All of a sudden the Sunset Strip was closed . . . ": Mark Spitz and Brendan Mullen, *We Got the Neutron Bomb: The Untold Story of L.A. Punk,* p. 17.

"With punk rock, people were so . . . ": Mario Maglieri, Interview by Authors, 8/12/99.

Chapter 14

"When we went on the air . . . ": Tom McGrath, *MTV: The Making of a Revolution.*

"We'd made videos in . . . ": Slim Jim Phantom, Interview by Authors, 10/22/02.

"What was cool about MTV . . . ": Slim Jim Phantom, Interview by Authors, 10/22/02.

"I had never been . . . ": Slim Jim Phantom, Interview by Authors, 10/22/02.

"The first day we arrived at . . . ": Slim Jim Phantom, Interview by Authors, 10/22/02.

"In '81, the kings . . . ": Chuck Klosterman, *Spin,* 9/02, pp. 86–94.

"Belinda and I . . . ": Chuck Klosterman, *Spin,* 9/02, pp. 86–94.

"MTV was no good to us at all . . . ": Chris Holmes, Interview by Authors, 10/29/02.

"Have you ever seen one . . . ": Chuck Klosterman, *Spin,* 9/02, pp. 86–94.

"Someone said I fucked the . . . ": Chris Holmes, Interview by Authors, 10/29/02.

"Another time this one girl . . . ": Anonymous, Interview by Authors, 8/11/99.

"The party outside . . . ": Maria Perdue, Interview by Authors, 8/11/99.

"It was like every night was the . . . ": Frank Sedloev, Interview by Authors, 9/12/99.

"We started playing in . . . ": Chuck Klosterman, *Spin,* 9/02, pp. 86–94.

Chapter 15

"I had nothing but respect . . . ": Bret Michaels, Interview by Authors, 10/25/02.

"We were what I called . . . ": Bret Michaels, Interview by Authors, 10/25/02.

"We spent all of our effort . . . ": Bret Michaels, Interview by Authors, 10/25/02.

"Bands were putting flyers . . . ": Slim Jim Phantom, Interview by Authors, 10/22/02.

"We had a huge tryout . . . ": Bret Michaels, Interview by Authors, 10/25/02.

"Poison was sort of the . . . ": Chuck Klosterman, *Spin*, 9/02, pp. 86–94.

"Our second video, 'Talk Dirty . . . '": Bret Michaels, Interview by Authors, 10/25/02.

"Poison was the first band . . . ": Bret Michaels, Interview by Authors, 10/25/02.

"When I first saw the . . . ": Chuck Klosterman, *Spin*, 9/02, pp. 86–94.

"What happened . . . ": Bret Michaels, Interview by Authors, 10/25/02.

"The second scene that we . . . ": Brent Muscat, Interview by Authors, 9/23/02.

"Rock 'n' roll is the ultimate . . . ": Brent Muscat, Interview by Authors, 9/23/02.

"The girls at the Rainbow . . . ": Bret Michaels, Interview by Authors, 10/25/02.

"I unfortunately never got to do . . . ": Bret Michaels, Interview by Authors, 10/25/02.

"Underwear was not very popular . . . ": Mandy Lion, Interview by Authors, 8/18/99.

"The '80s hair bands were a . . . ": Jim Ladd, Interview by Authors, 9/17/02.

"Poison never had a fight with . . . ": Bret Michaels, Interview by Authors, 10/25/02.

"All these L.A. bands that were . . . ": Bret Michaels, Interview by Authors, 10/25/02.

"I always dug the whole . . . ": Slim Jim Phantom, Interview by Authors, 10/22/02.

"I had my birthday party . . . ": Bret Michaels, Interview by Authors, 10/25/02.

Chapter 16

"Playing the Whisky is a . . . ": Greg Martin, Interview by Authors, 10/18/02.

"We grew up in small towns . . . ": Dan Noonan, Interview by Authors, 9/8/02.

"It was an acknowledgment . . . ": Jeremy Penick, Interview by Authors, 9/8/02.

"The Strip's definitely where it . . . ": Gordon Heckaman, Interview by Authors, 9/8/02.

"I noticed that A&R . . . ": Jeremy Penick, Interview by Authors, 9/8/02.

"That's how we got our . . . ": Ryan Burchfield, Interview by Authors, 9/8/02.

"The Strip's more like Times . . . ": Jim Ladd, Interview by Authors, 9/17/02.

"Now the Hollywood scene . . . ": Henry Rollins, Interview by Authors, 10/11/02.

"I started off doing raves . . . ": Mike Maglieri Jr., Interview by Authors, 8/7/99.

"With the clubs, it's all . . . ": Mike Maglieri Jr., Interview by Authors, 8/7/99.

"My goal is to bring the . . . ": Mike Maglieri Jr., Interview by Authors, 8/7/99.

"I'm in a very fortunate position . . . ": Nic Adler, Interview by Authors, 10/2/02.

"After Guns N' Roses . . . ": Nic Adler, Interview by Authors, 10/2/02.

"The fire department will show up . . . ": Nic Adler, Interview by Authors, 10/2/02.

"I know I'm pushing . . . ": David Kamp, "Live at the Whisky," *Vanity Fair,* 11/00, p. 254.

"Mario is amazing . . . ": Nic Adler, Interview by Authors, 10/2/02.

"The Whisky is still there . . . ": Jim Ladd, Interview by Authors, 9/17/02.

"The Whisky is a landmark . . . ": Mario Maglieri, Interview by Authors, 8/12/99.

ADDITIONAL SOURCES

Arnold, Gina, "Pop Perfect: The Monterey Pop Festival of 1967 . . . ," *Silicon Valley Metro Newspaper,* 14 June 2001.

Baker, Glenn A. "Johnny Rivers: The Singer Not the Song." *Goldmine Magazine,* no. 290 (1982): transcript from Whisky Archives *(www.whisky agogo.com).*

Balfour, Victoria. *Rock Wives: The Hard Lives and Good Times of the Wives, Girlfriends, and Groupies of Rock and Roll.* New York: Beech Tree Books, William Morrow and Company, 1986.

Bardsley, Marilyn. "Where Are They Now: Charles Manson." *(www.crime library.com/manson/mansonhel.htm).*

Barger, Ralph. "Sonny." *Hell's Angel: The Life and Times of Sonny Barger and the Hell's Angels Motorcycle Club.* New York: HarperCollins, 2000.

Bergman, Georgia. "Snapshots from the Road." *Gimme Shelter Exploration* (liner notes). Criterion, 2000. DVD.

Booth, Stanley. *The True Adventures of the Rolling Stones.* Chicago: A Capella Books, reprint, 2000.

Burks, John and Jerry Hopkins. "Groupies and Other Girls." *Rolling Stone,* no. 27 (1969): 72–73.

Caserta, Peggy and Dan Knapp. *Goin' Down with Janis.* New York: Dell, published by arrangement with Lyle Stuart, Inc., 1973.

Chandler, Carmen Ramos, "Police Caught Unprepared for Rock Fans, Question Handling of Ticket Sale," *Los Angeles Daily News,* 7 July 1992: transcript from Whisky Archives *(www.whiskyagogo.com).*

Cheshire, Godfrey, "The 'Demonic Charisma' of Gimme Shelter," *New York Press,* 9 August 2000.

Cromelin, Richard and Michele Meyer. "Rainbow." *Interview Magazine,* February 1976: 36–37.

Cuda, Heidi Siegmund. "Club Review." *Los Angeles Magazine.* October 1999: 14.

Cuda, Heidi Siegmund, "On the Rox Rebounds to Its Glory," *Los Angeles Times,* 27 June 1996: transcript from Whisky Archives *(www.whiskyagogo.com).*

Daunt, Tina, "'Gramps' on the Strip," *Los Angeles Times,* 11 September

1991: transcript from Whisky Archives *(www.whiskyagogo.com)*.

Daunt, Tina, "Interview with Mario Maglieri," *Los Angeles Times,* 4 November 1993: transcript from Whisky Archives *(www.whiskyagogo.com)*.

Davis, Stephen. *Hammer of the Gods: The Led Zeppelin Saga.* New York: Ballantine Books, 1985.

Densmore, John. *Riders on the Storm: My Life with Jim Morrison and the Doors.* New York: Bloomsbury Publishing, 1991.

Des Barres, Pamela. *I'm with the Band: Confessions of a Groupie.* New York: Jove Books, 1987.

Duff, S.L. "Sunset Strip as Memory Lane." *Music Connection* (9 March 1988).

Evans, David and Scott Michaels. *Rocky Horror: From Concept to Cult.* London: Sanctuary Publishing, 2002.

Everett, Todd, "Revenge of the Waitresses; Roxettes Turn Tables to Star in Nightclub Revue," *Los Angeles Herald-Examiner*, April 1985: transcript from Whisky Archives *(www.whiskyagogo.com)*.

Farrell, Tom and Paola Palazzo. "Strip Clubs Earmarked for Historical Status; Future Lease Arrangements for Roxy and Rainbow Uncertain." *Music Connection* (September 1991): transcript from Whisky Archives, *(www.whiskyagogo.com)*.

Fein, Art. *The L.A. Music Industry Tour: A Guide to Rock 'n' Roll Landmarks of Los Angeles.* London: Faber and Faber, 1990.

Ferrell, David, "Golden Sunset; Glittering Boulevard L.A.'s Unique Blend of Glamour and Panache," *Los Angeles Times*, 8 September 1991.

"Find the Monkees Interview." *(www.geocities.com/Hollywood/Set/9847/findthe.html)*.

Fink, Mitchell, "Whisky's Closing Is Another Sign of Decay in the Music Biz," *Los Angeles Times,* 29 December 1979: transcript from Whisky Archives *(www.whiskyagogo.com)*.

Freek, Jim. "Good Night at the Whisky." *BAM Magazine* (12 February 1999): 11.

Friedenberg, Edward Z. and Anthony Bernhard. "The Battle of Sunset Strip." *The New York Review of Books* (9 March 1967). Reprinted in *The*

California Dream, edited by Dennis Hale and Jonathan Eisen, New York: Collier Books, 1968.

Gittelson, Gerry. "Mario Maglieri: A Story from Rock to Riches." *Rock City News*, May 1992: 34–36.

Gold, Jonathan, "The Loudest Job Interviews in Town," *Los Angeles Times*, 18 March 1990: transcript from Whisky Archives (*www.whiskyagogo.com*).

Hillburn, Robert, "The L.A. Rock Scene: A Dramatic Resurgence," *Los Angeles Times*, 24 July 1979: transcript from Whisky Archives (*www.whiskyagogo.com*).

Hillburn, Robert, "Homegrown Punk," *Los Angeles Times*, 4 January 1977: transcript from Whisky Archives (*www.whiskyagogo.com*).

Hillburn, Robert, "Nostalgia Night at the Whisky," *Los Angeles Times*, 21 July 1982: transcript from Whisky Archives (*www.whiskyagogo.com*).

Hillburn, Robert, "Where the Wild Things Lived," *Los Angeles Times*, 15 December 1996: transcript from Whisky Archives (*www.whiskyagogo.com*).

Hinkle, Warren. "A Social History of the Hippies." *Ramparts* (March 1967). Reprinted in *The California Dream*, edited by Dennis Hale and Jonathan Eisen, New York: Collier Books, 1968.

Hochman, Steven, "Taste of Vintage Whisky at Celebration," *Los Angeles Times*, 18 January 1999: transcript from Whisky Archives (*www.whiskya gogo.com*).

Hopkins, Jerry and Danny Sugerman, *No One Here Gets Out Alive*. New York: Warner Books, 1980 (revised edition, 1995).

Hoskyns, Barney. *Waiting for the Sun: Strange Days, Weird Scenes and the Los Angeles Sound*. New York: St. Martin's Griffin. 1999.

Hunt, Dennis, "A Guessing Game at the Whisky," *Los Angeles Times*, 27 October 1972: transcript from Whisky Archives (*www.whiskyagogo.com*).

Hunt, Dennis, "Whisky, On Rocks, to Become Disco," *Los Angeles Times*, 25 March 1975: transcript from Whisky Archives (*www.whiskyagogo.com*).

Kamp, David. "Live at the Whisky." *Vanity Fair* (November 2000): 255–270.

Klosterman, Chuck. *Spin* (September 2002): 86–94.

Levin, Eric. "John Belushi's Final Hours." *People Weekly* (22 March 1982): 84–88.

Lydon, Michael. "The Decade That Spawned Altamont." *Gimme Shelter Exploration* (liner notes). Criterion, 2000. DVD.

Maguire, Tom. "Welcome to the World Famous Rainbow Bar and Grill." *Shockwaves Magazine* (June 1997).

McGrath, Tom, *MTV: The Making of a Revolution.*

Mojo, (May 2000): *(www.groupiecentral.com/articlespameladb.html).*

Nejman, Michael R., "L.A. Rock," *Chicago Sun-Times*, 12 February 1991: transcript from Whisky Archives *(www.whiskyagogo.com).*

Nilsen, Per and Dorothy Sherman. *The Wild One: The True Story of Iggy Pop.* London: Omnibus Press, 1988.

Noxon, Christopher. "The King and Prince of Sunset Strip." *West Hollywood Independent* (12 August 1996): transcript from Whisky Archives *(www.whiskyagogo.com).*

Overend, William, "When the Sun Set on the Strip: Many See Street in Decline; Others Have Hope," *Los Angeles Times*, 4 November 1981: transcript from Whisky Archives *(www.whiskyagogo.com).*

"Pamela Des Barres on Pamela Des Barres." *Playboy* (March 1989): 121–124.

Parrent, Joanne with Liza, Linda, Tiffany, and Robin. *You'll Never Make Love in This Town Again.* New York: Newstar Press. 1995.

"Random Notes." *Rolling Stone*, no. 807 (1999): 31.

"Roxy: Pop-Rock Takes a Step Uptown," *Los Angeles Times,* 22 September 1975: transcript from Whisky Archives *(www.whiskyagogo.com).*

Sandow, Gregory, "Bowie for the '90s Emerges at Roxy," *Los Angeles Herald-Examiner,* 12 February 1991: transcript from Whisky Archives *(www.whisky agogo.com).*

Schneider, Sue. "Life and Times at the Rainbow." *Daily News Magazine* (April 1984).

Schneider, Susan and Anne Moore. "Mario Maglieri: A Rock 'n' Roll Legend." *Monsters of Rock* (Fall 1992): 87–92.

Scott, Jane, "Sunset Strip: End of Rock Rainbow," *Sunday Plain Dealer* (Cleveland, Ohio), 27 August 1978: transcript from Whisky Archives (*www.whiskyagogo.com*).

Scott, John L., "At Whisky A Go-Go, Athletic Mayhem in Motion," *Los Angeles Times,* 15 March 1965: transcript from Whisky Archives (*www.whiskyagogo.com*).

Sims, Judith. "Neil Young Opens the Roxy Theatre." *Rolling Stone,* no. 146 (1973): 27.

Slash. Interview from *True Hollywood Story: Sunset Strip.* E! Entertainment Channel, 2 November 1999.

Spitz, Mark and Brendan Mullen. *We Got the Neutron Bomb: The Untold Story of L.A. Punk.* New York: Three Rivers Press, 2001.

Taubin, Amy. "Rock and Roll Zapruder." *Gimme Shelter Exploration* (liner notes). Criterion, 2000. DVD.

"Toasting Twenty-five Years at the Whisky; Owners Recall Glory Days at Famous Club," *Los Angeles Times,* 13 March 1989: transcript from Whisky Archives (*www.whiskyagogo.com*).

Tobler, John. *This Day in Rock: Day by Day Record of Rock's Biggest News Stories.* New York: Carlton, 1993.

Trakin, Roy, "A Special Time in Rock: 1966 on the Sunset Strip," *Los Angeles Times,* 7 April 1991: transcript from Whisky Archives (*www.whiskyagogo.com*).

"Under the Rock, an Exciting Crop of Newcomers," *Los Angeles Times,* 27 November 1977: transcript from Whisky Archives (*www.whiskyagogo.com*).

Whiteside, Johnny, "Pleasure Pits on Parade: A Romp Through L.A.'s Rock, Blues and Country Clubs," *L.A. Weekly,* 25 June 1999: 27–32.

INDEX